Gold

Peter Tillessen
Gold

Lars Müller Publishers

Aktionskünstler / Action Artists

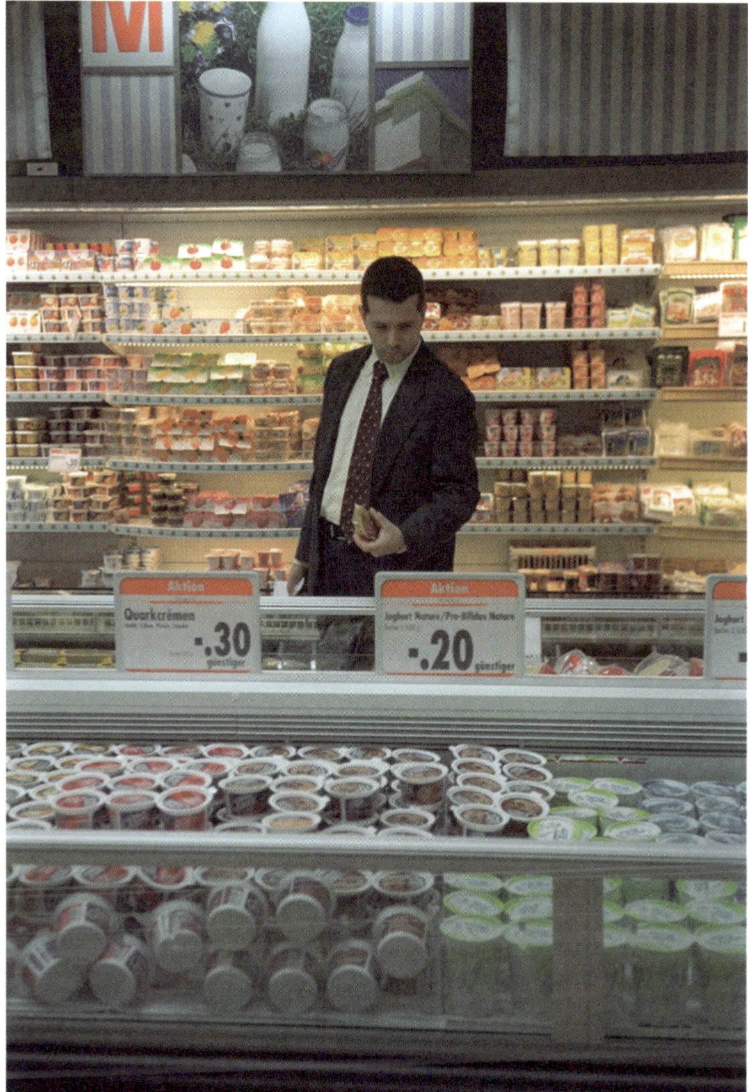

Aktion
Quarkcrèmen
–.30 günstiger
Aktion
Joghurt Nature / Pro-Bifidus Nature
–.20 günstiger

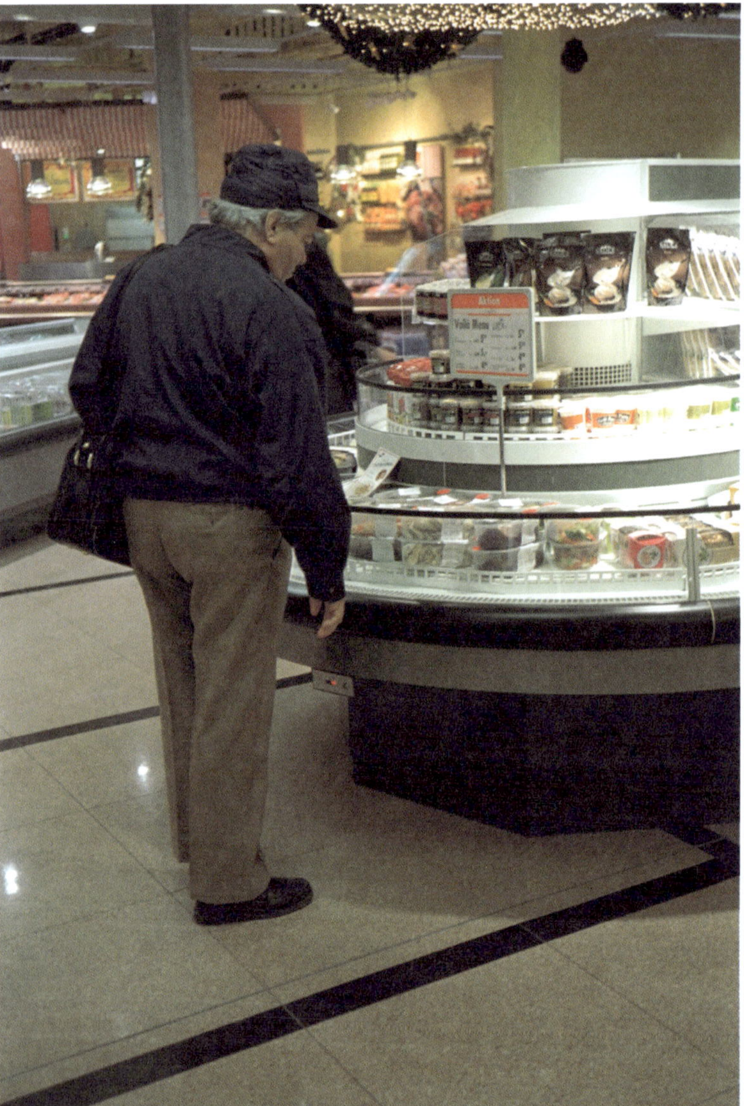

Aktion

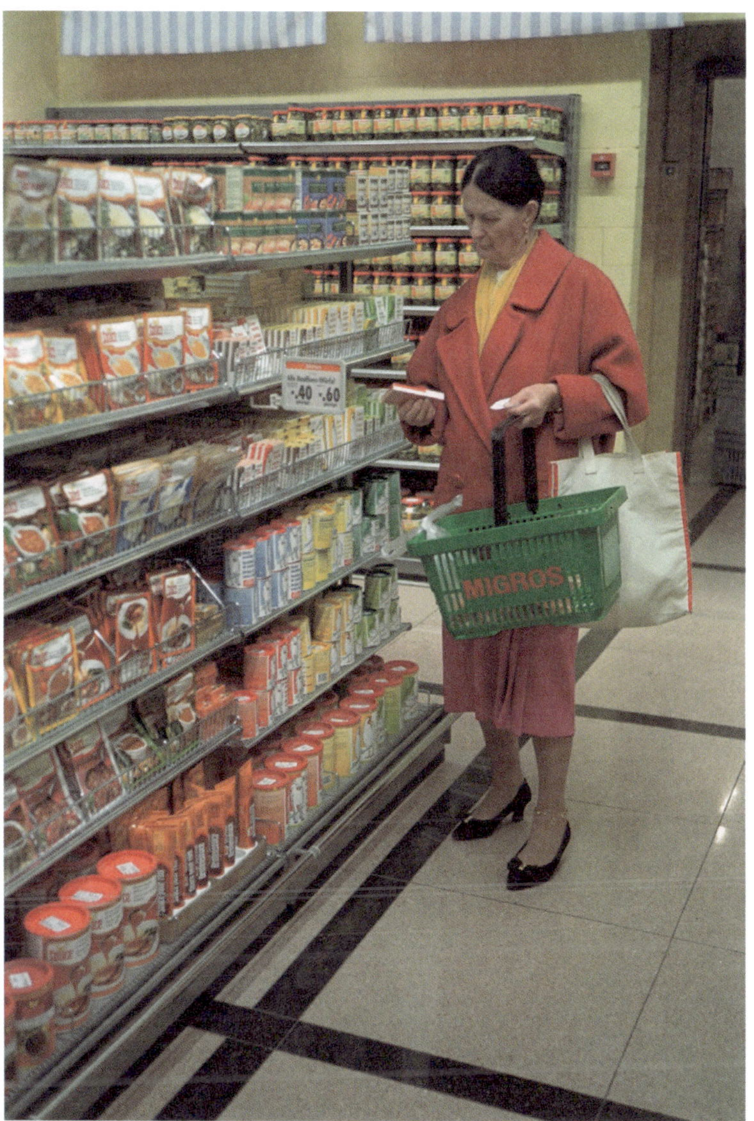

MIGROS

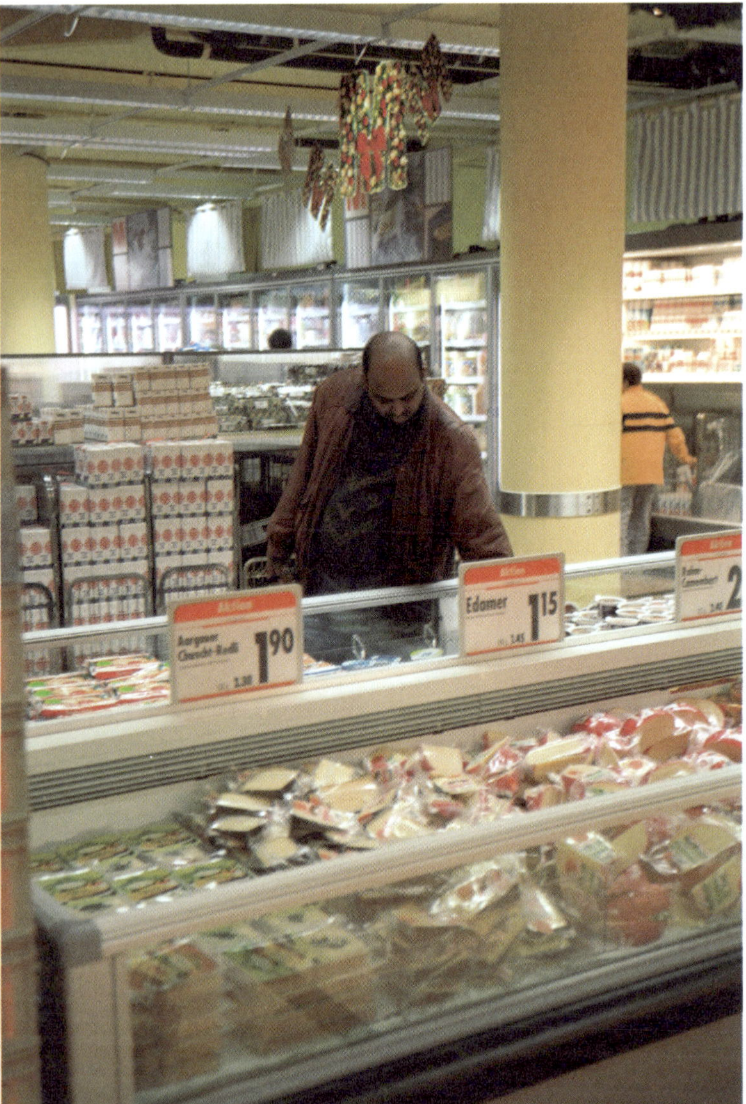

Aargauer Cheschi-Rudli 1.90
Edamer 1.15

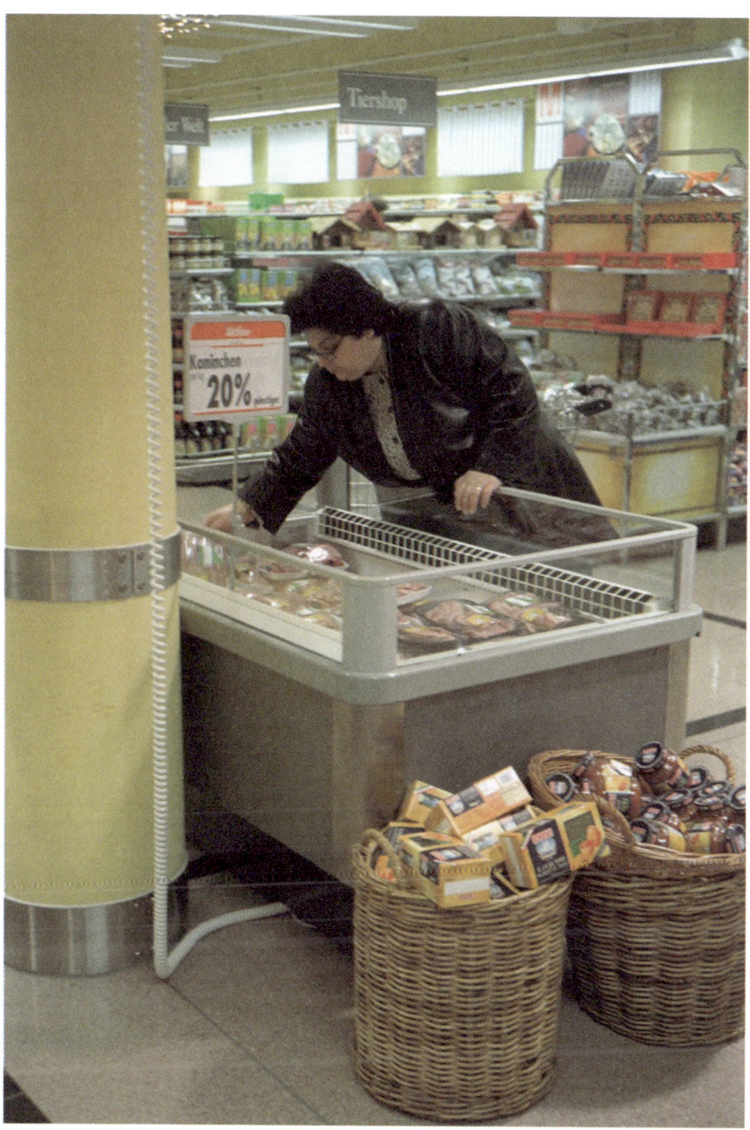
Tiershop
Kaninchen
20% günstiger

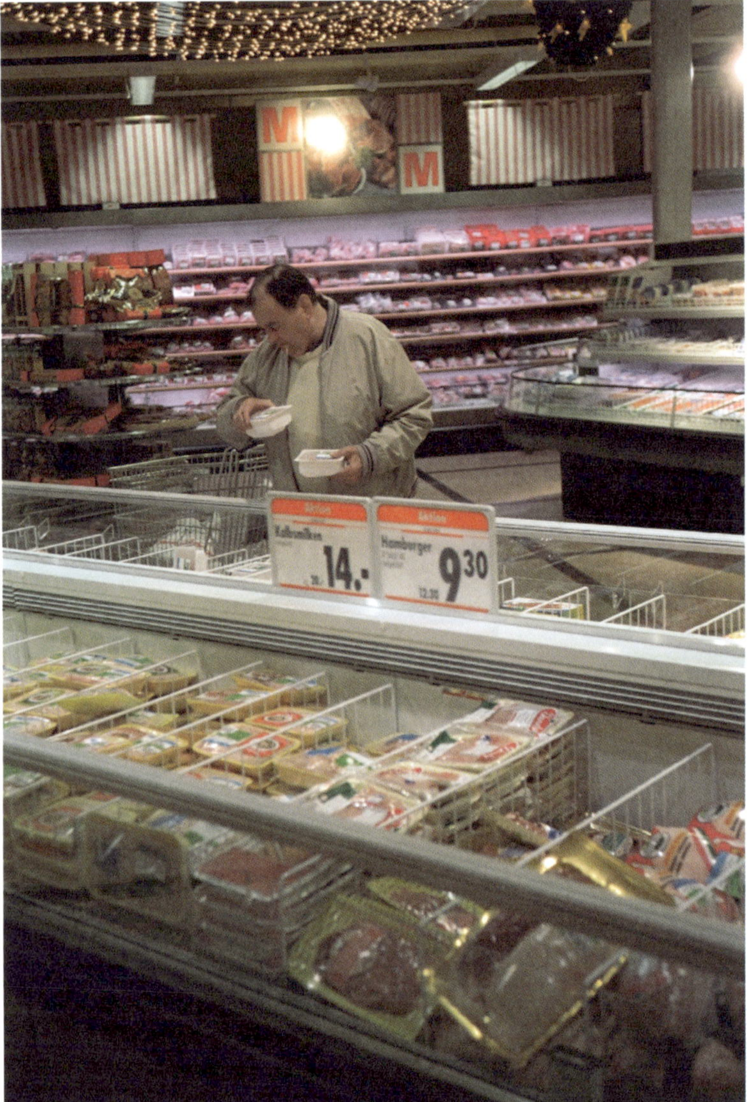
14.-
9 30

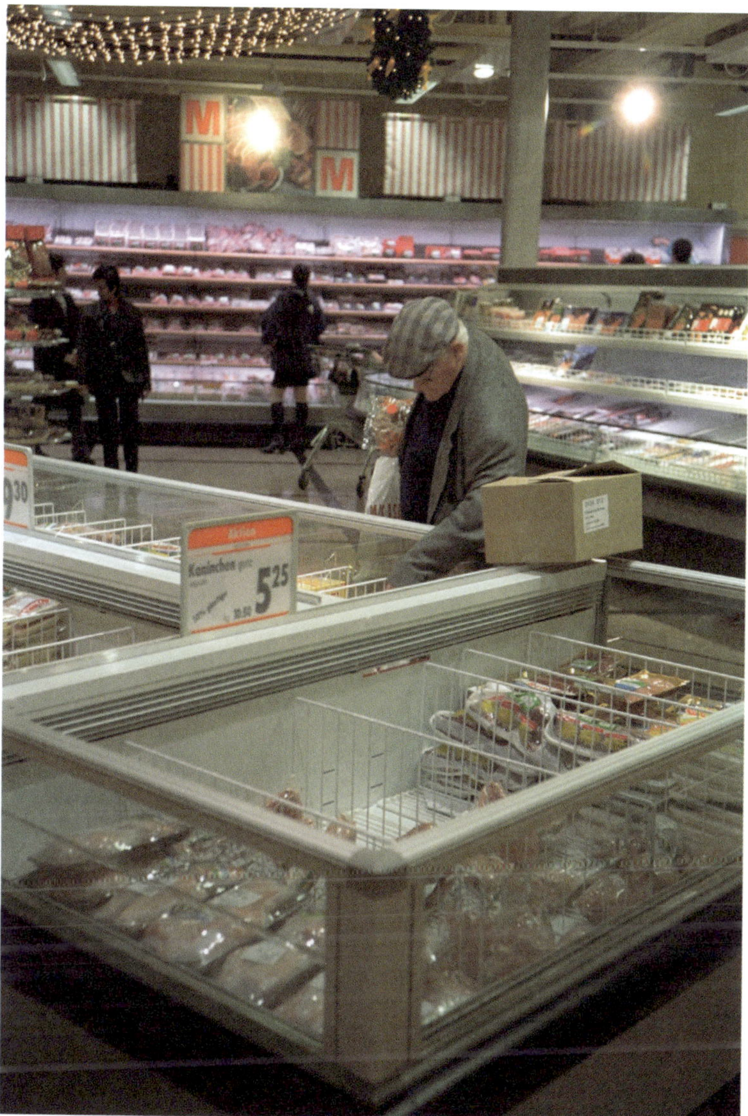
Aktion
Kaninchen
5 25

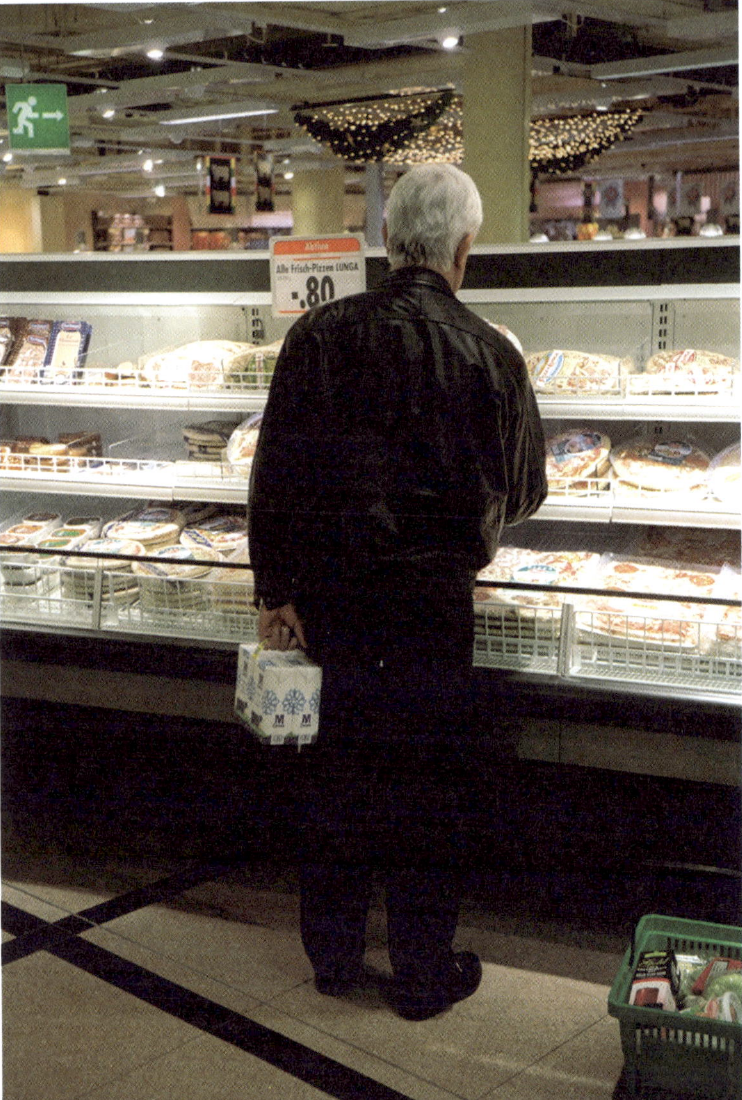

Aktion
Alle Frisch-Pizzen LUNGA
.80

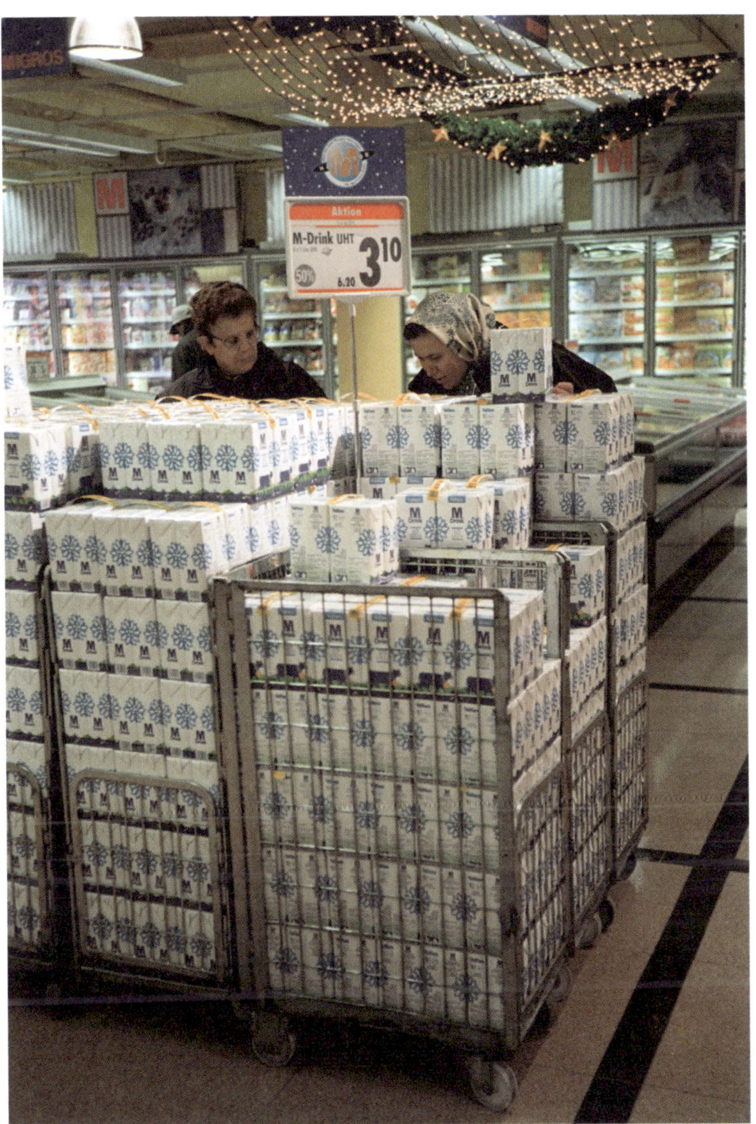
Aktion
M-Drink UHT
3 10
6.20
50%

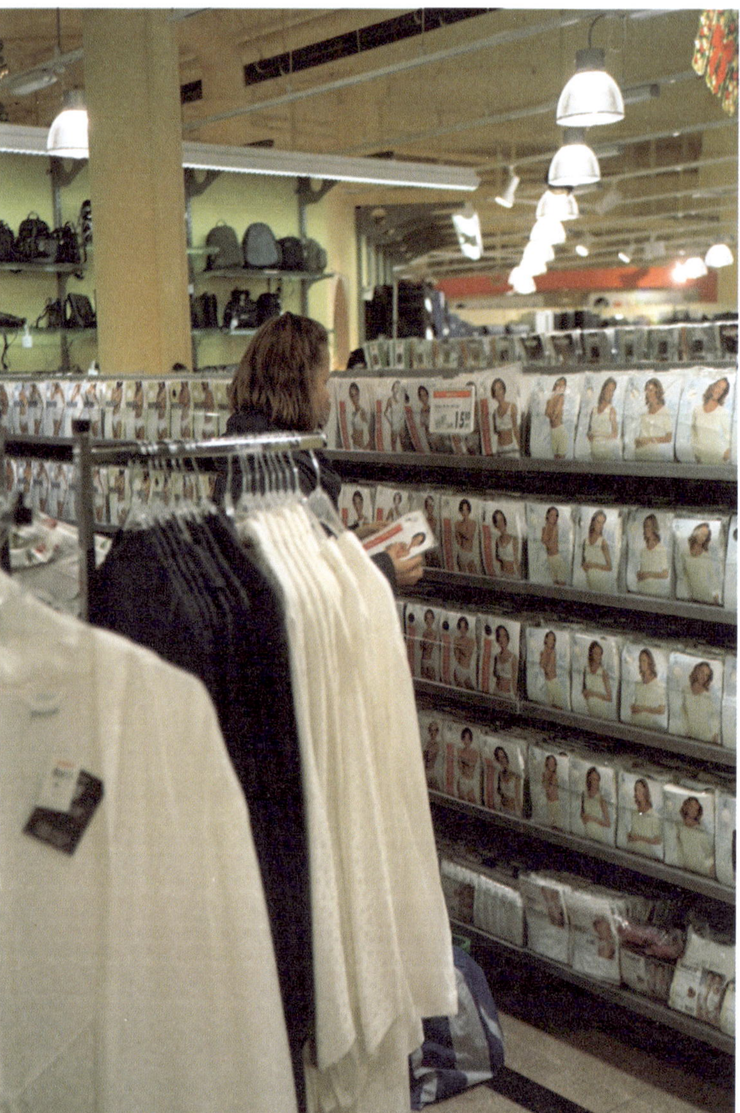

Kunst am Bau 1 /Art for Buildings 1

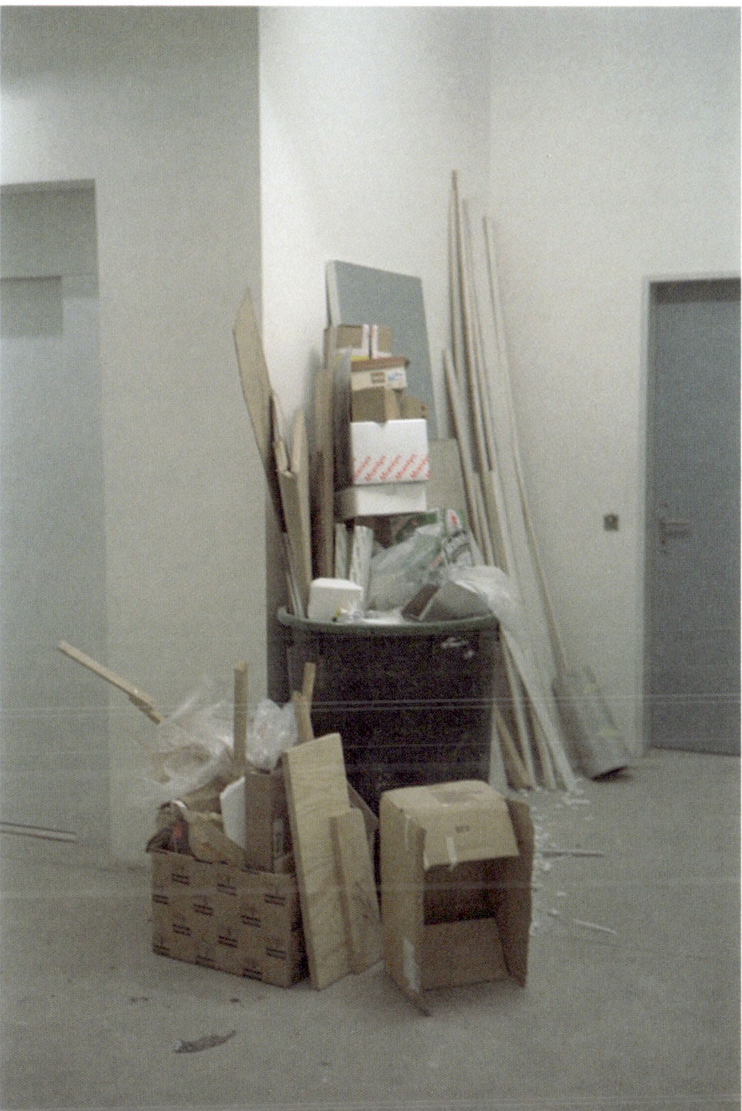

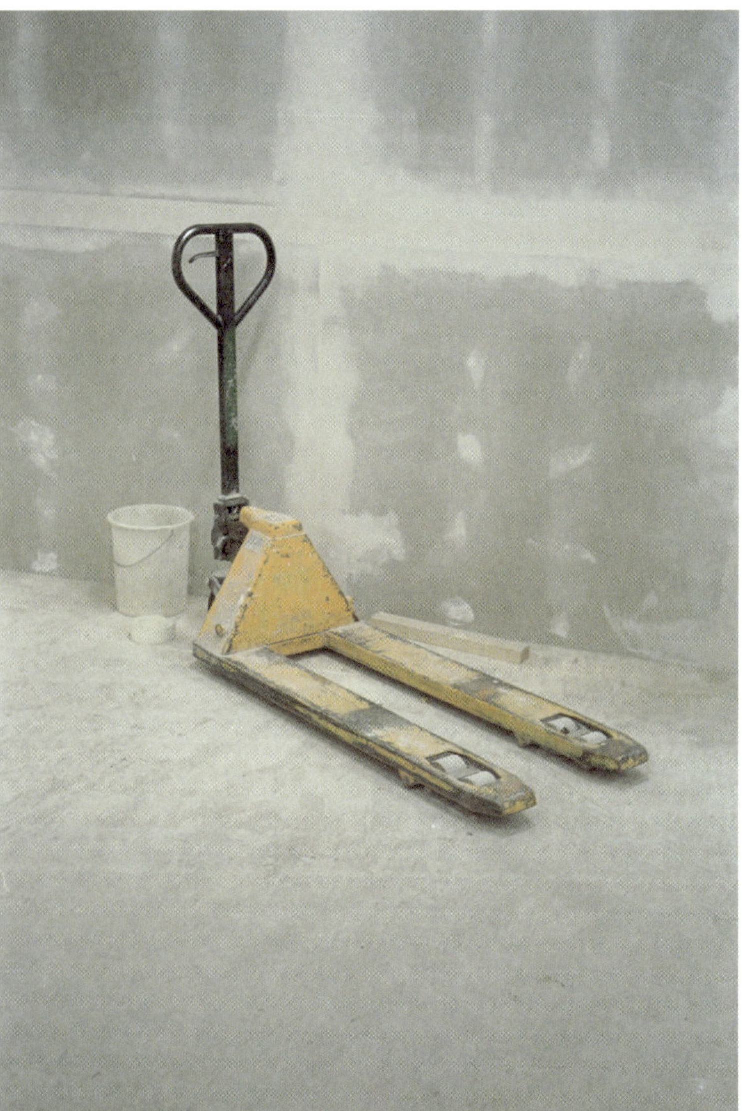

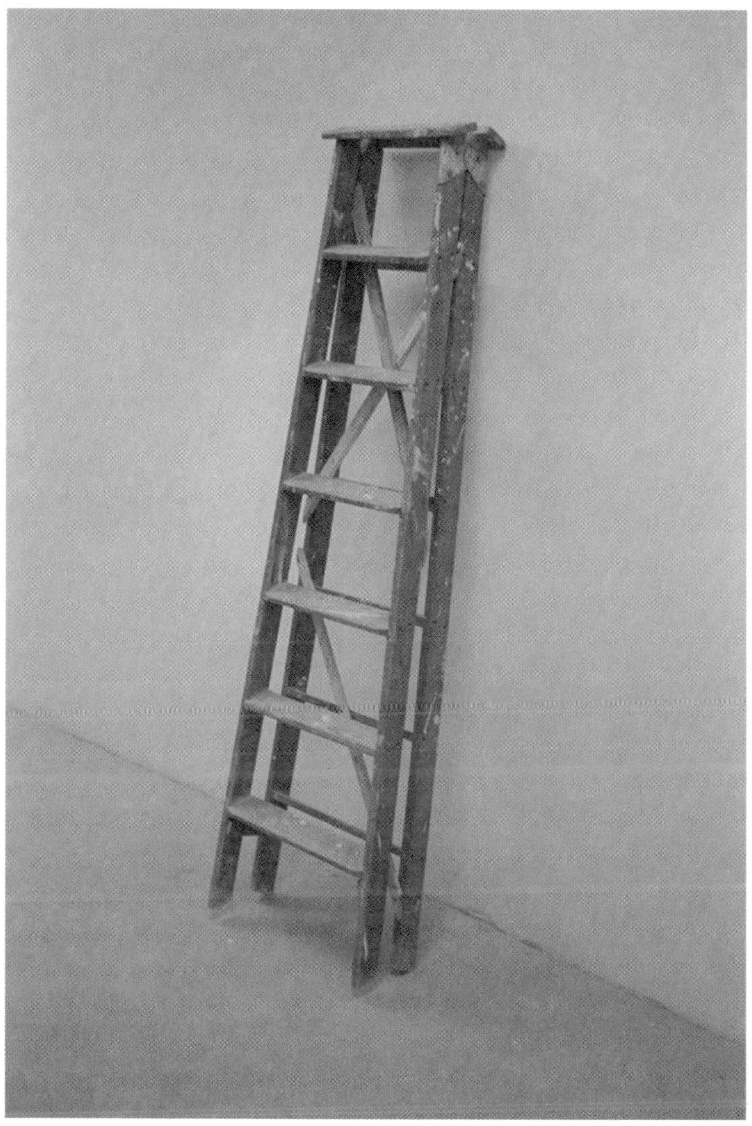

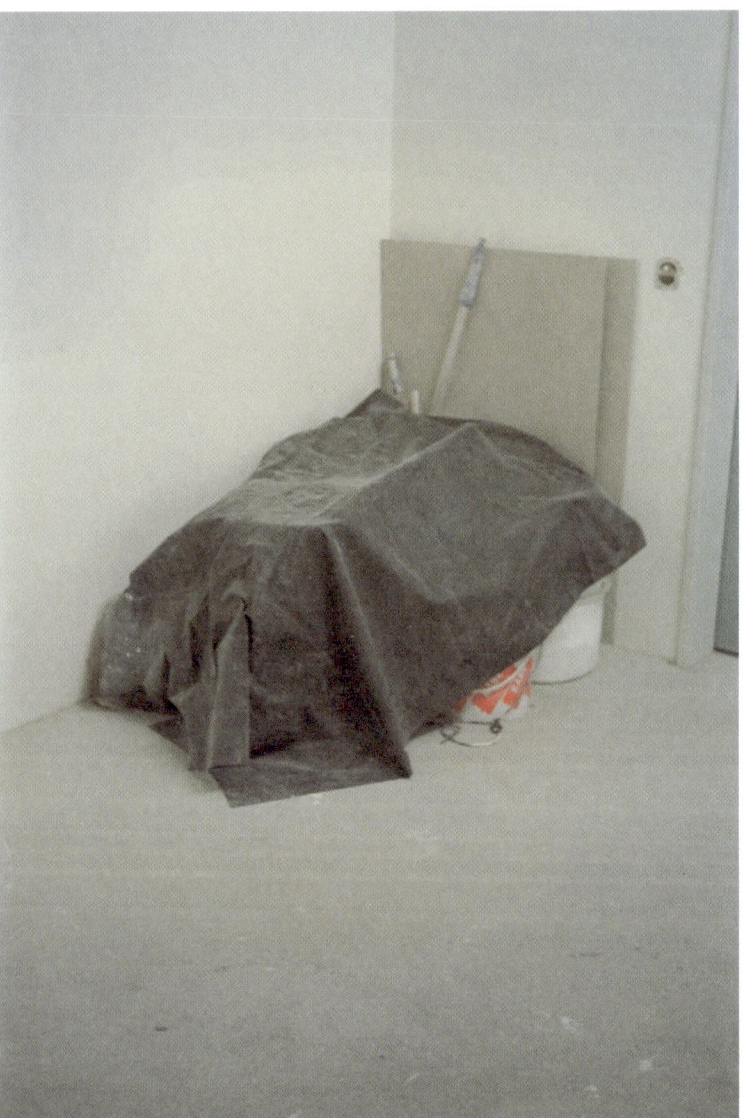

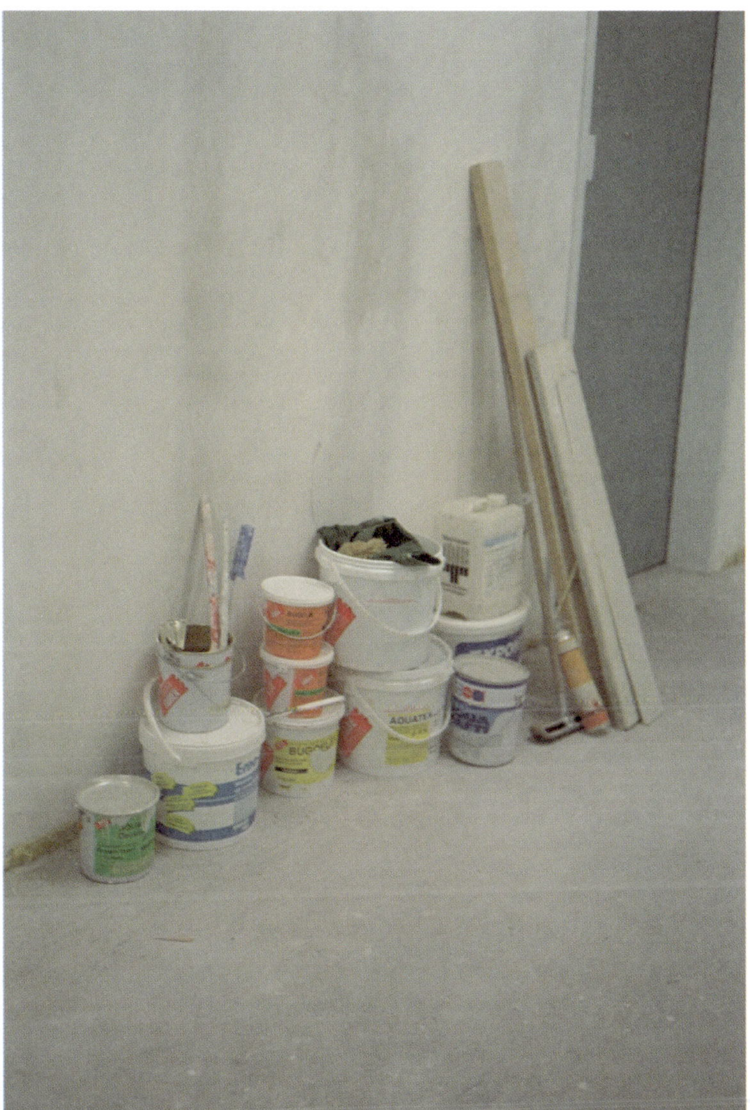

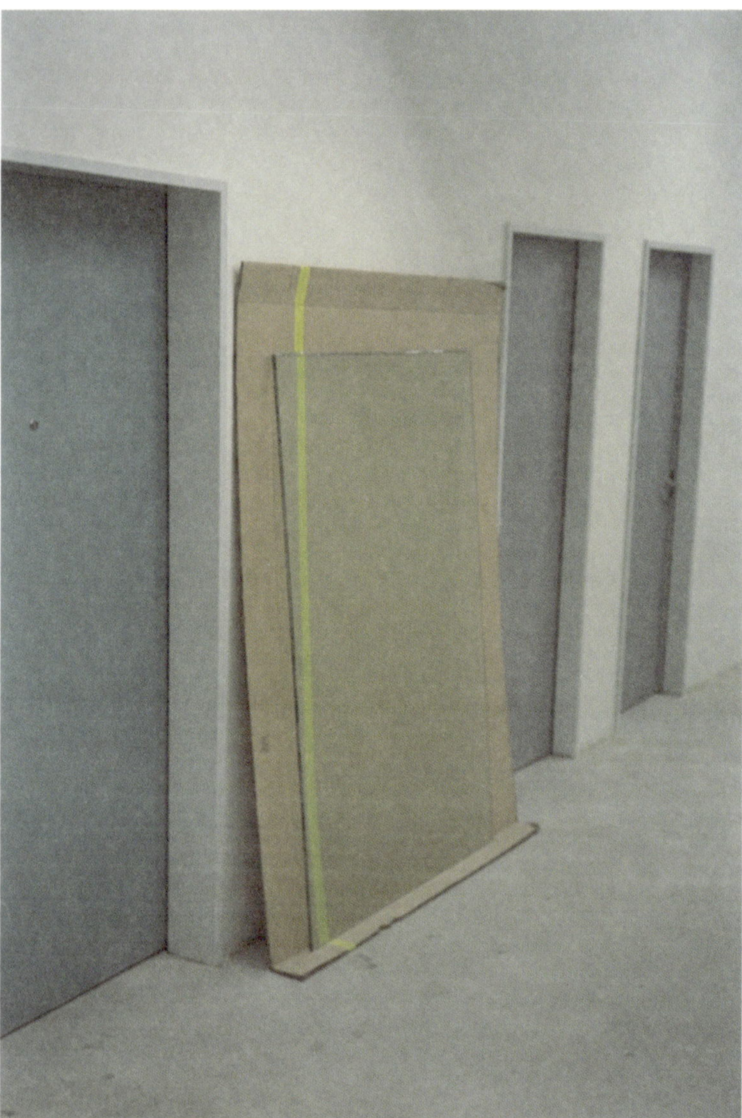

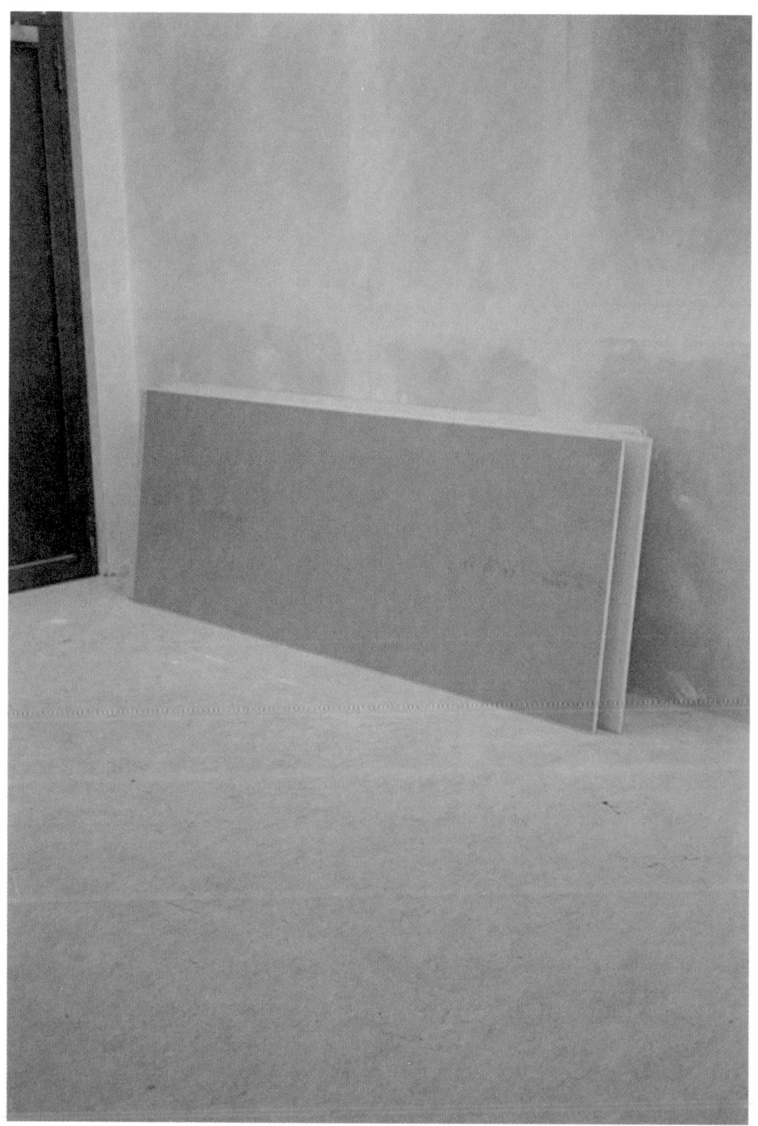

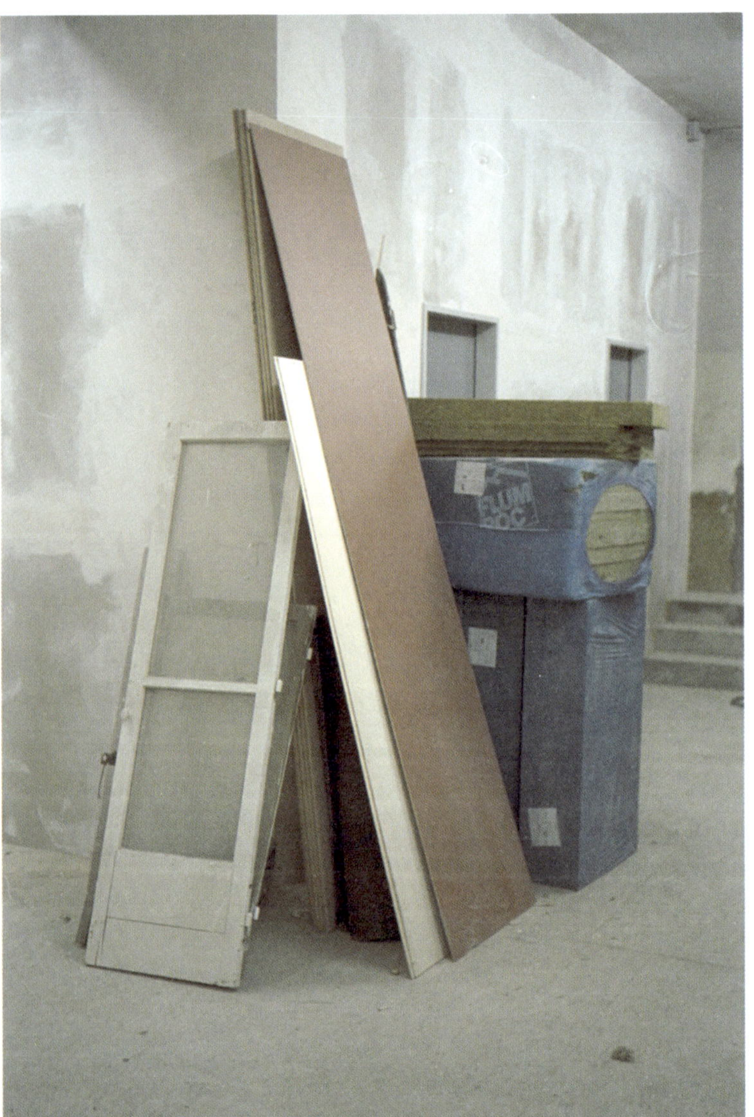

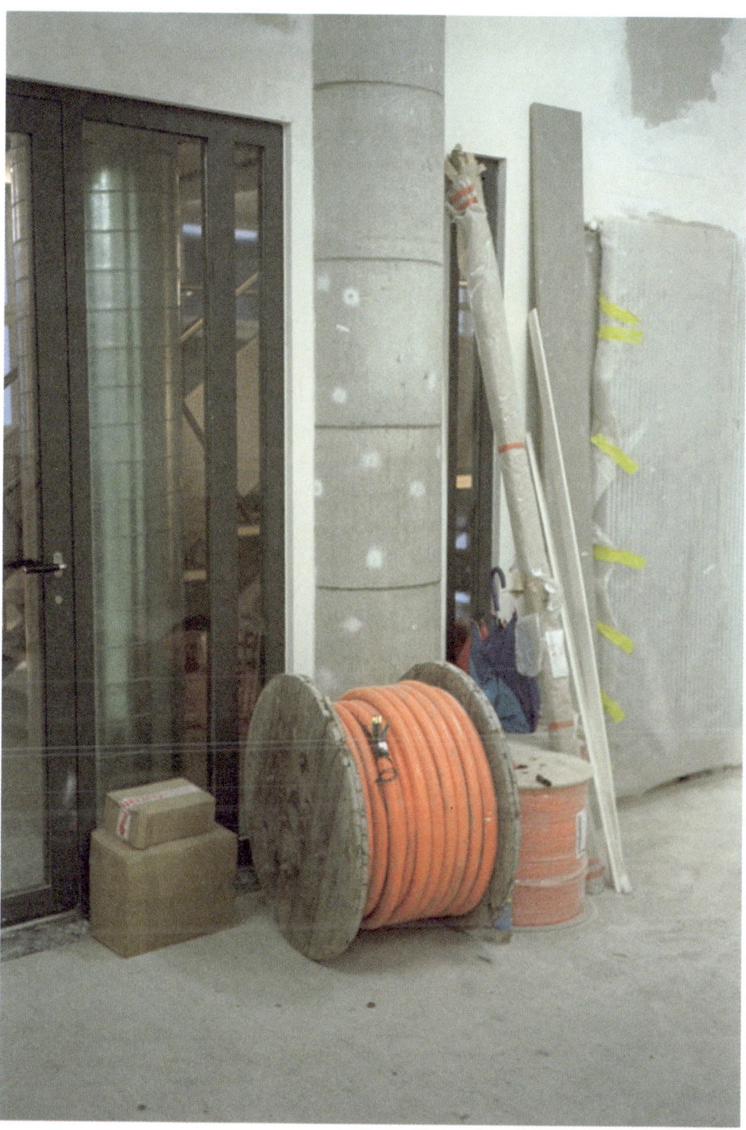

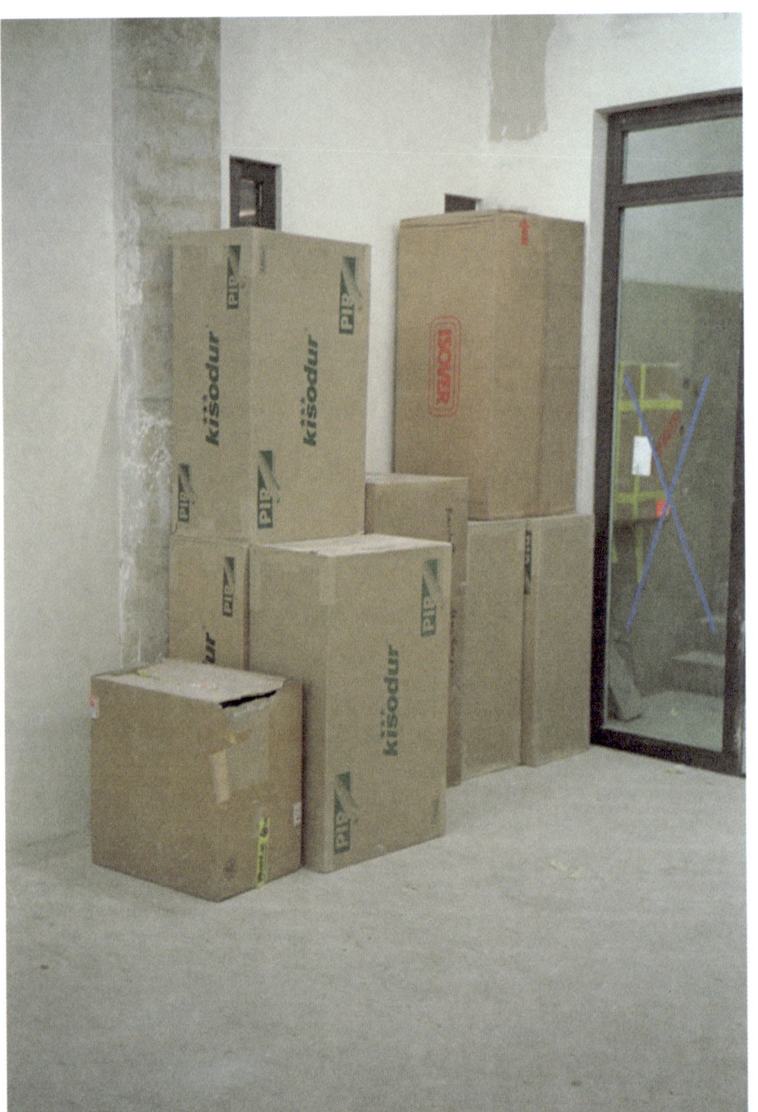

PIP
kisodur
ISOVER

Degenerative Bilder 1/ Degenerative Pictures 1

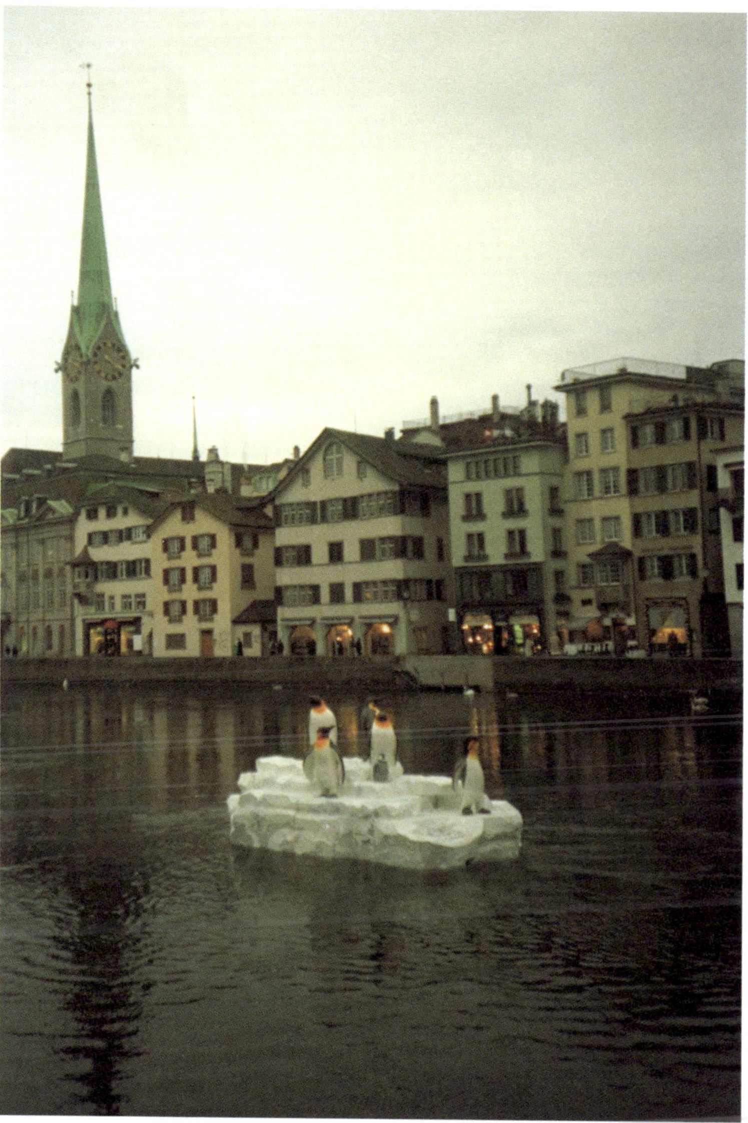

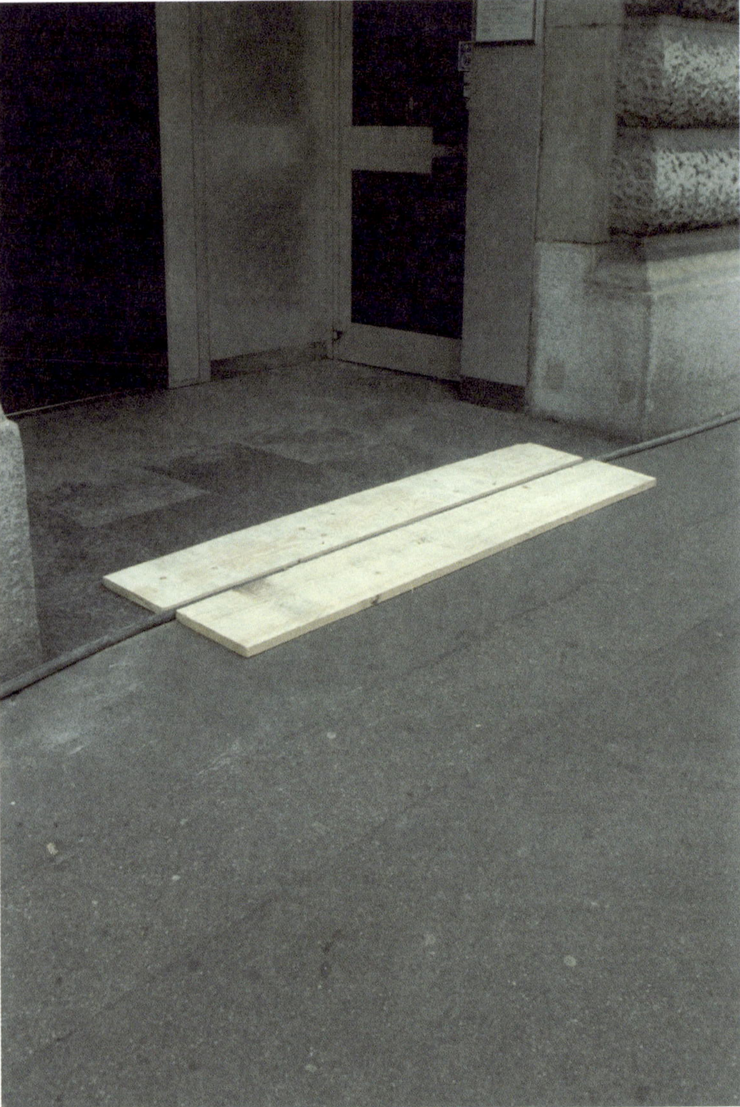

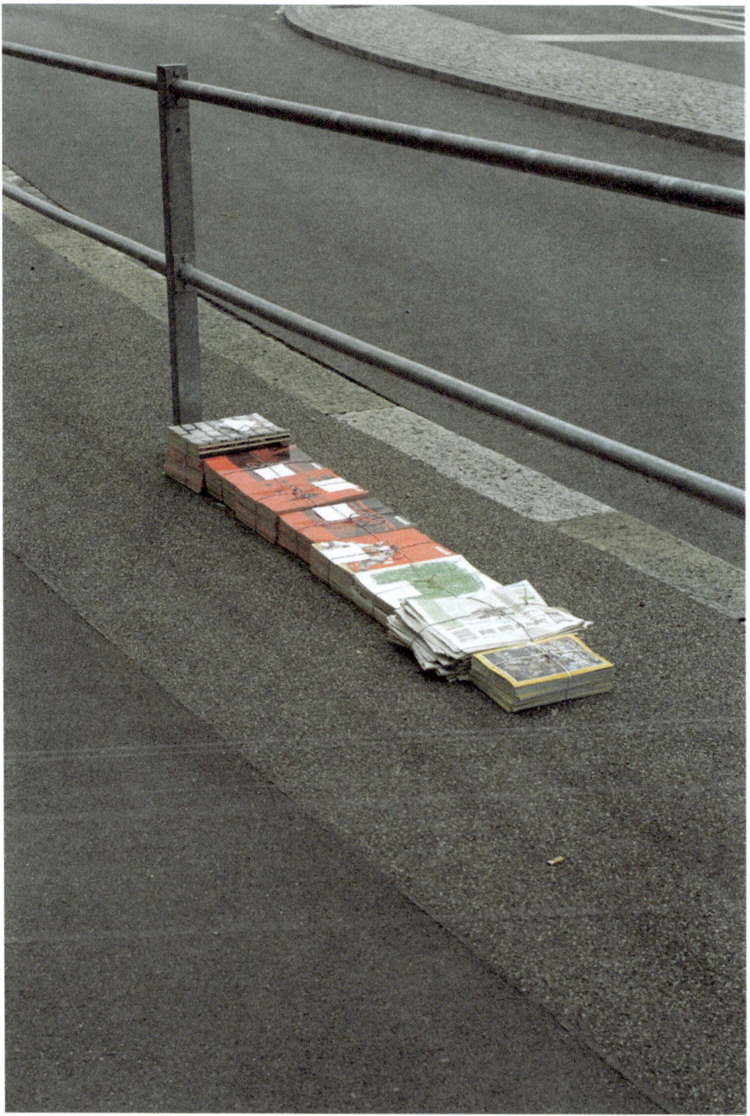

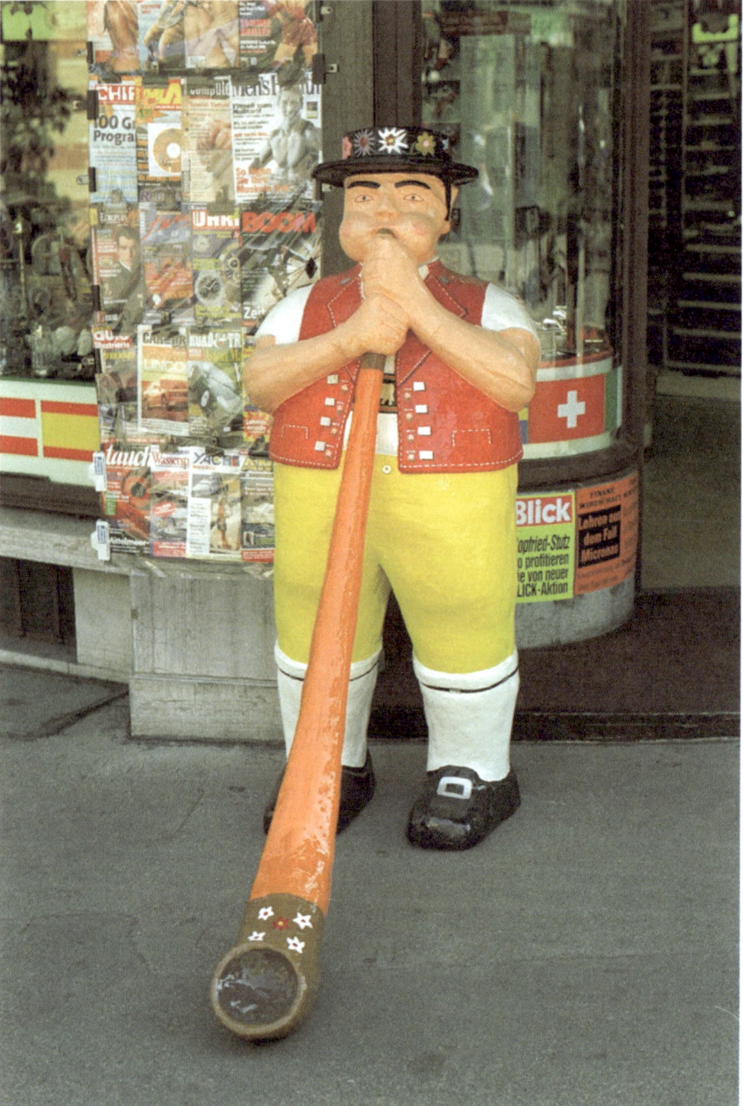

CHIP
100 G
Program
BOOM
Blick
opfried-Stutz
profitieren
e von neuer
LICK-Aktion

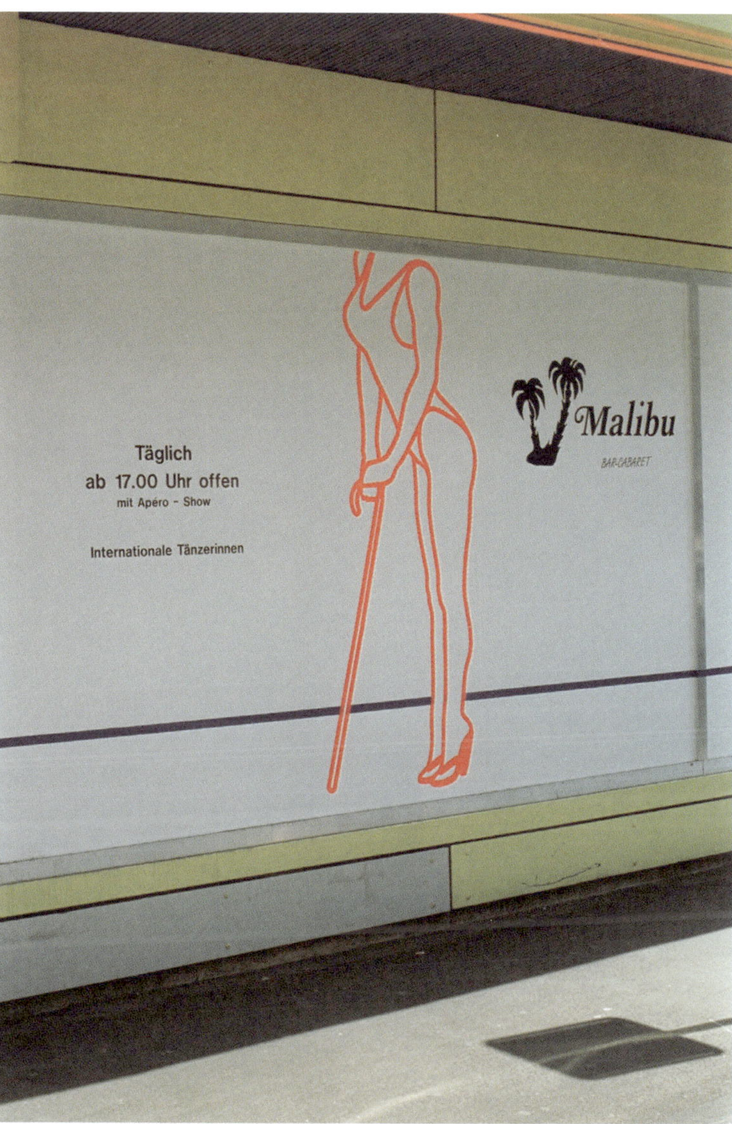

Täglich
ab 17.00 Uhr offen
mit Apéro - Show

Internationale Tänzerinnen

Malibu
BAR-CABARET

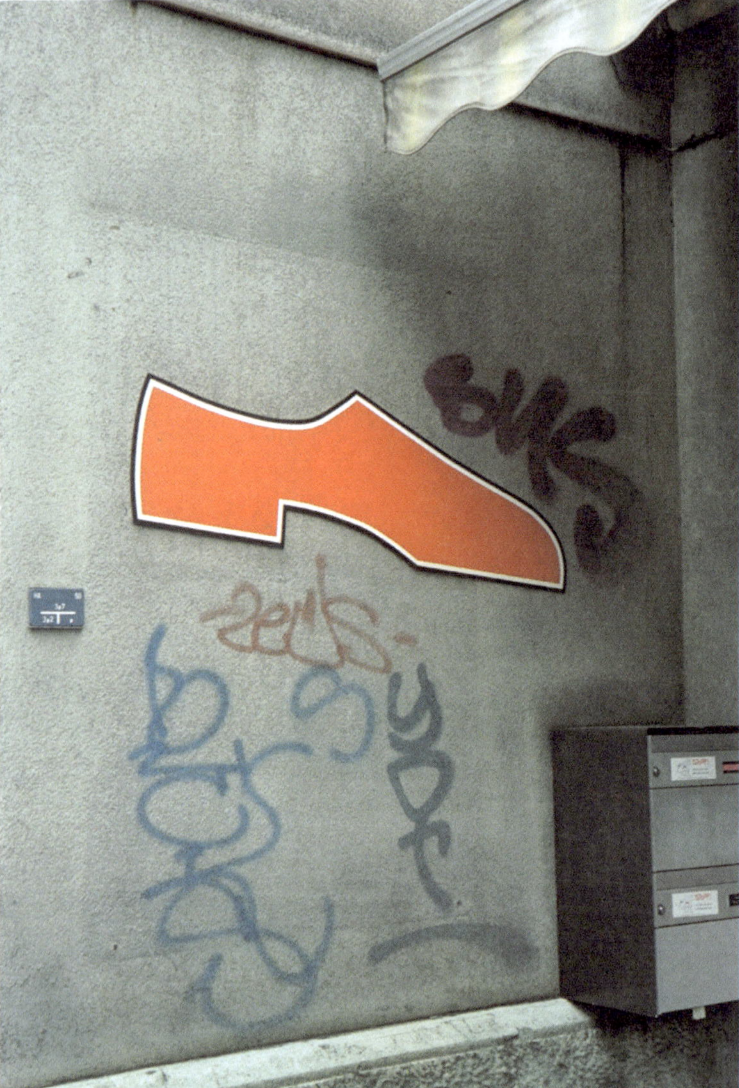

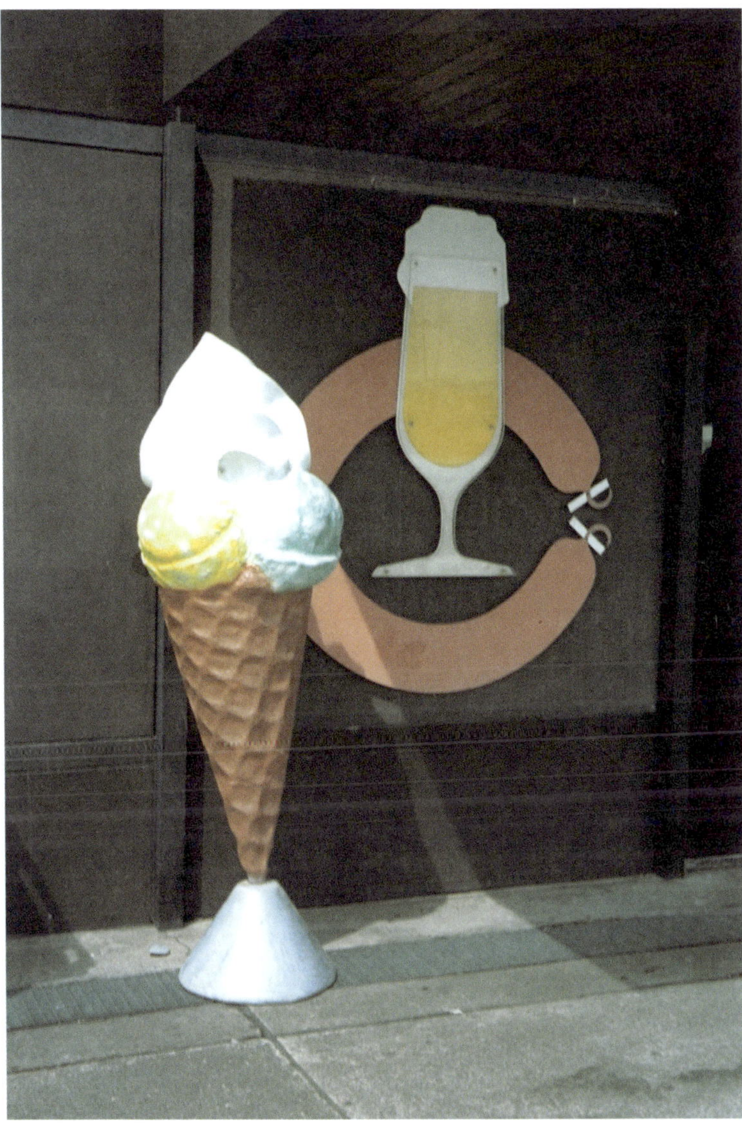

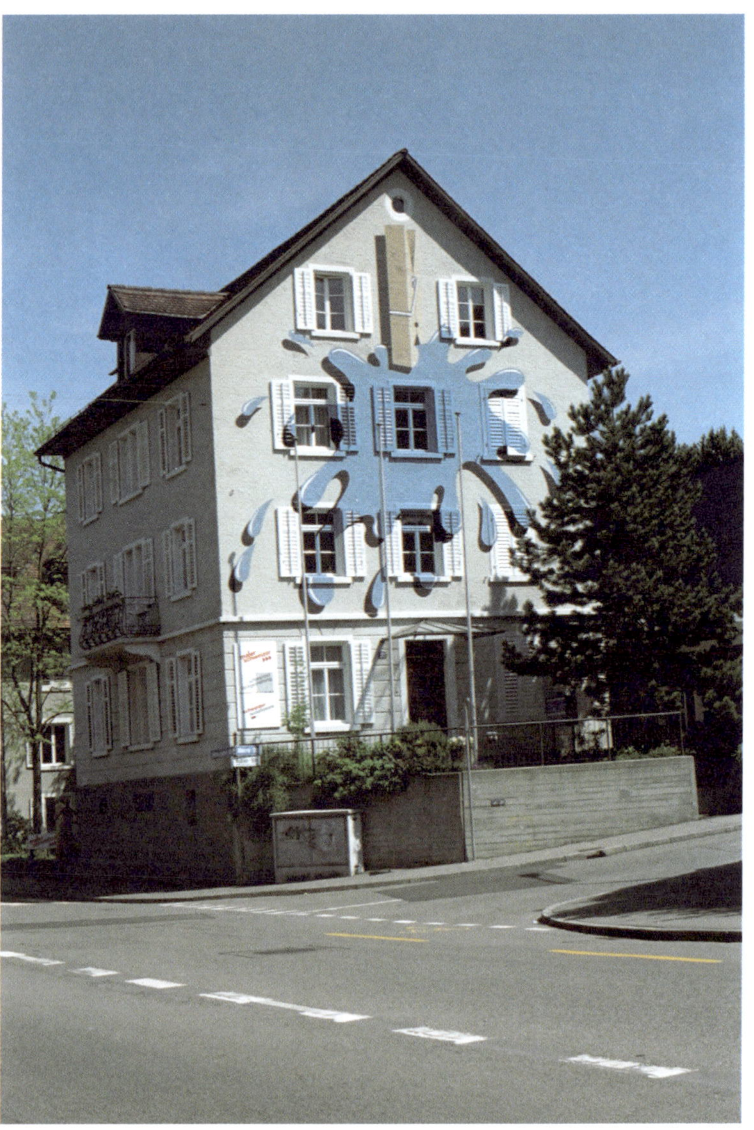

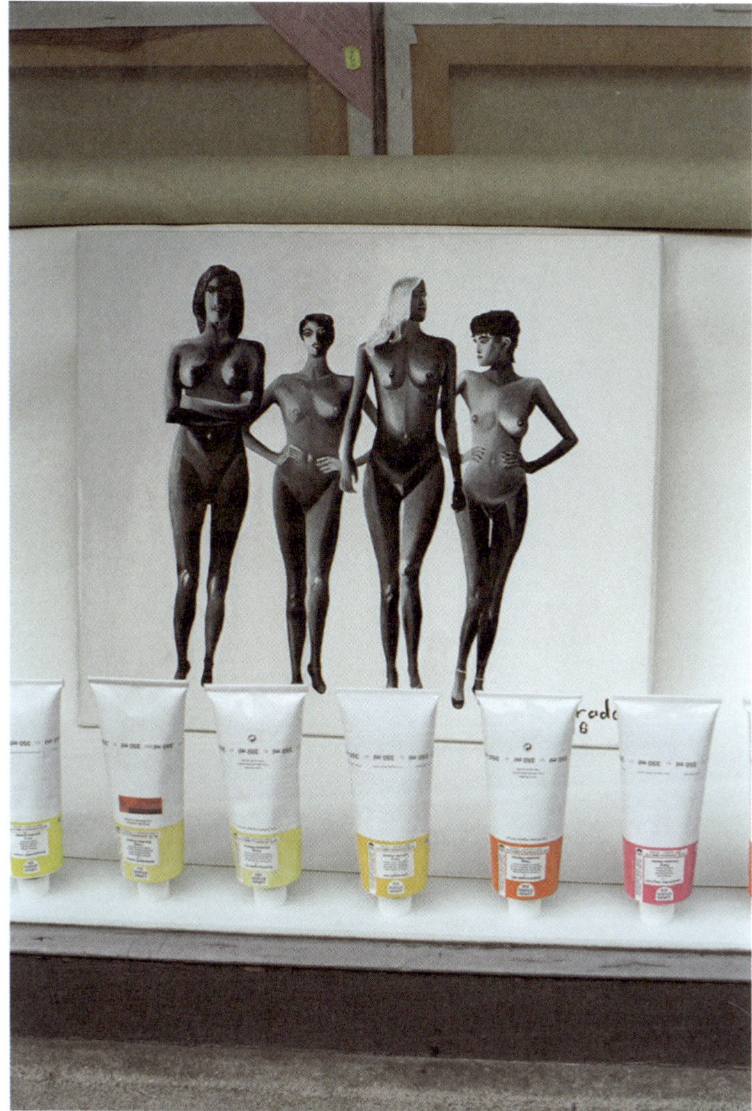

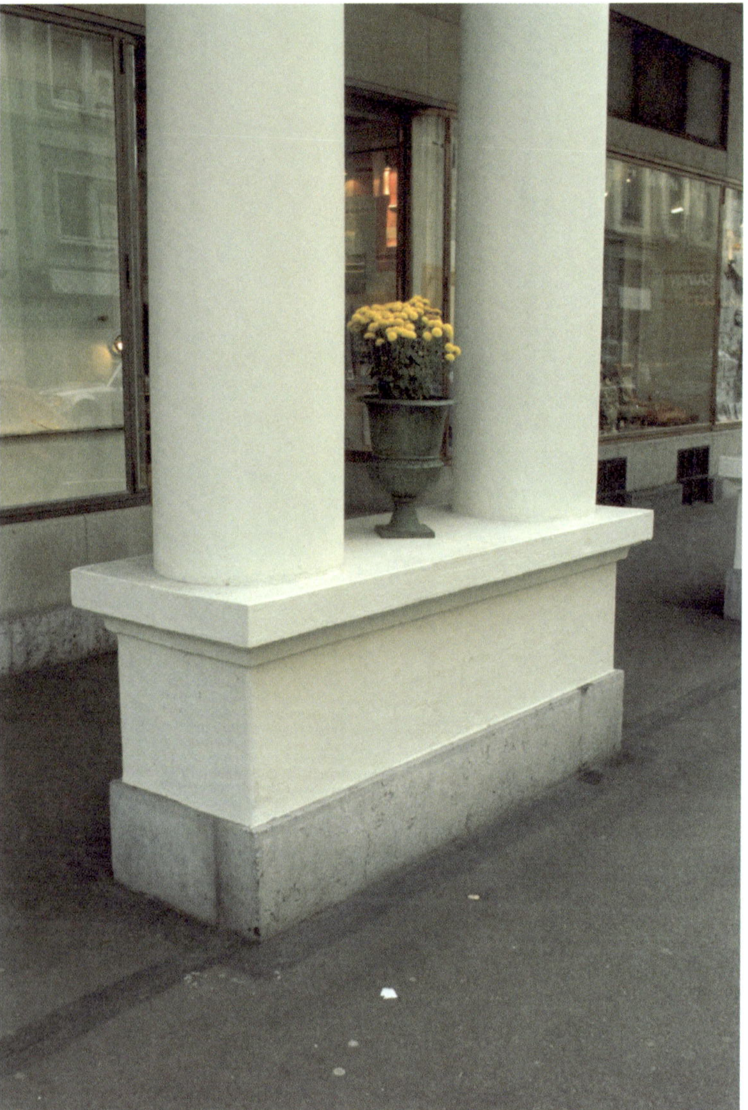

Goldrausch 1/Gold Rush 1

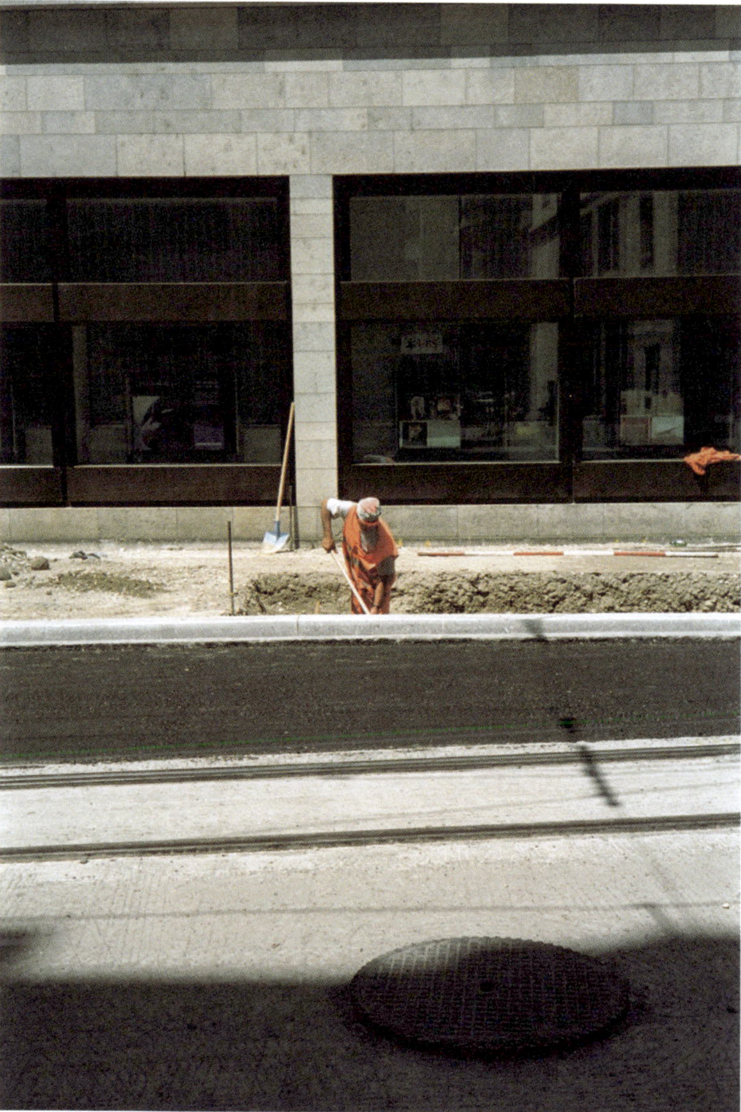

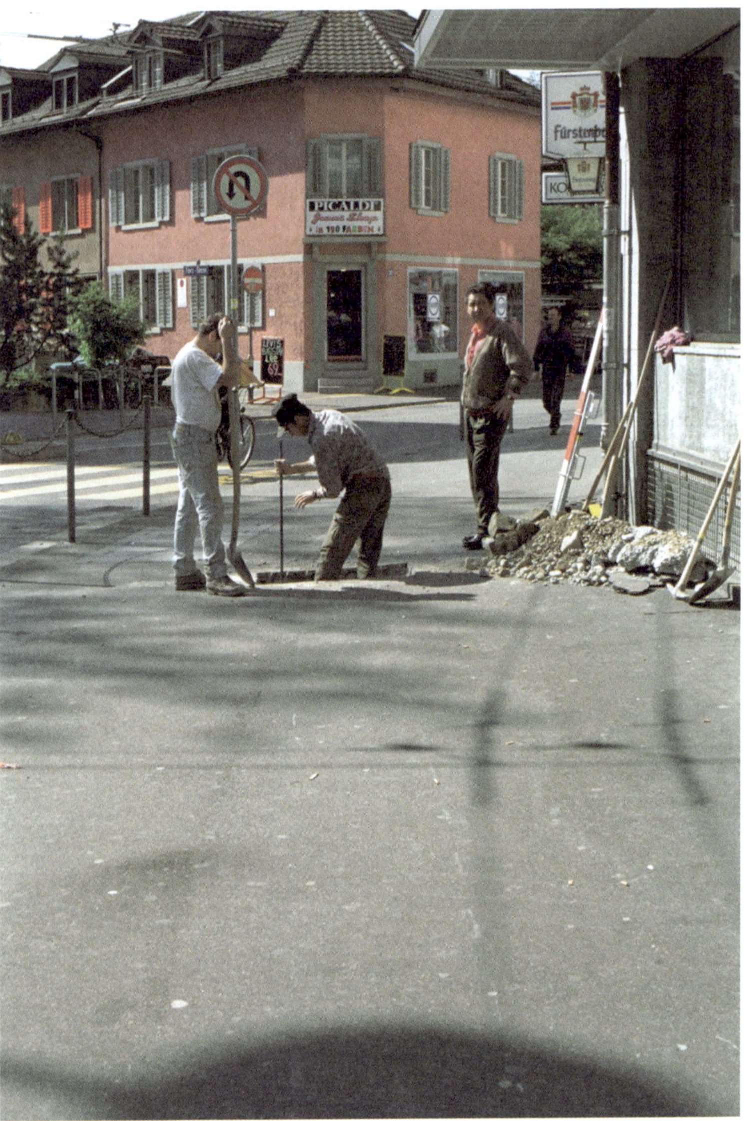
PICALDI
in 100 FARBEN
Fürstenbe
KO

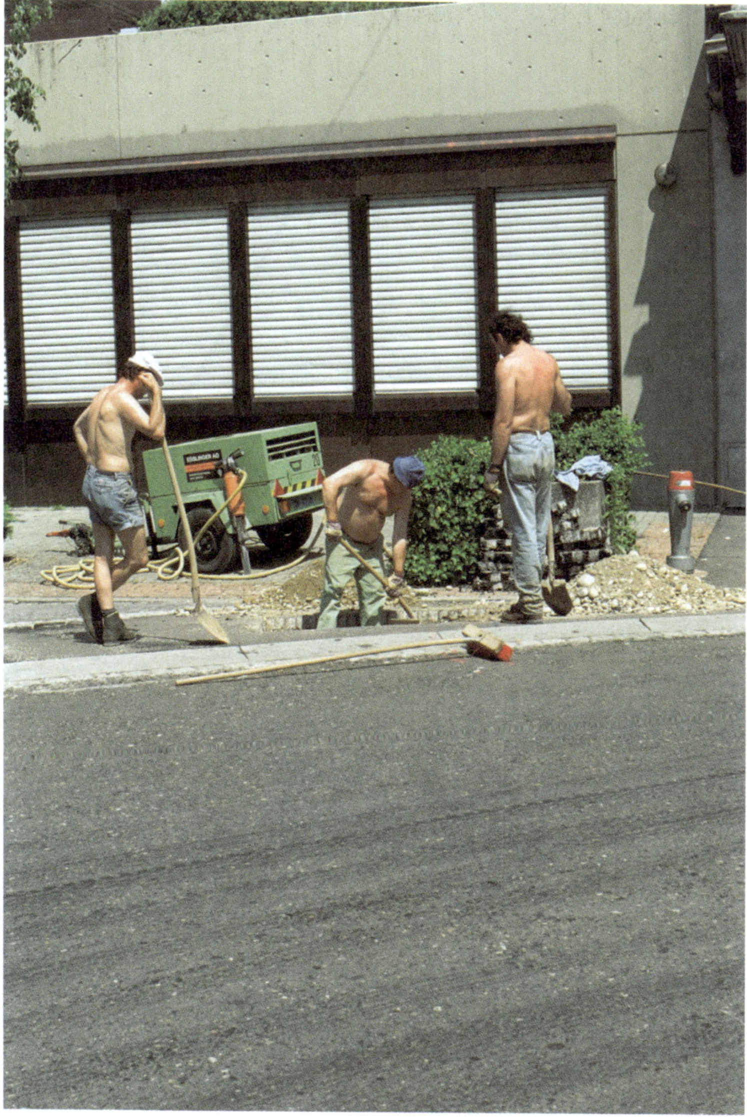

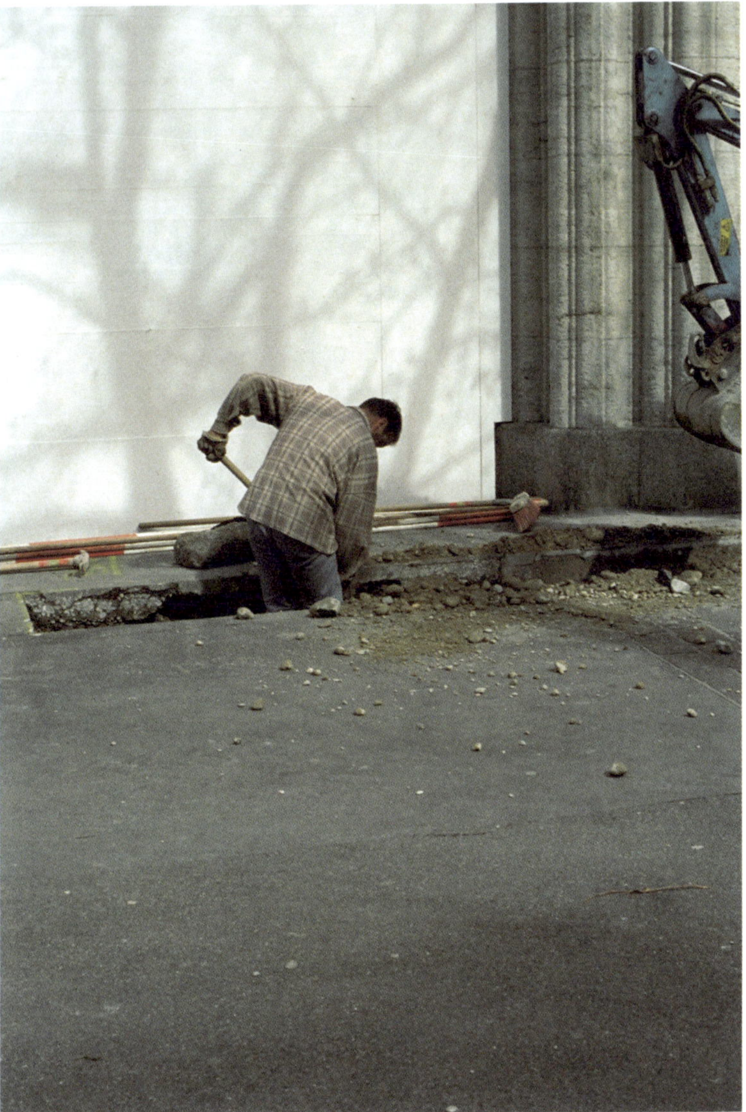

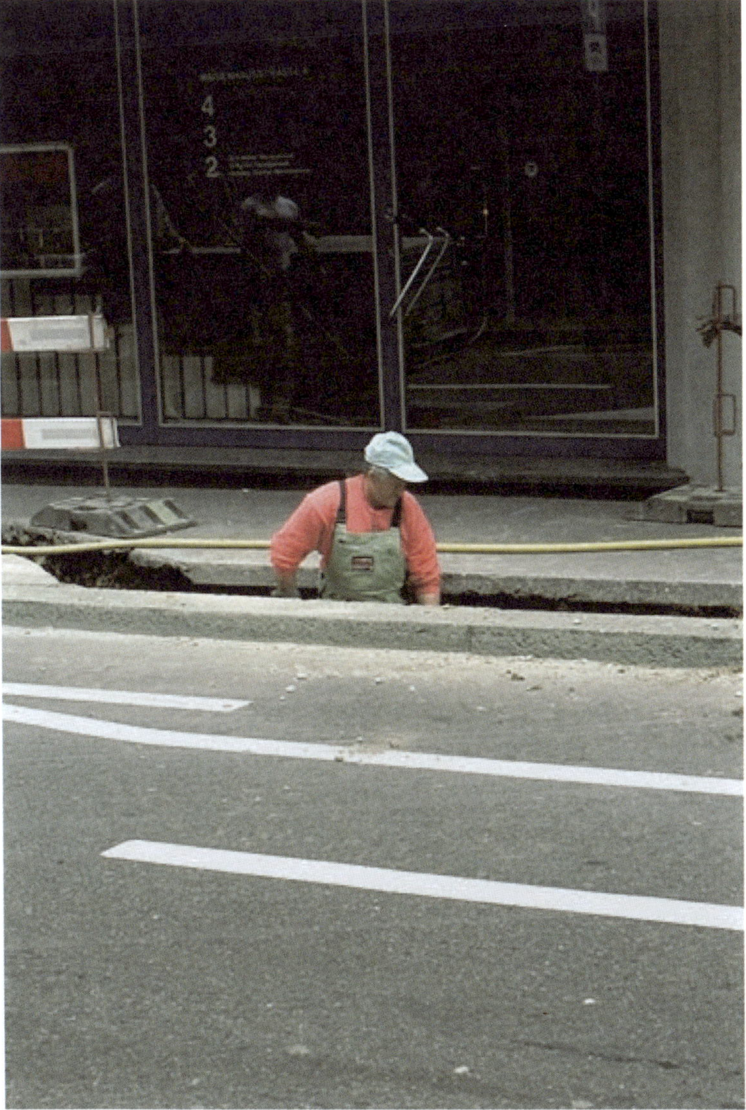

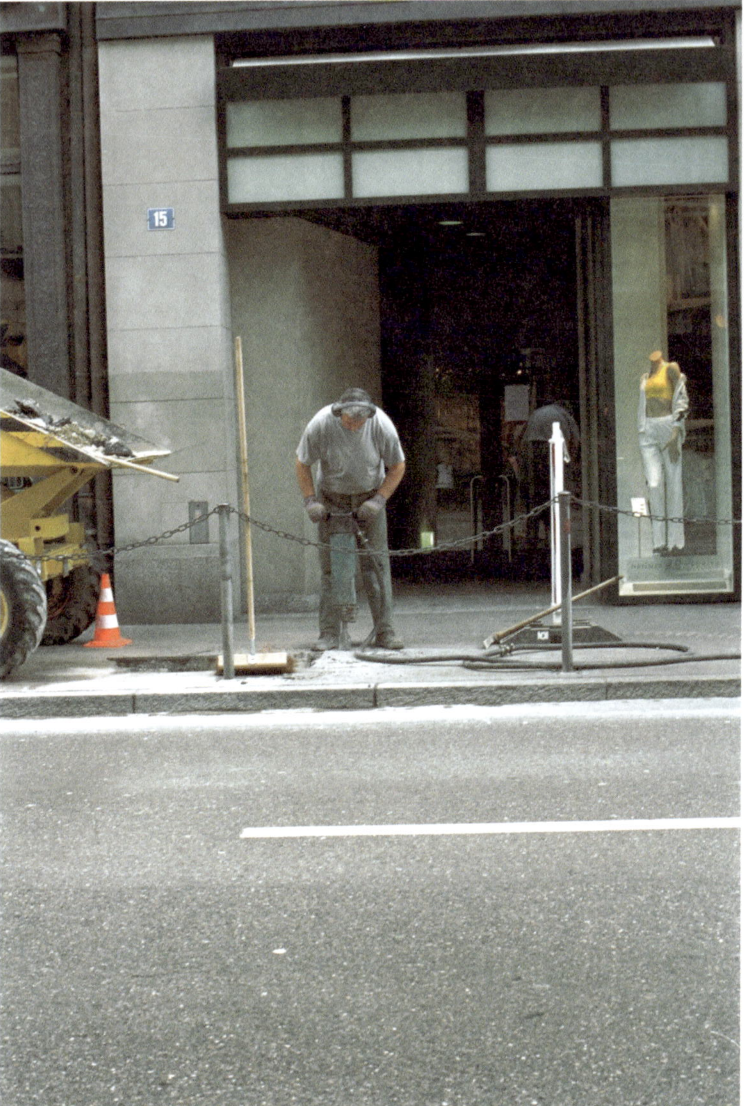

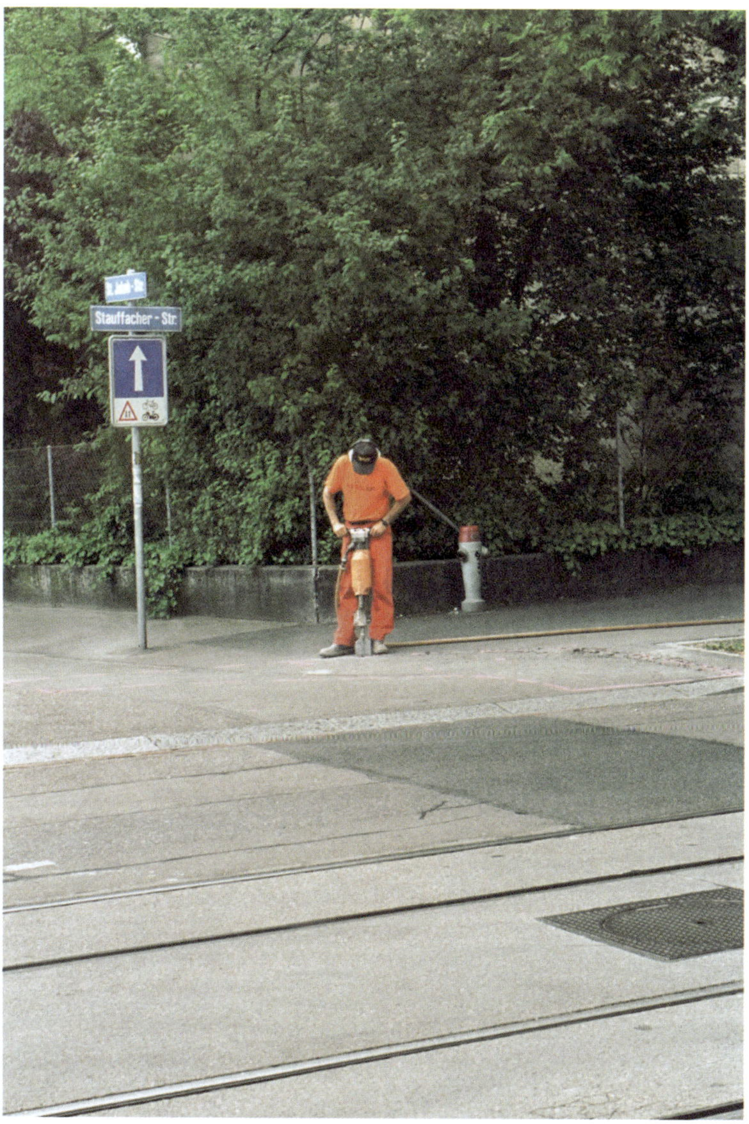
Stauffacher - Str.

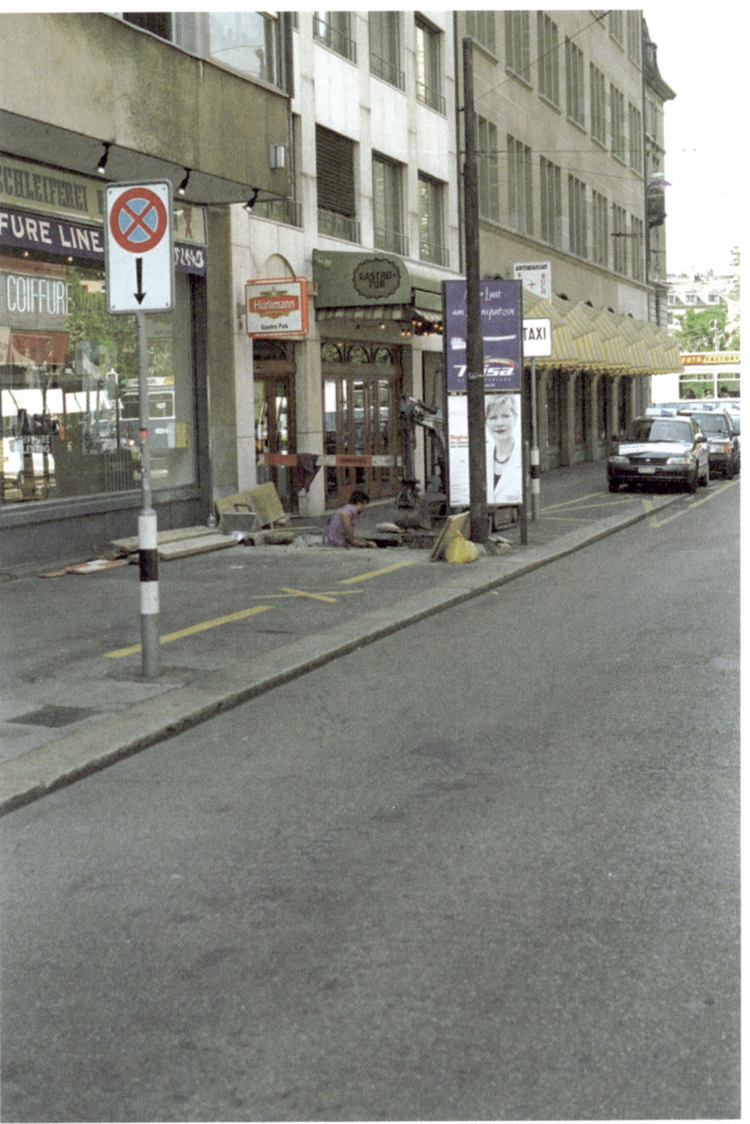
SCHLEIFEREI
FURE LINE
COIFFURE
COIFFURE LINE
Hürlimann
Gastro Pub
GASTRO-
PUB
ANTIQUARIAT
TAXI
FOTO FACTORY

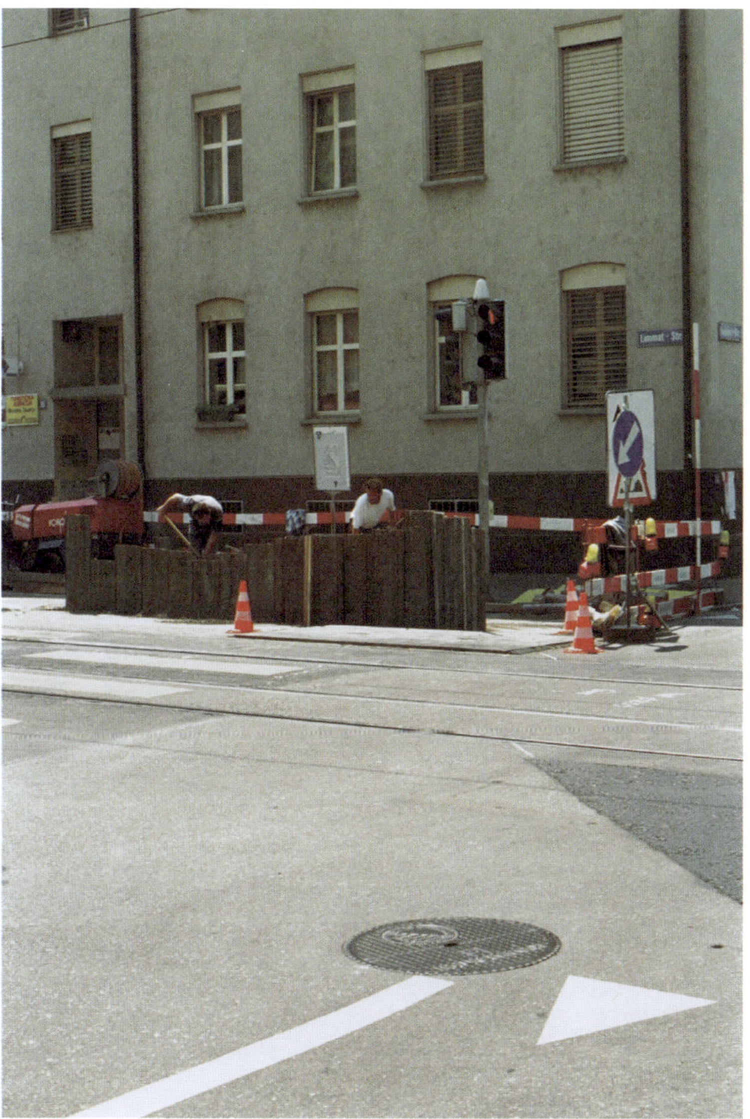

Limmat - Str

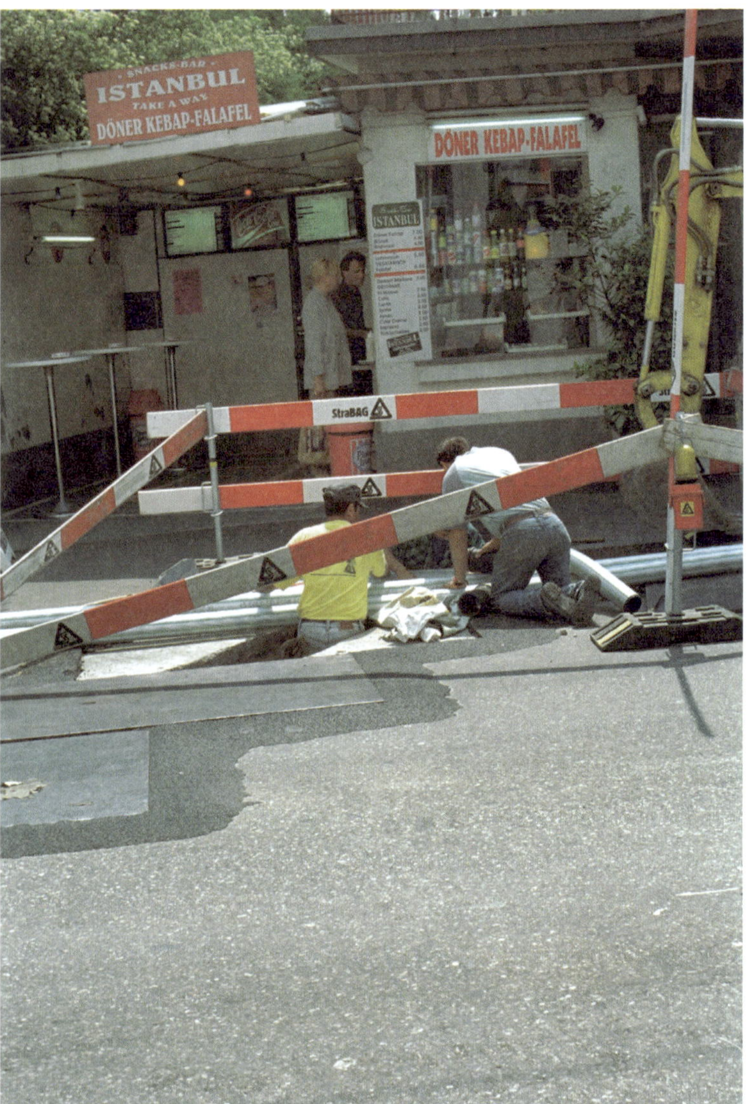

· SNACKS-BAR ·
ISTANBUL
TAKE A WAY
DÖNER KEBAP-FALAFEL
DÖNER KEBAP-FALAFEL
ISTANBUL
StraBAG

Inhalt und Form / Content and Form

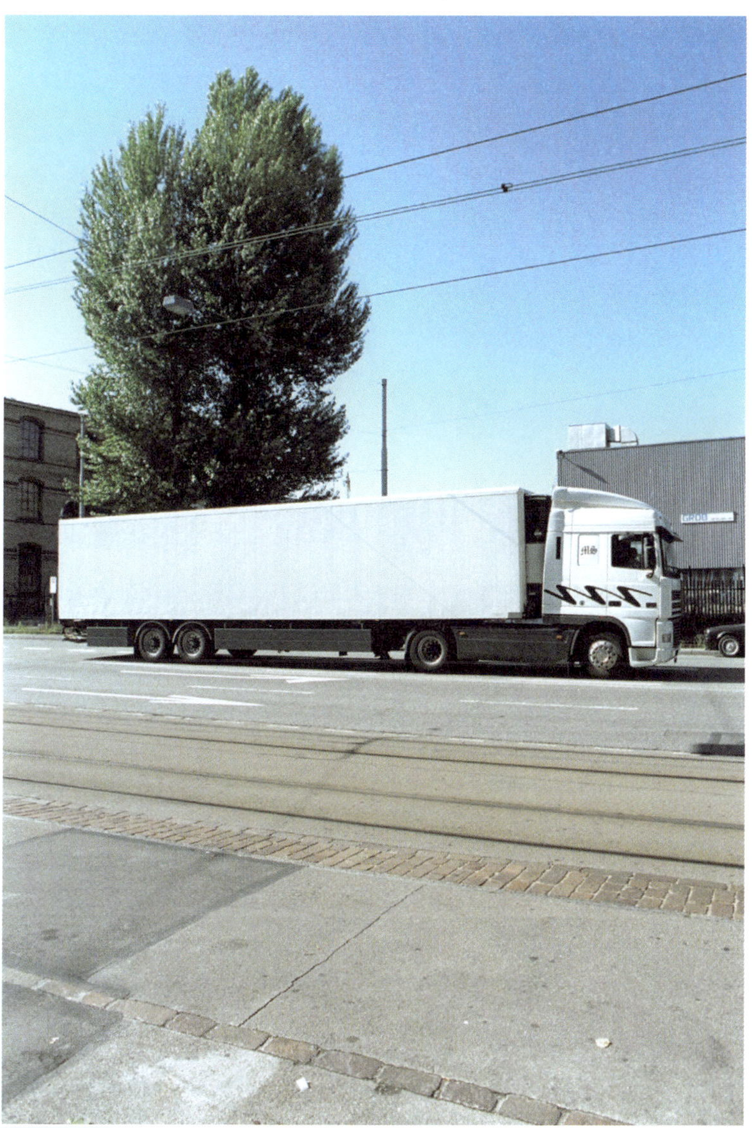

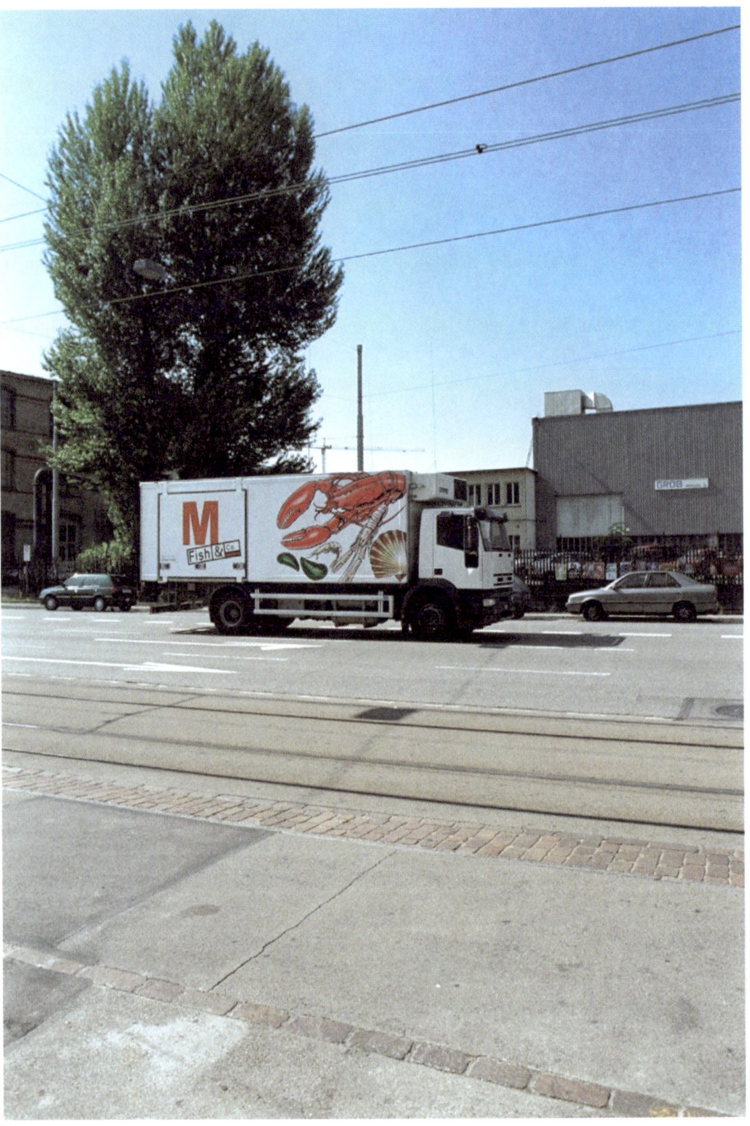
M
Fish & Co.
GROB

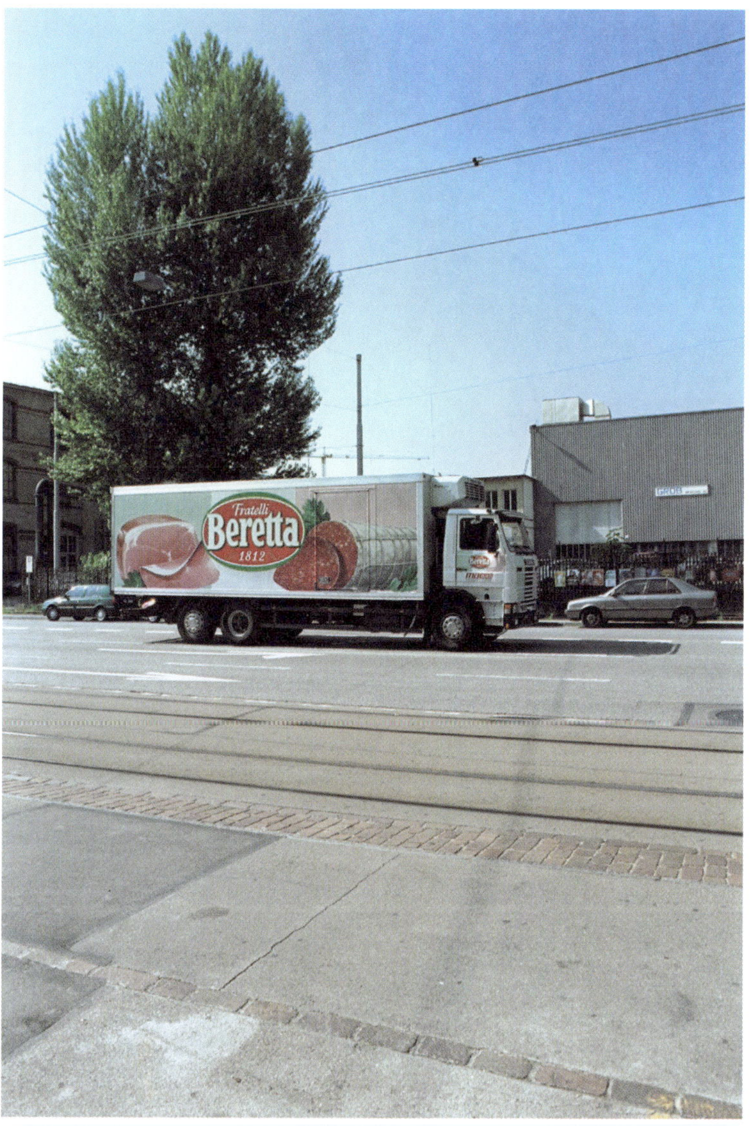
Fratelli
Beretta
1812

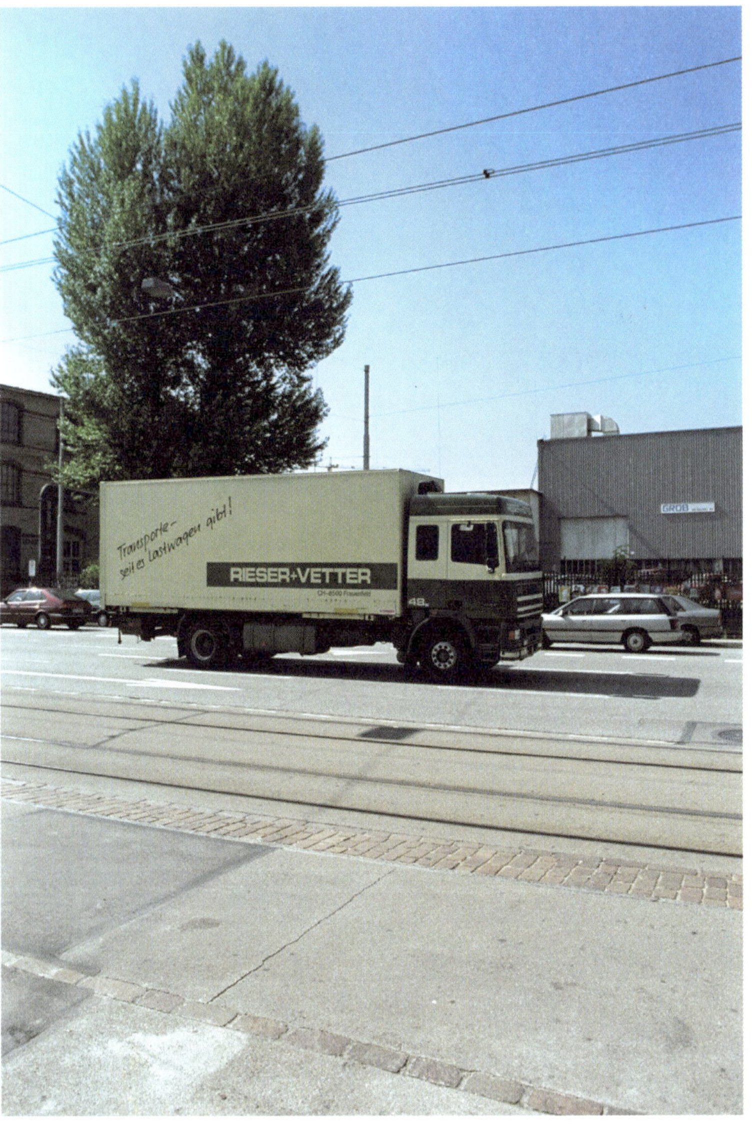

Transporte –
seit es Lastwagen gibt!
RIESER+VETTER
CH-8500 Frauenfeld
GROB

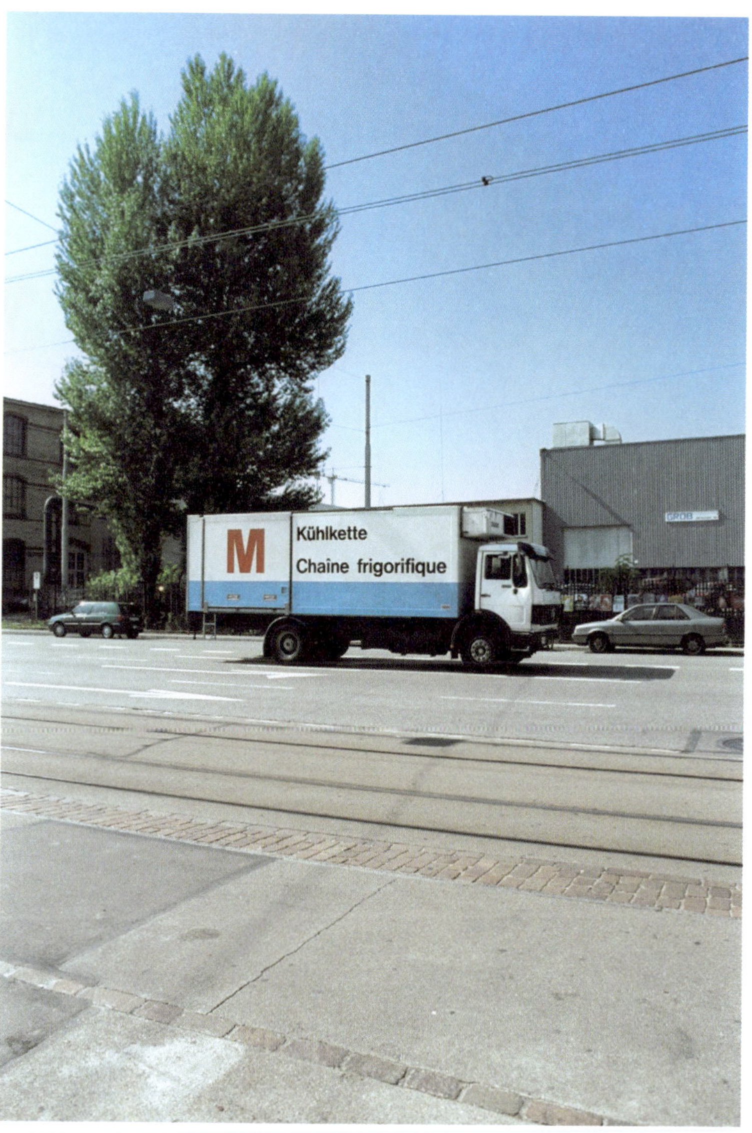

M
Kühlkette
Chaîne frigorifique
GROB

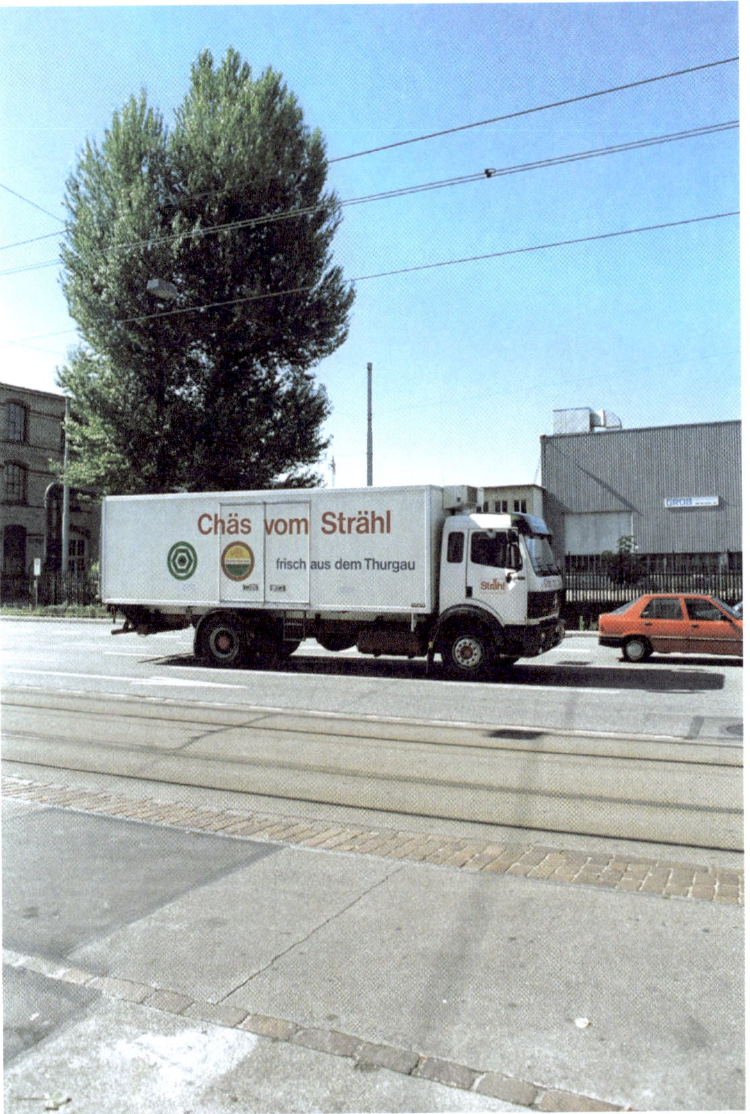
Chäs vom Strähl
frisch aus dem Thurgau
Strähl
GROB

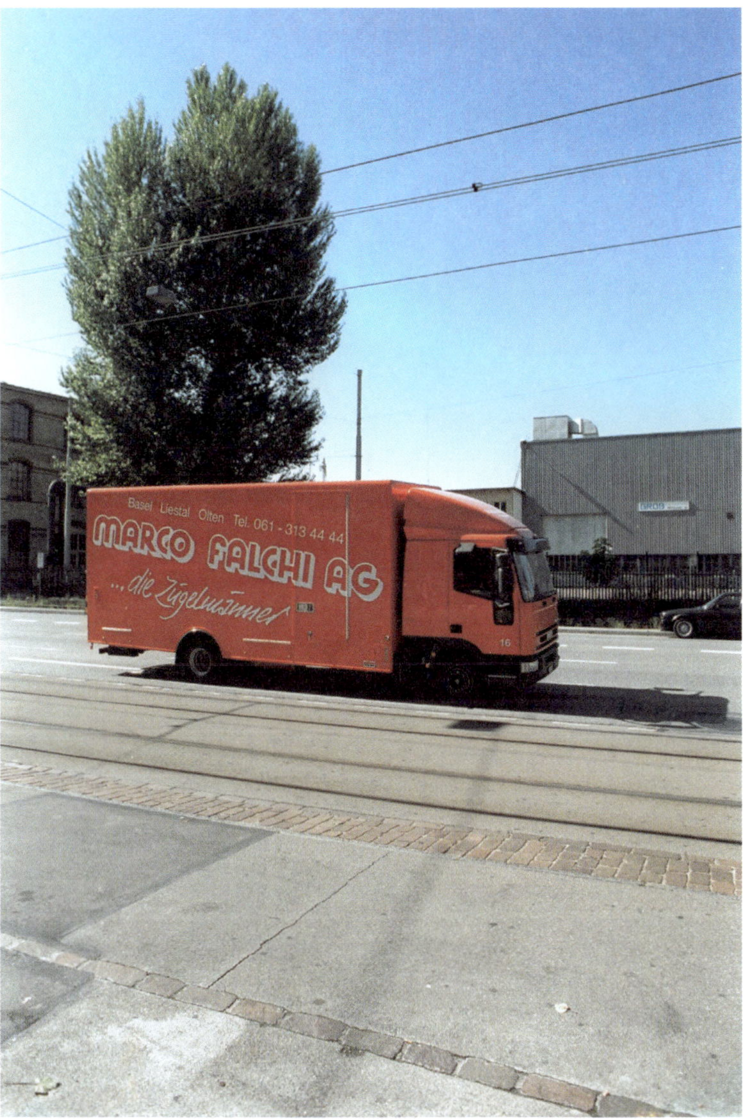
Basel Liestal Olten Tel. 061 - 313 44 44
MARCO FALCHI AG
...die Zügelmänner
16

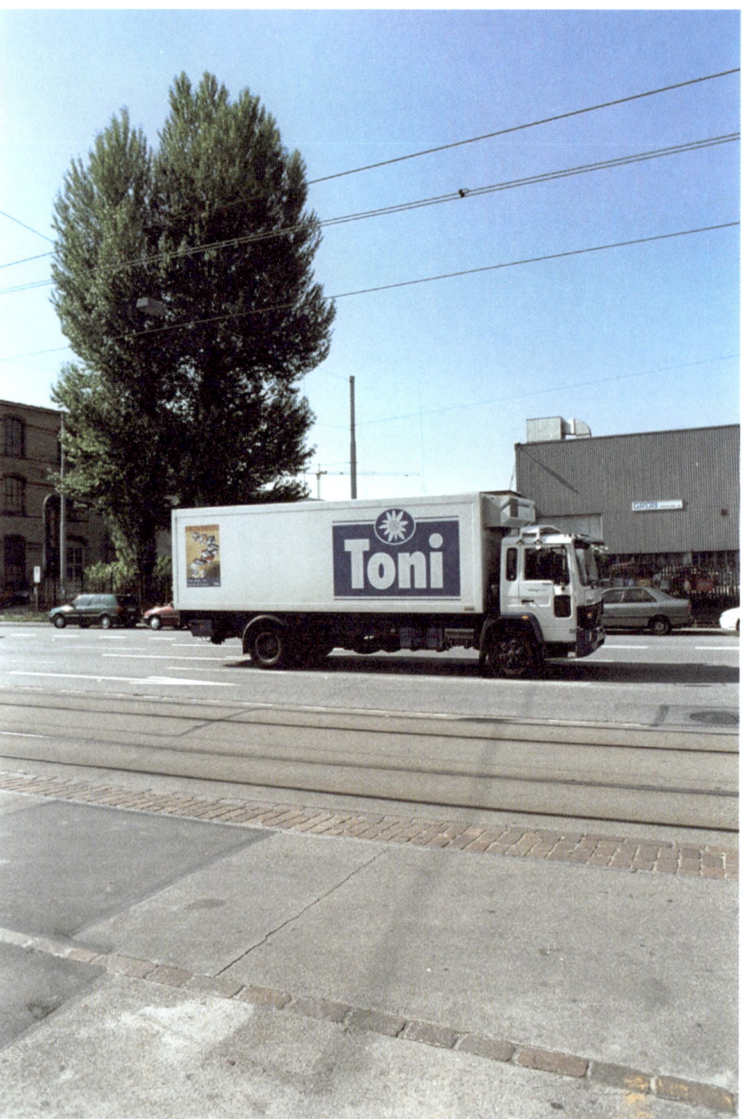

Toni
GROSS

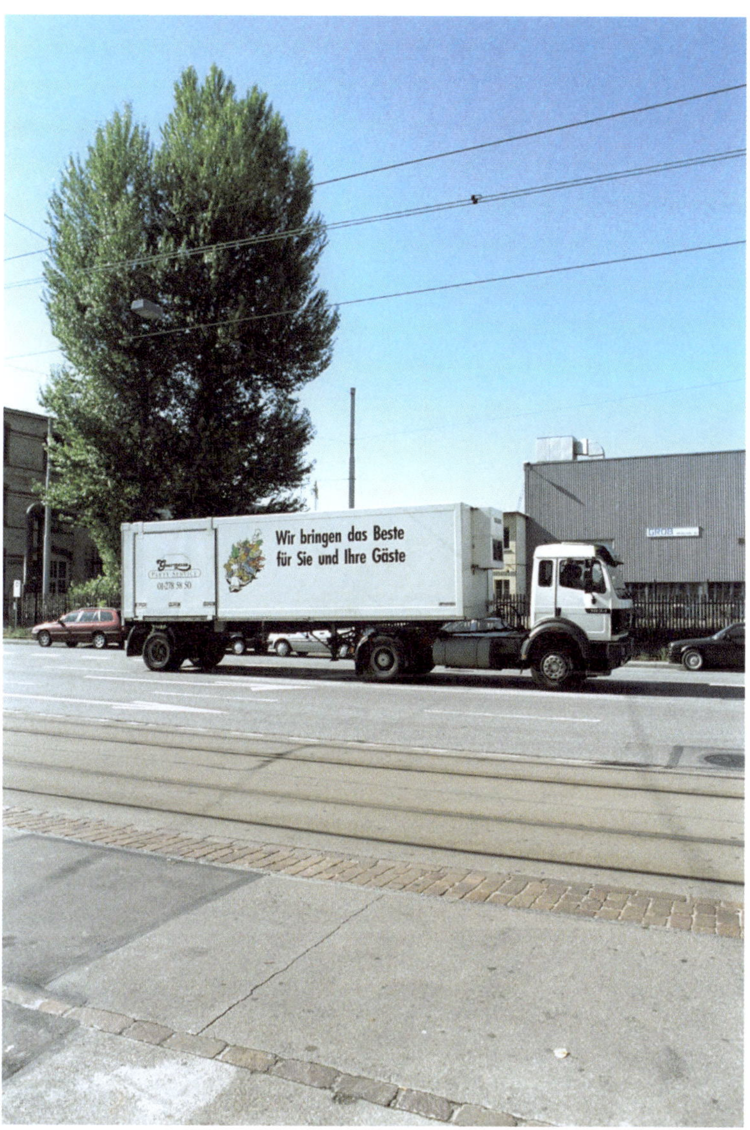
Party Service
01-278 98 50
Wir bringen das Beste
für Sie und Ihre Gäste

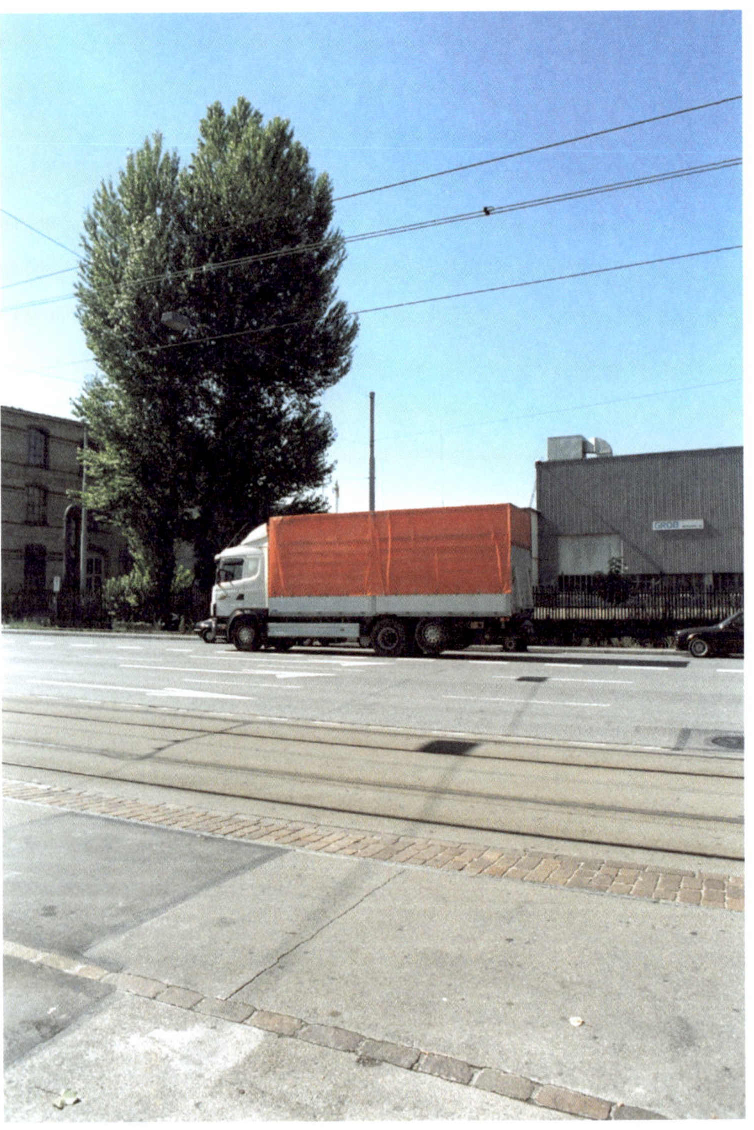
GROB

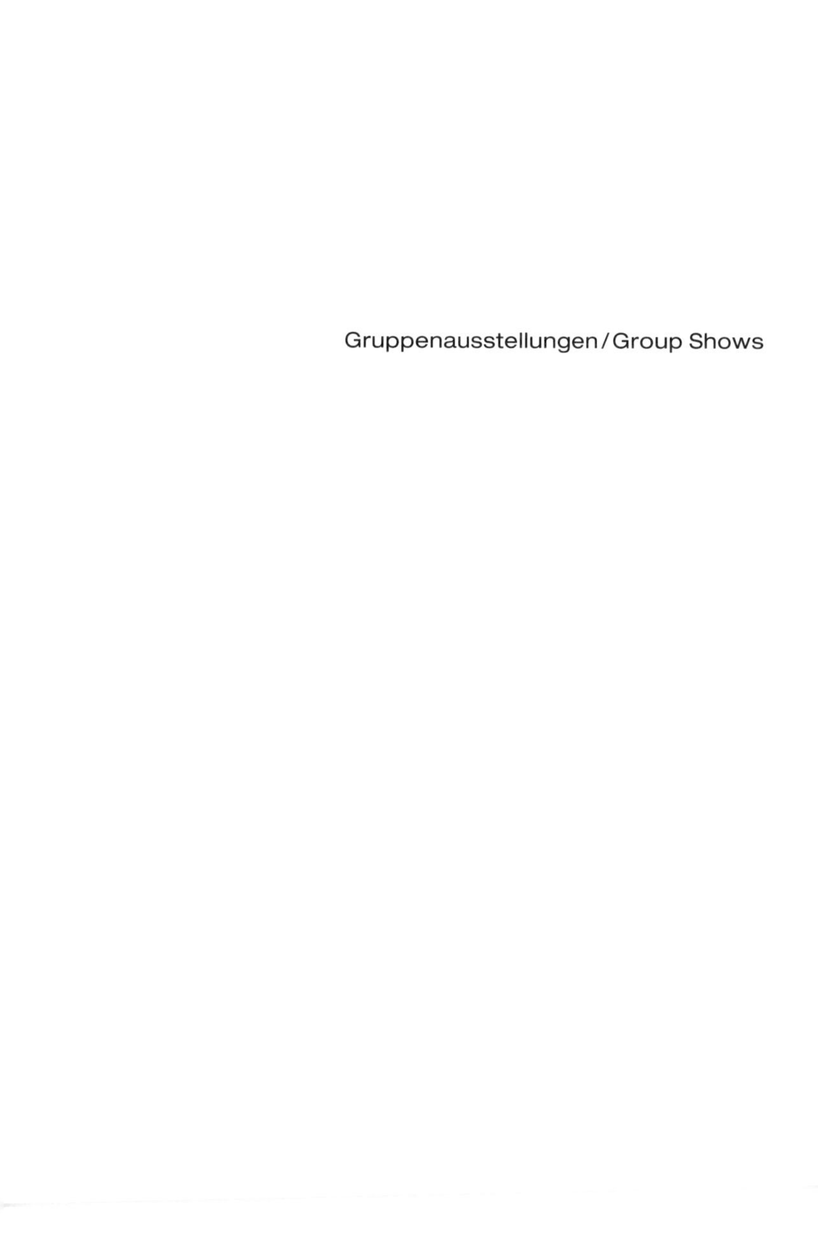

Gruppenausstellungen / Group Shows

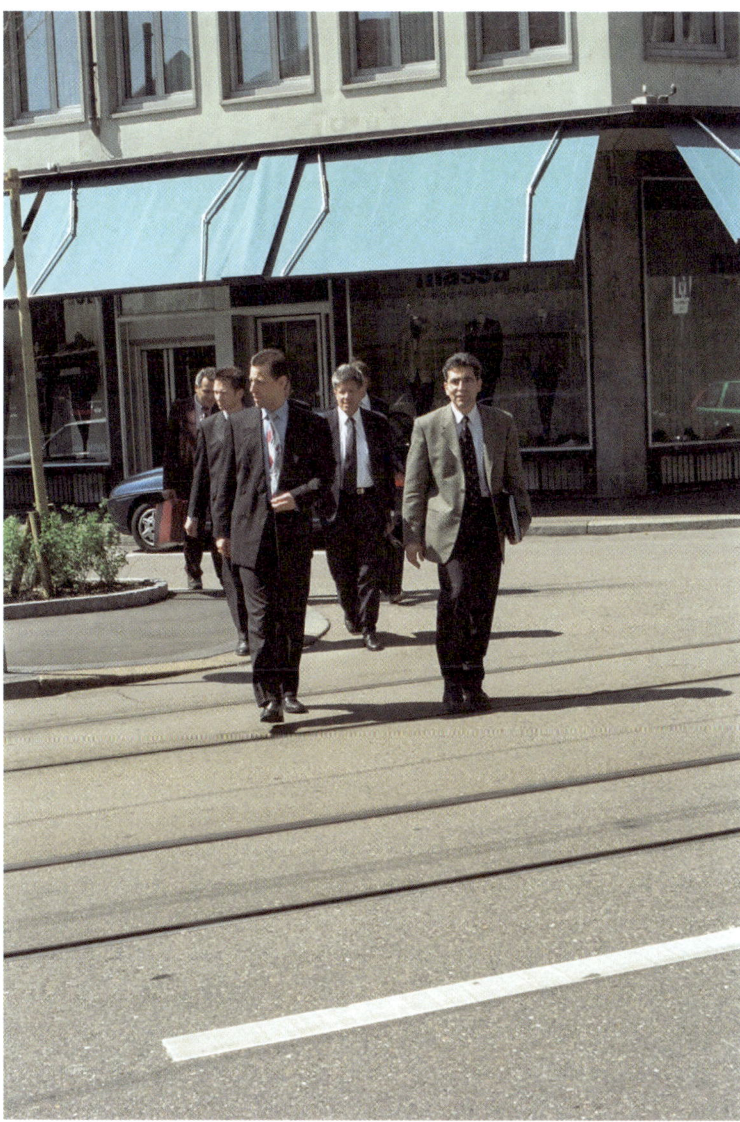

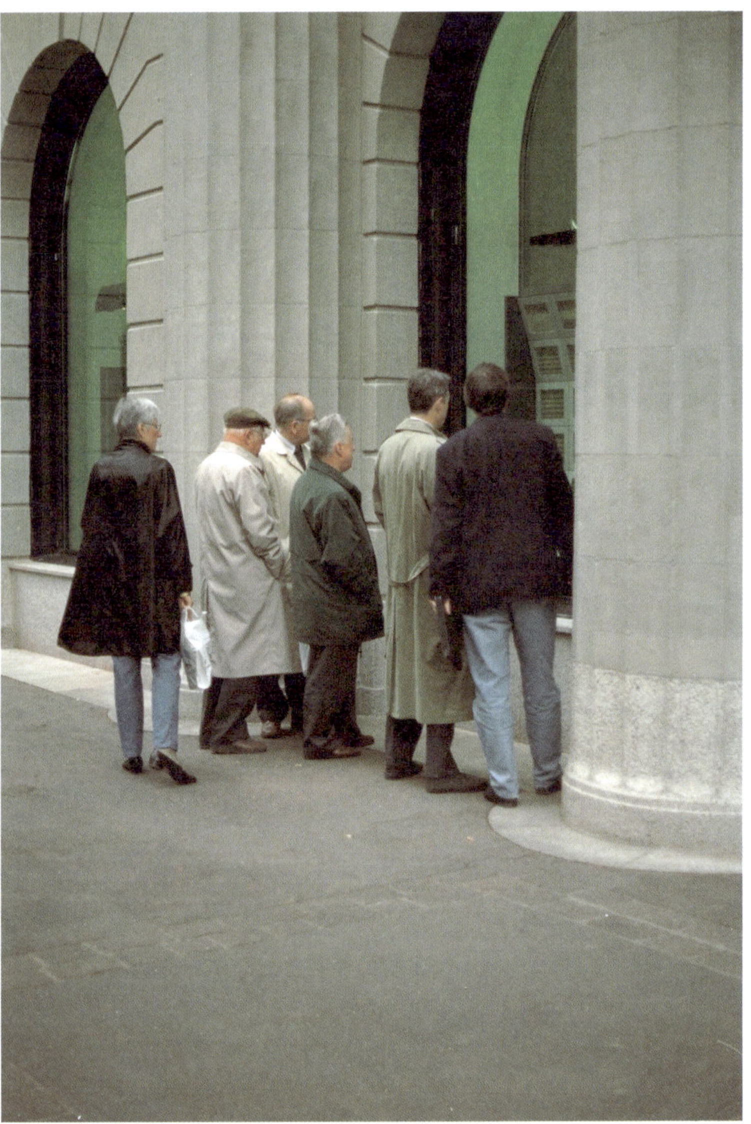

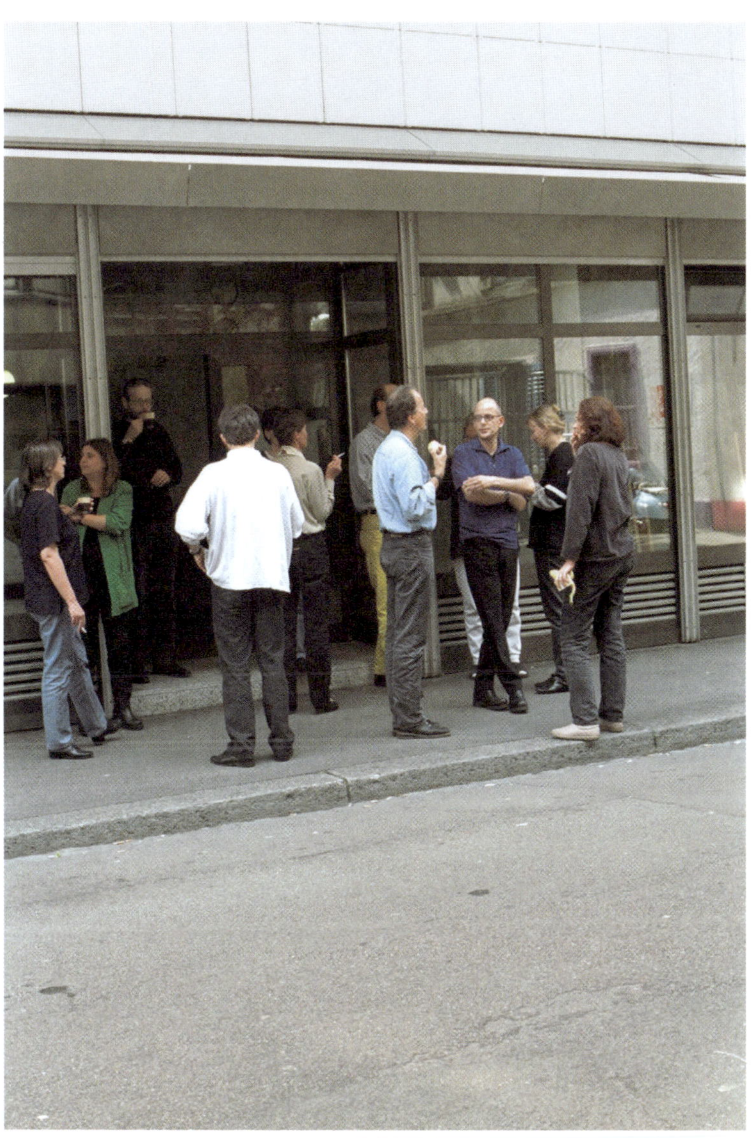

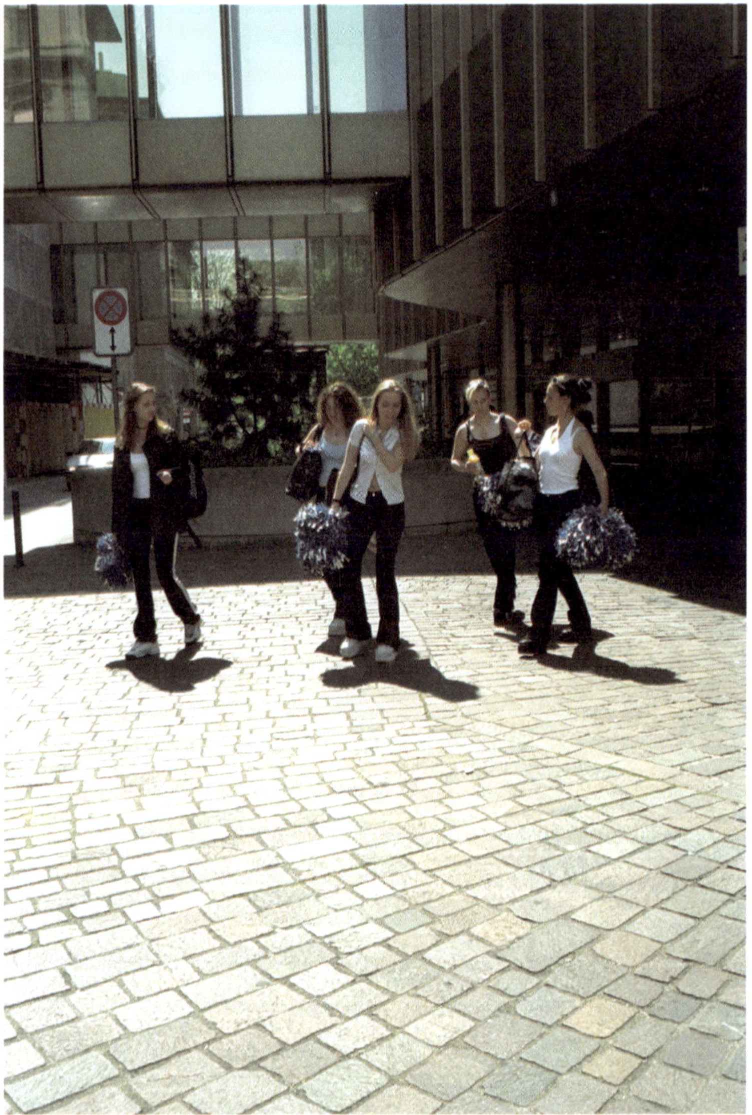

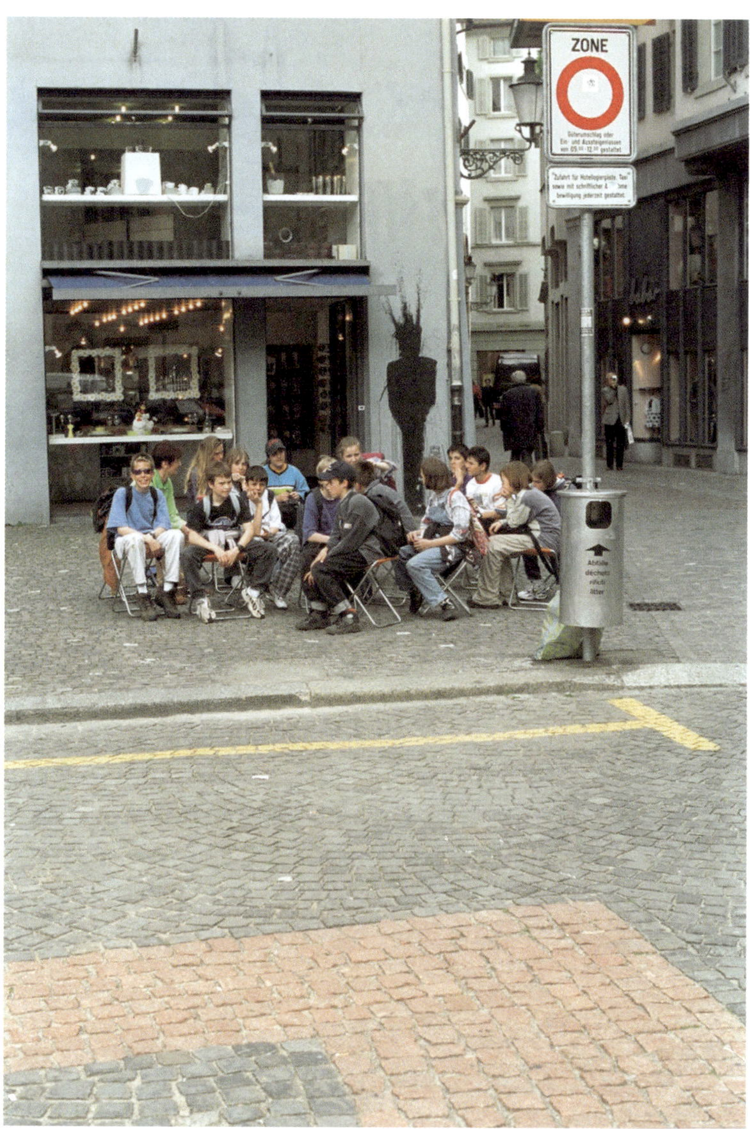

ZONE
Güterumschlag oder
Ein- und Aussteigenlassen
von 05.00 -12.00 gestattet
Zufahrt für Hotellogiergäste, Taxi
sowie mit schriftlicher &... one
bewilligung jederzeit gestattet.
Abfälle
déchets
rifiuti
litter

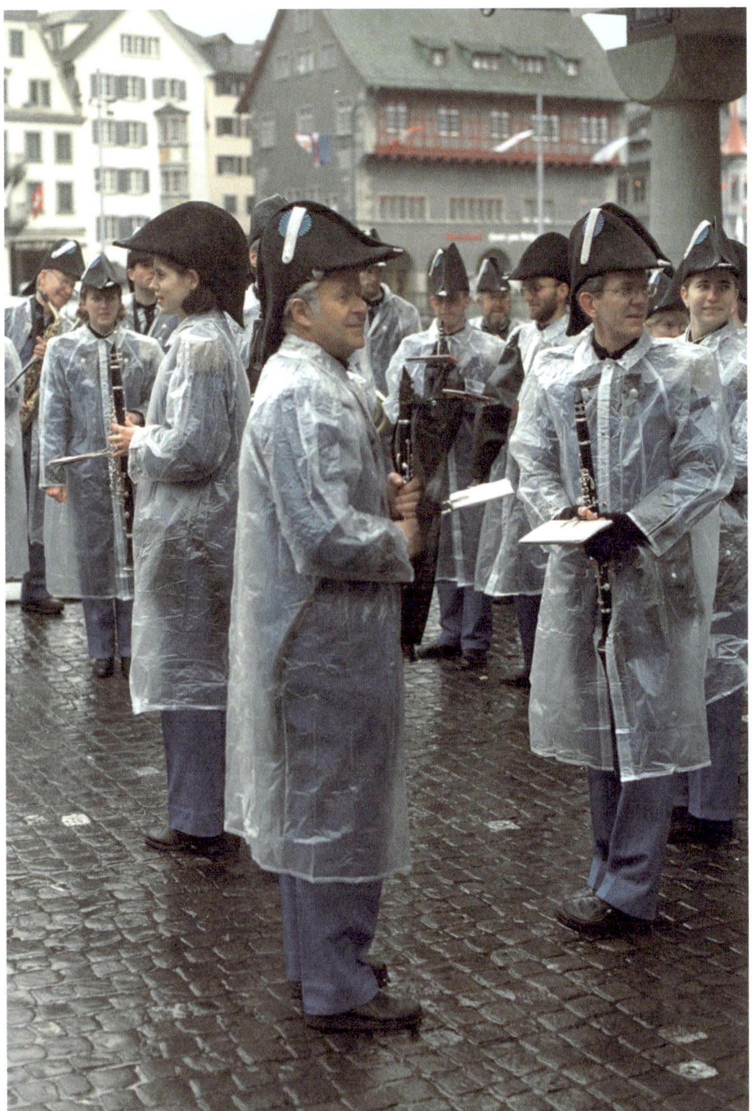

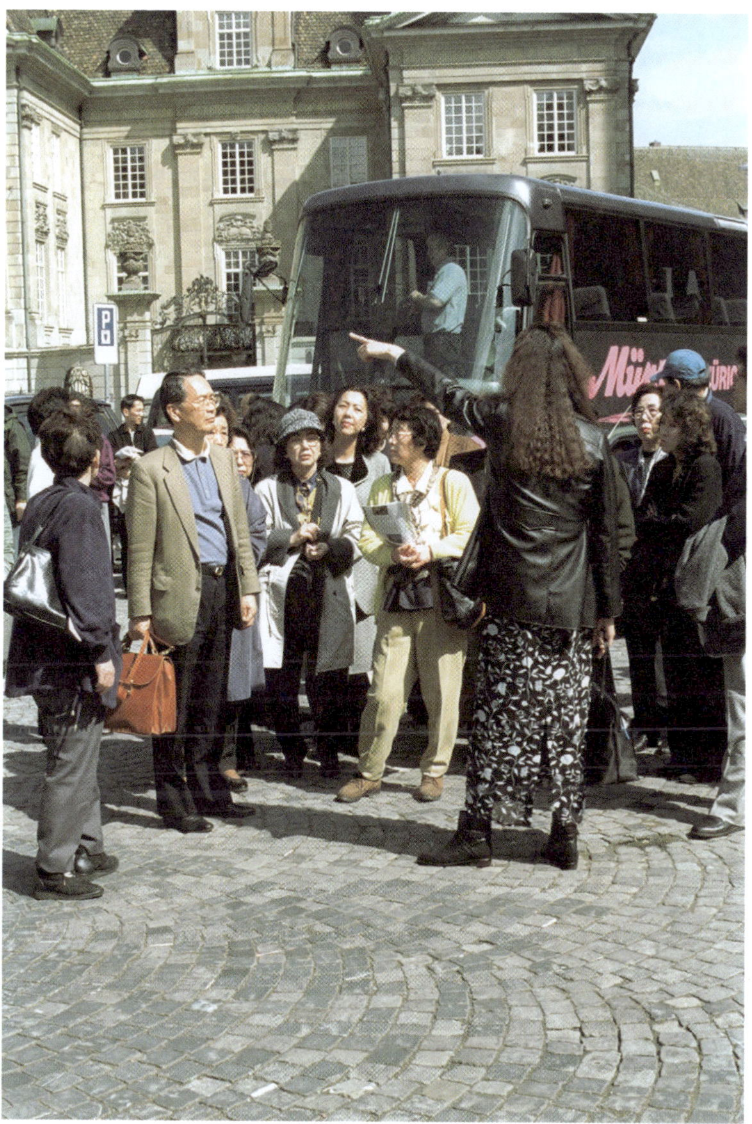

Mü
ürio

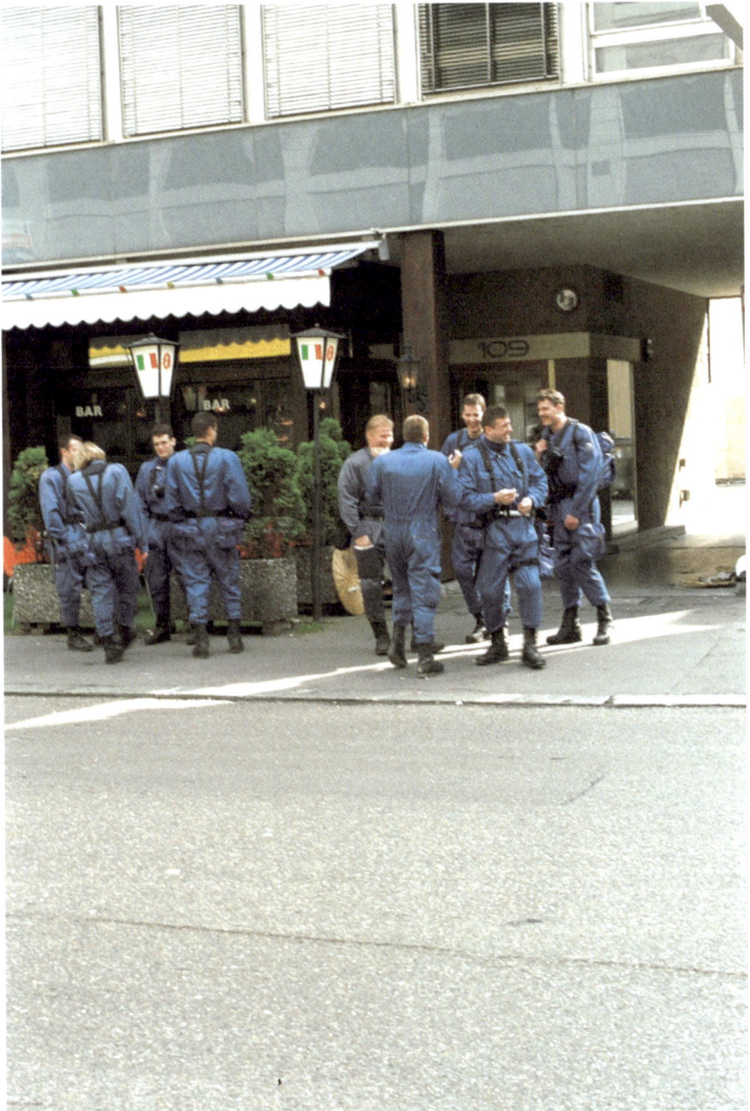

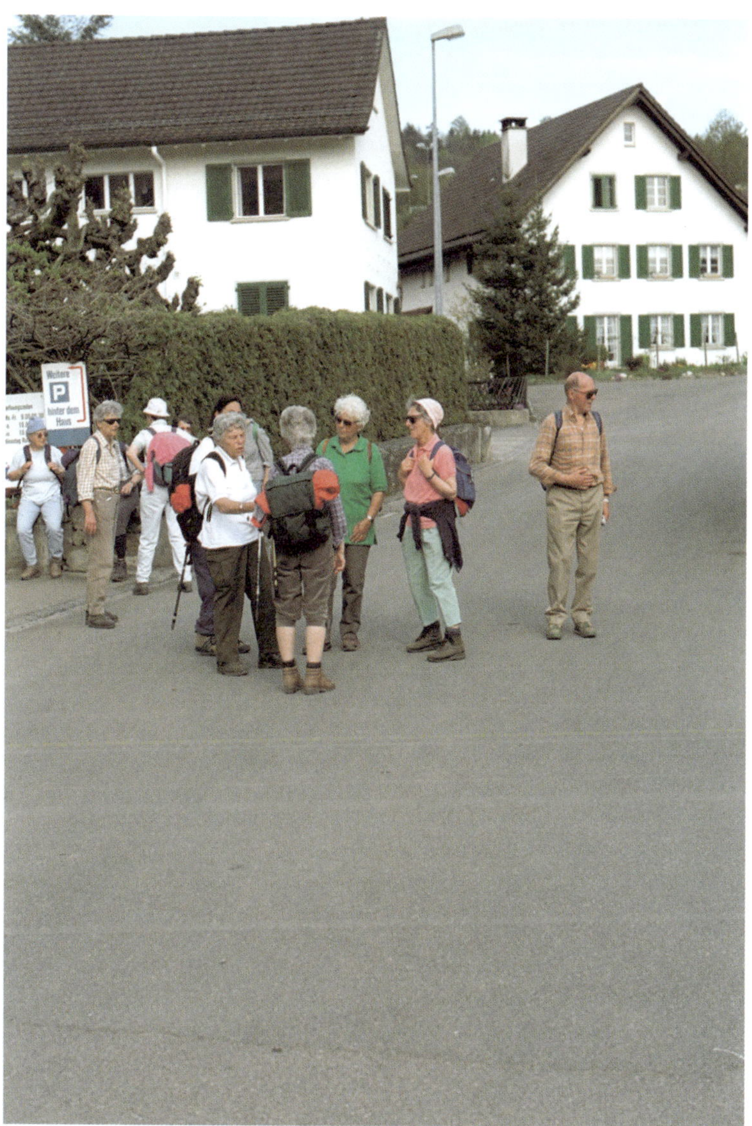
Weitere
P
hinter dem
Haus

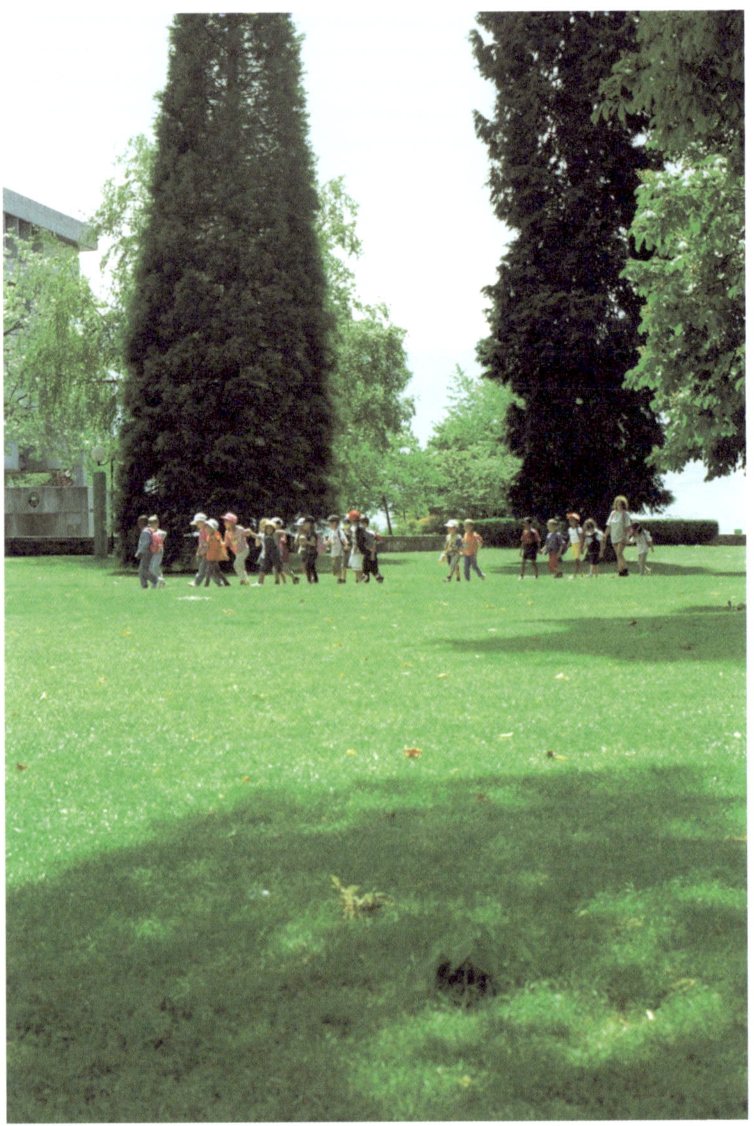

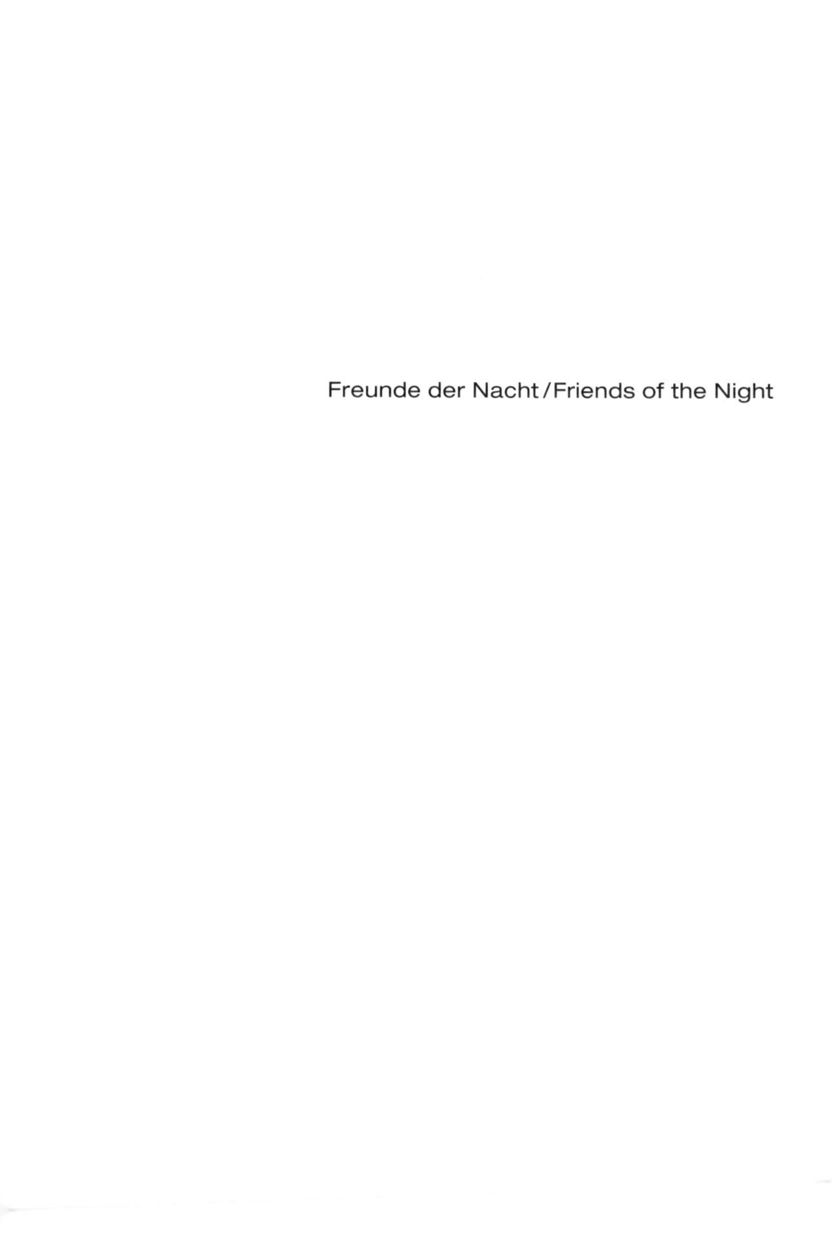

Freunde der Nacht / Friends of the Night

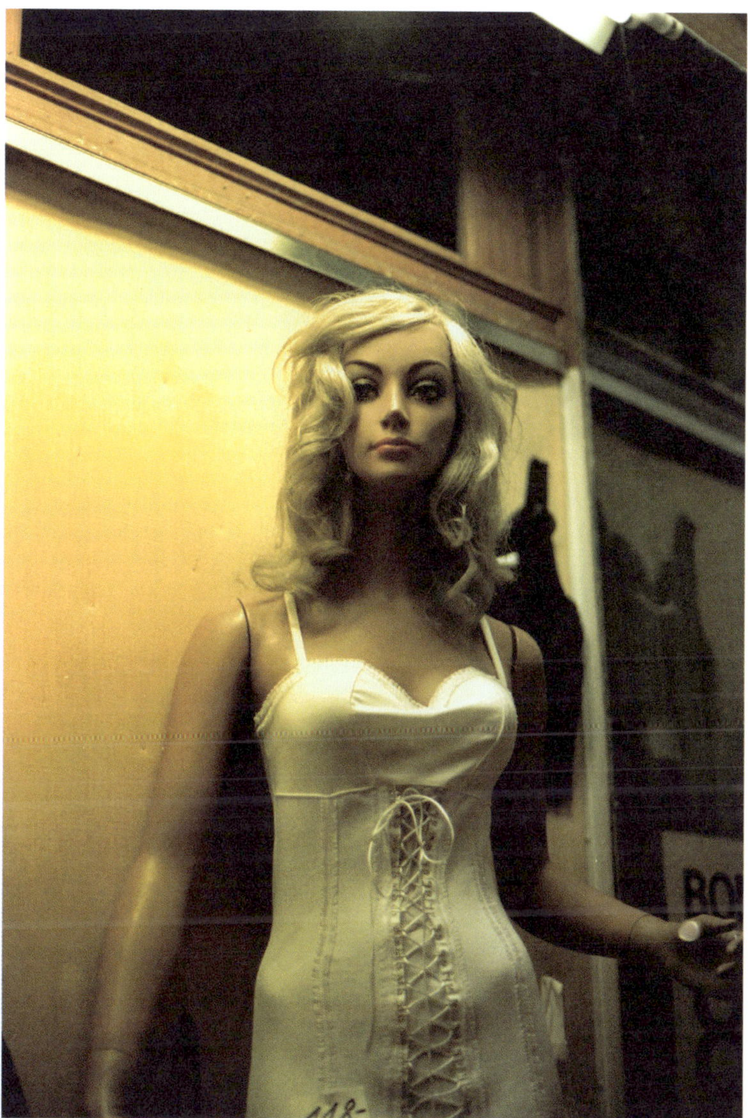
BO
118-

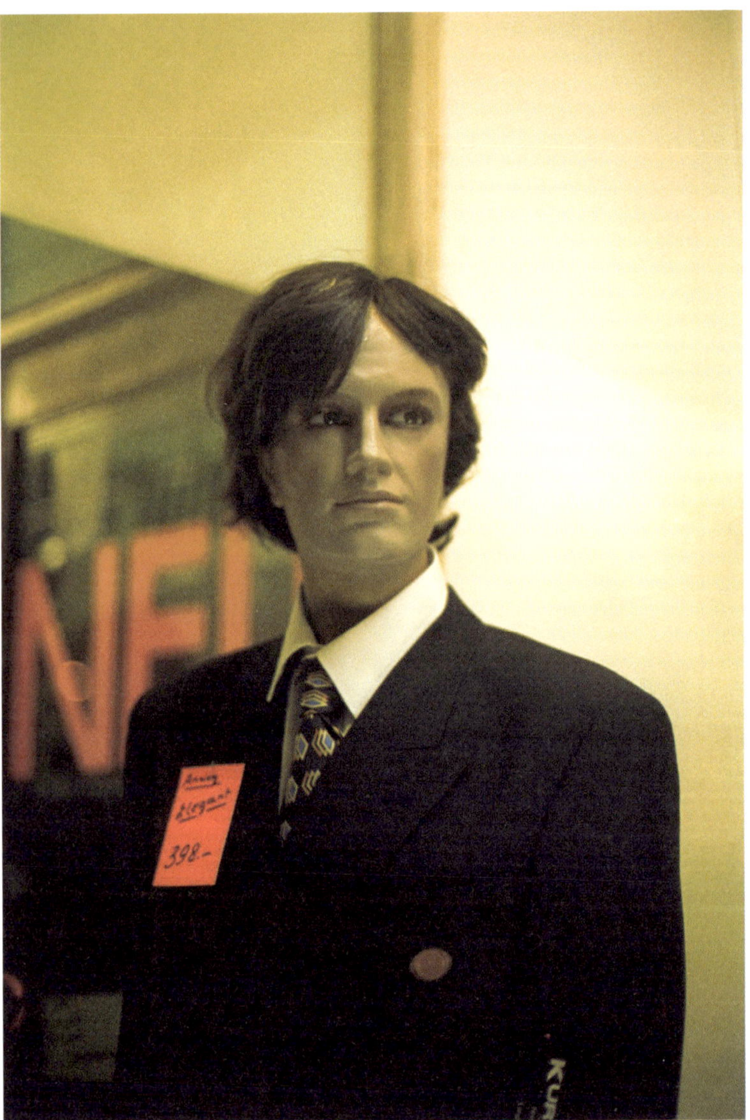

NFI
398.-

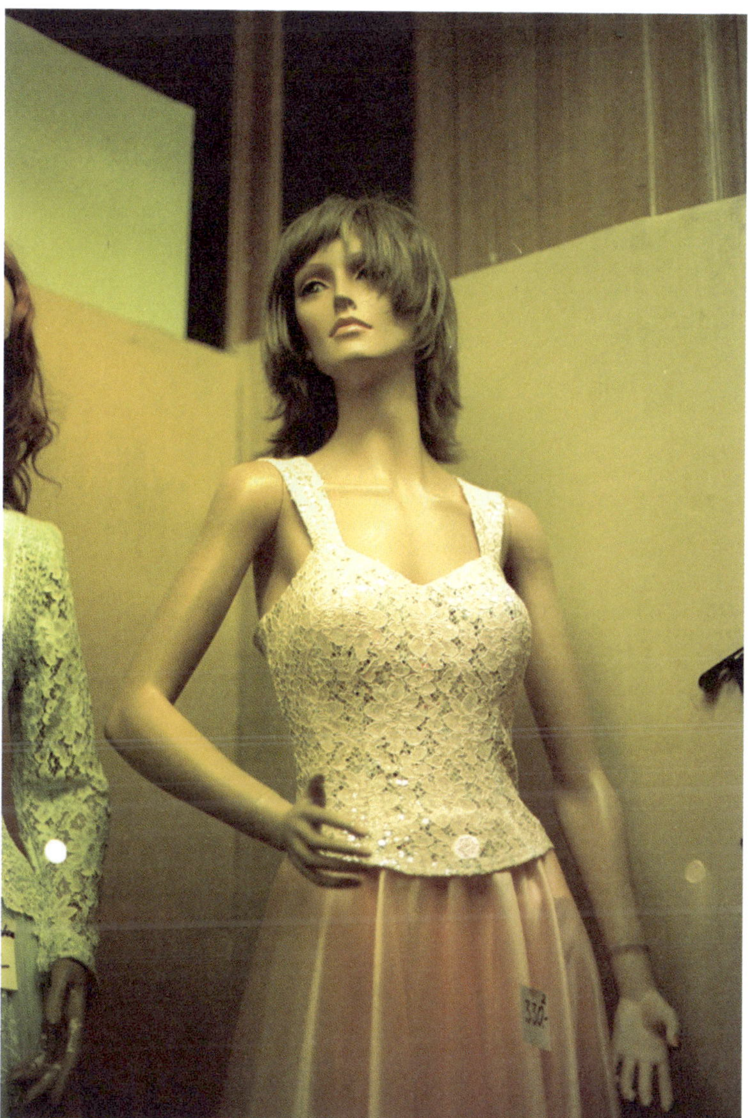

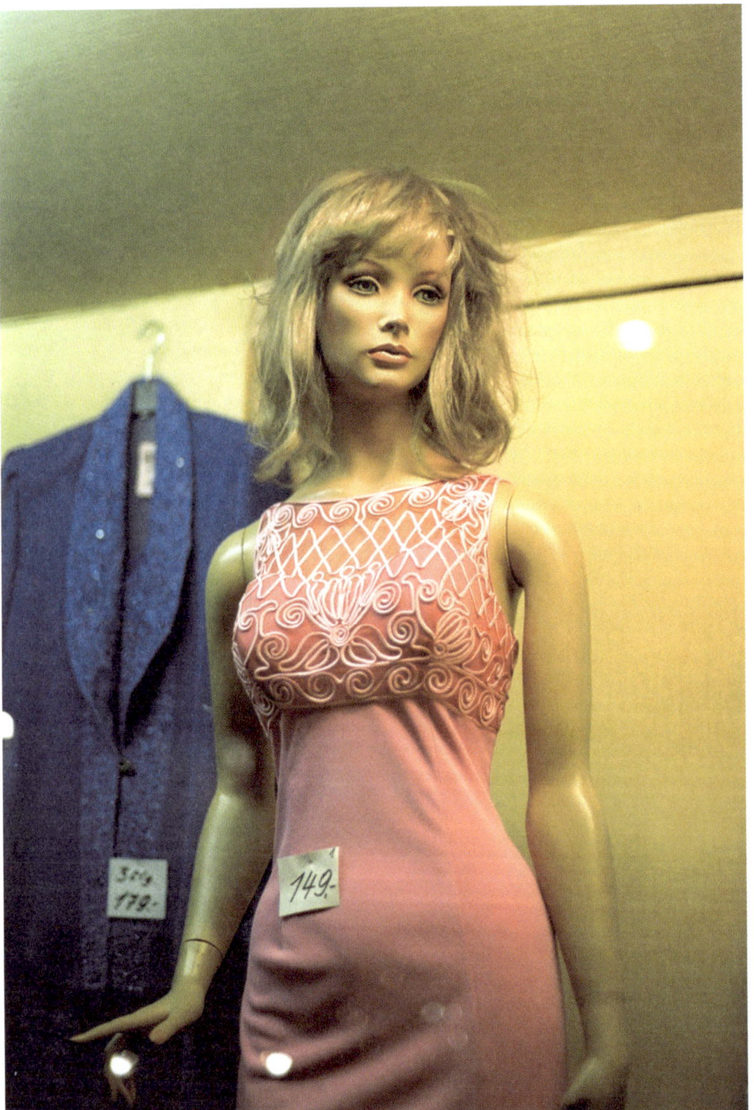
149.-
179.-

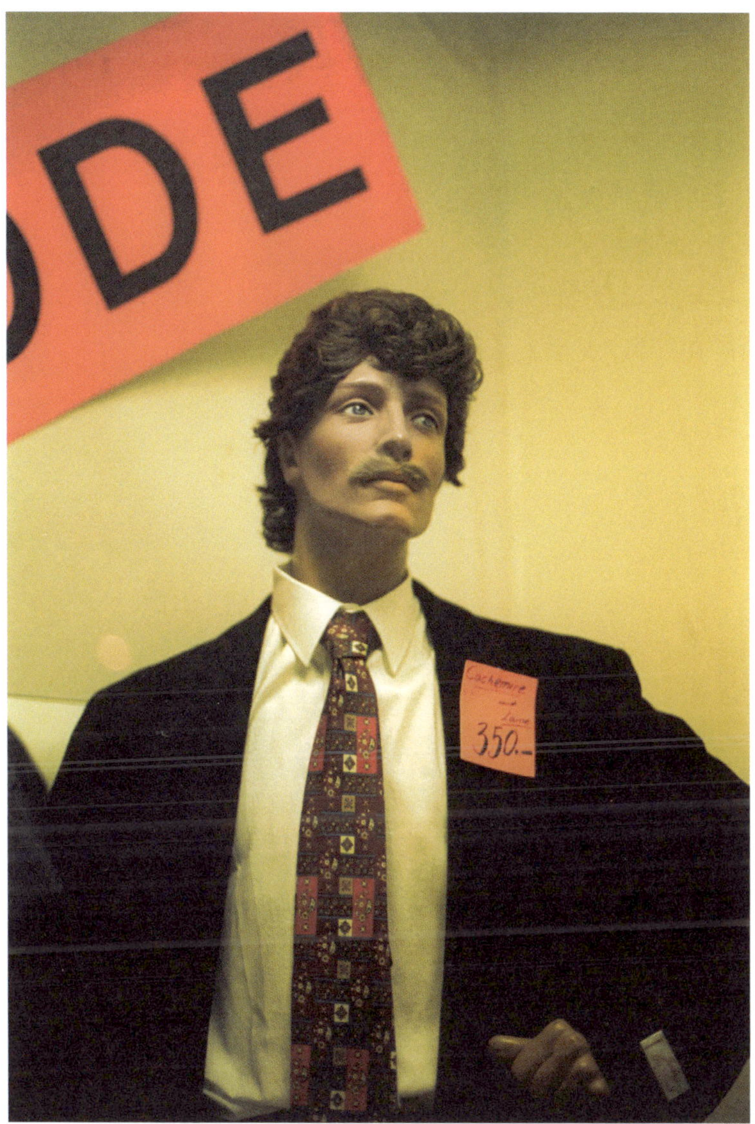

ODE
Cachemire
Lana
350.—

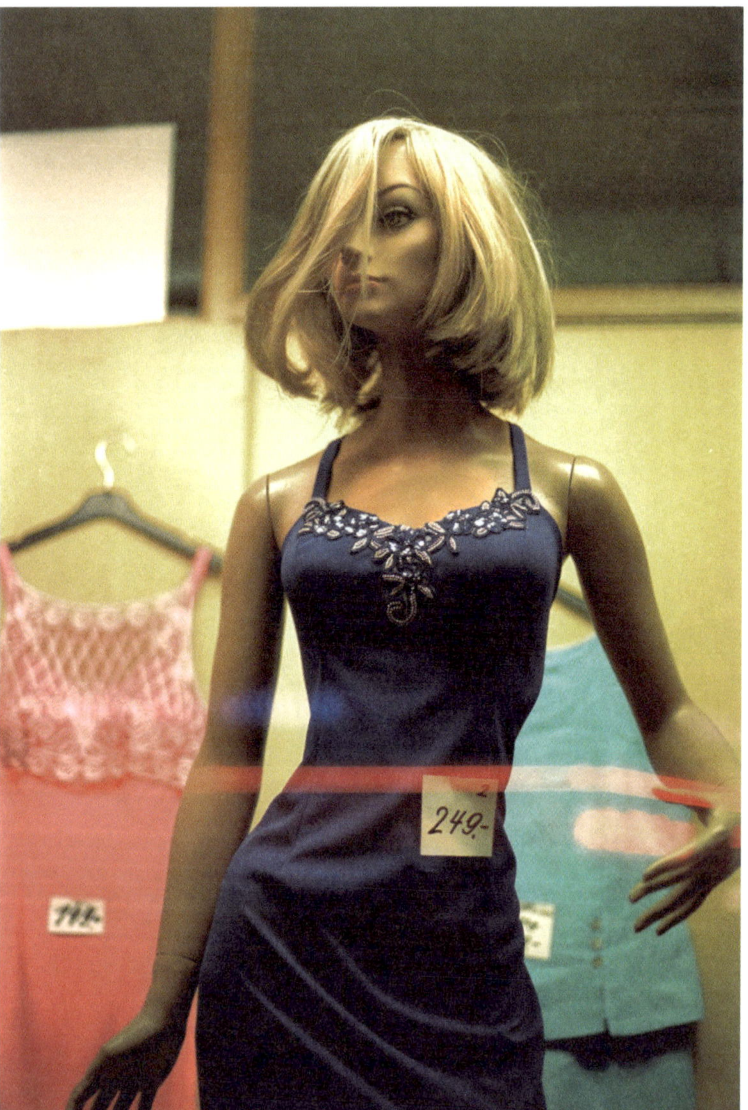

249.-

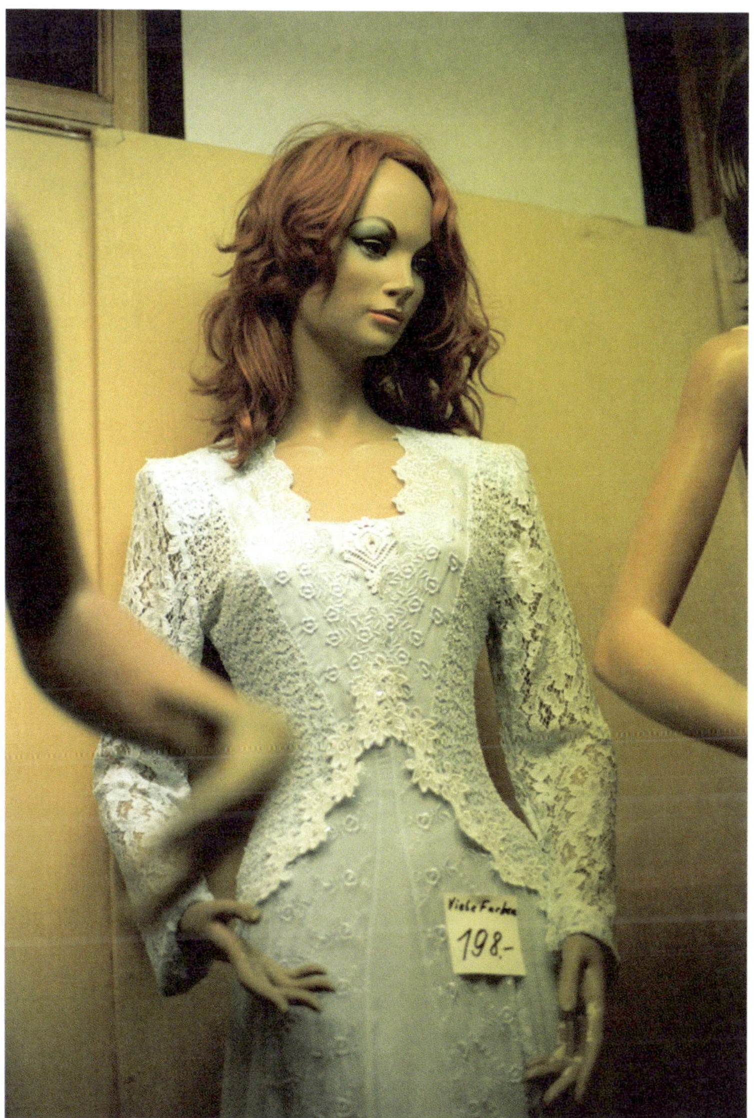
Viele Farben
198.-

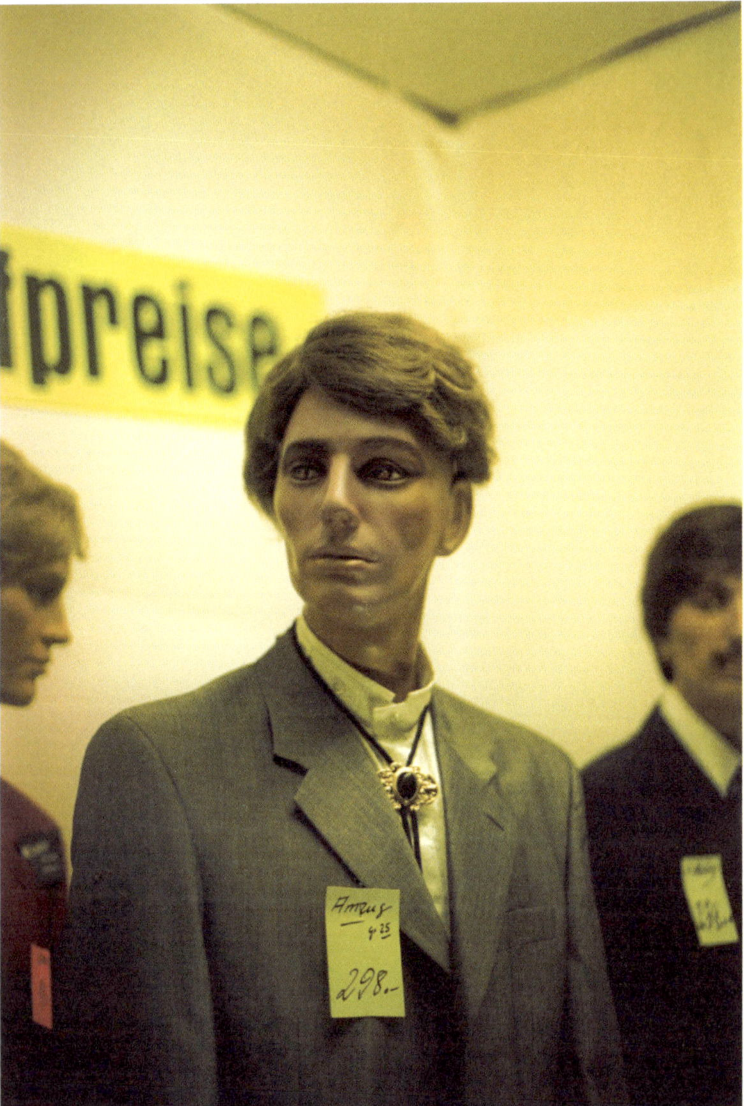

preise
Amrus
4·25
298.-

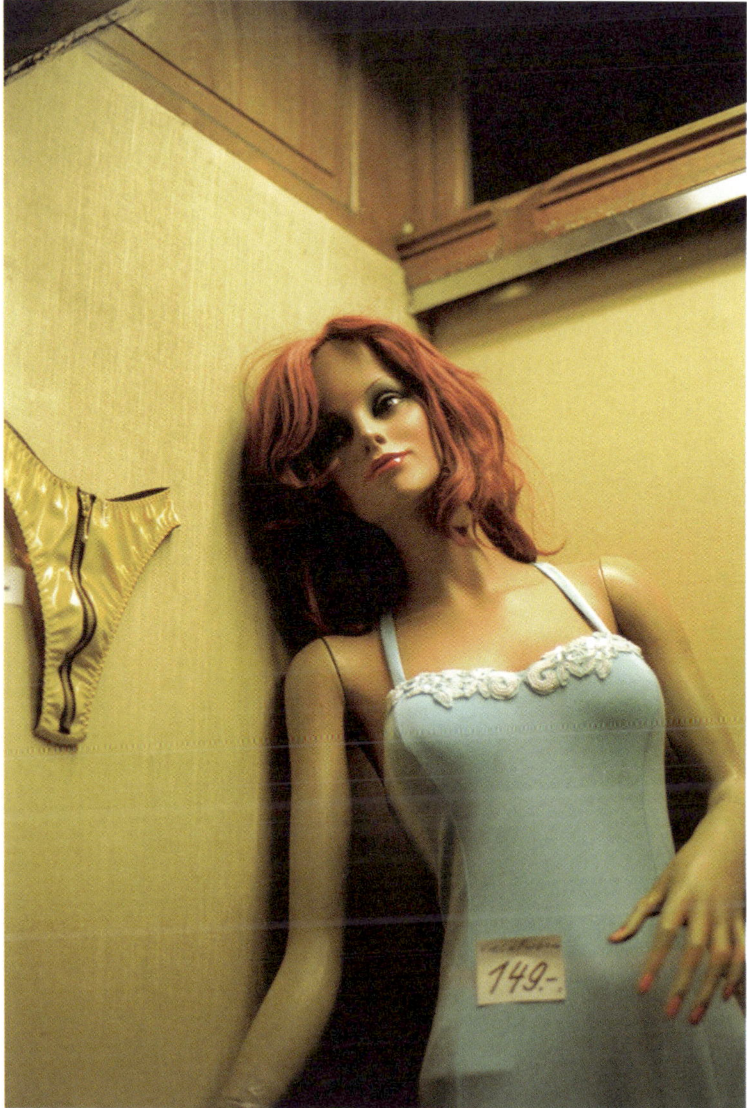

149.-

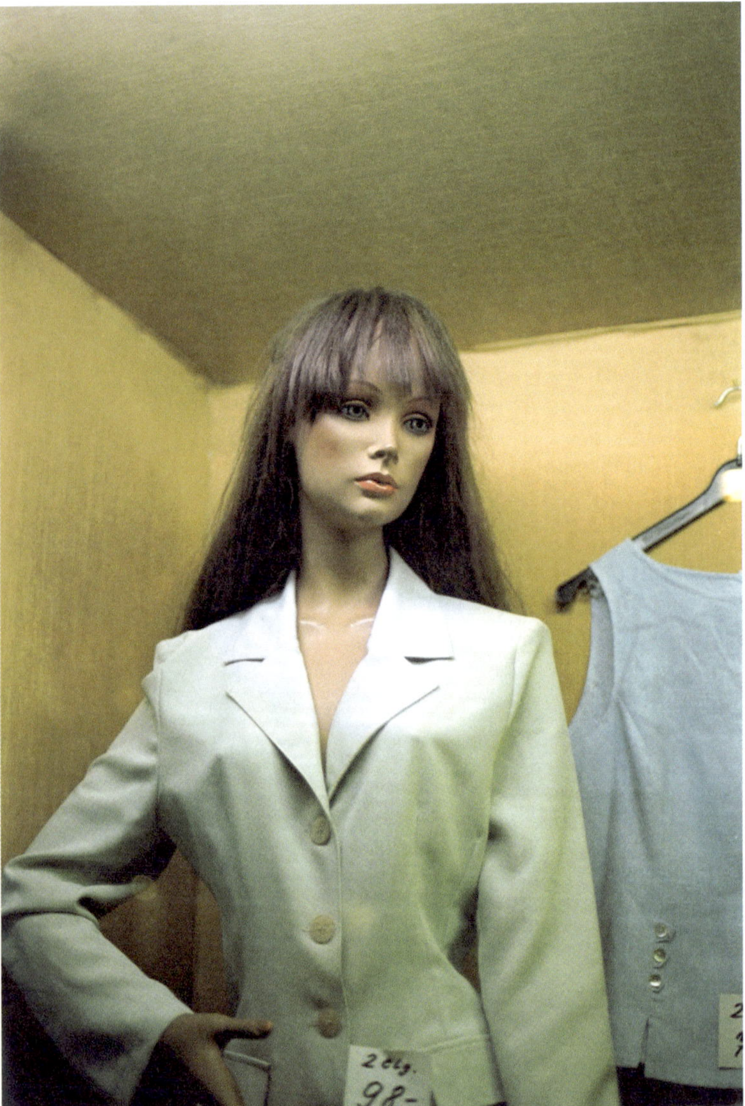
2tlg.
98.-
2
7

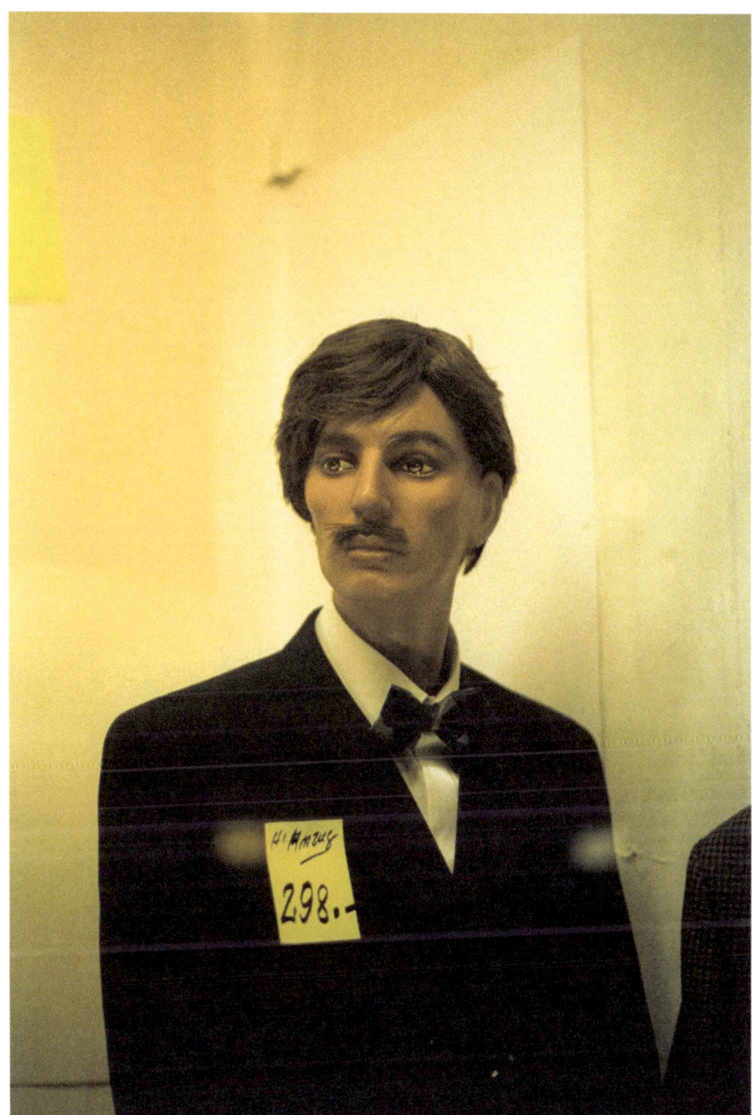
Hi Anzug
298.-

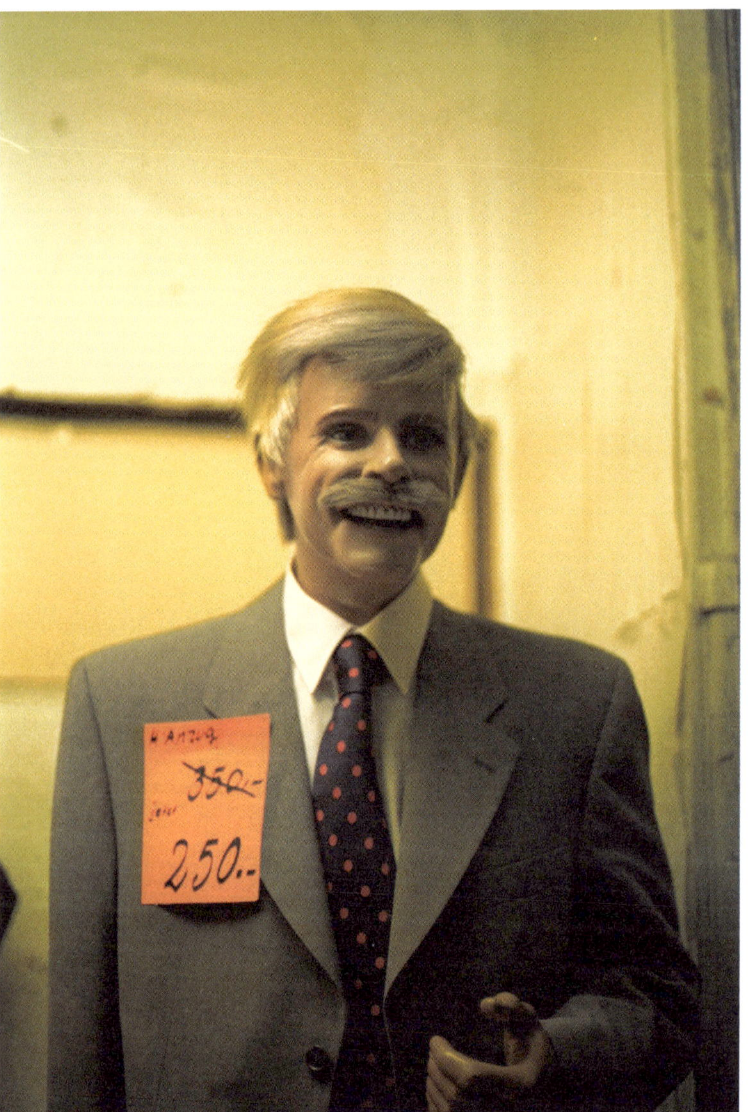
250.--

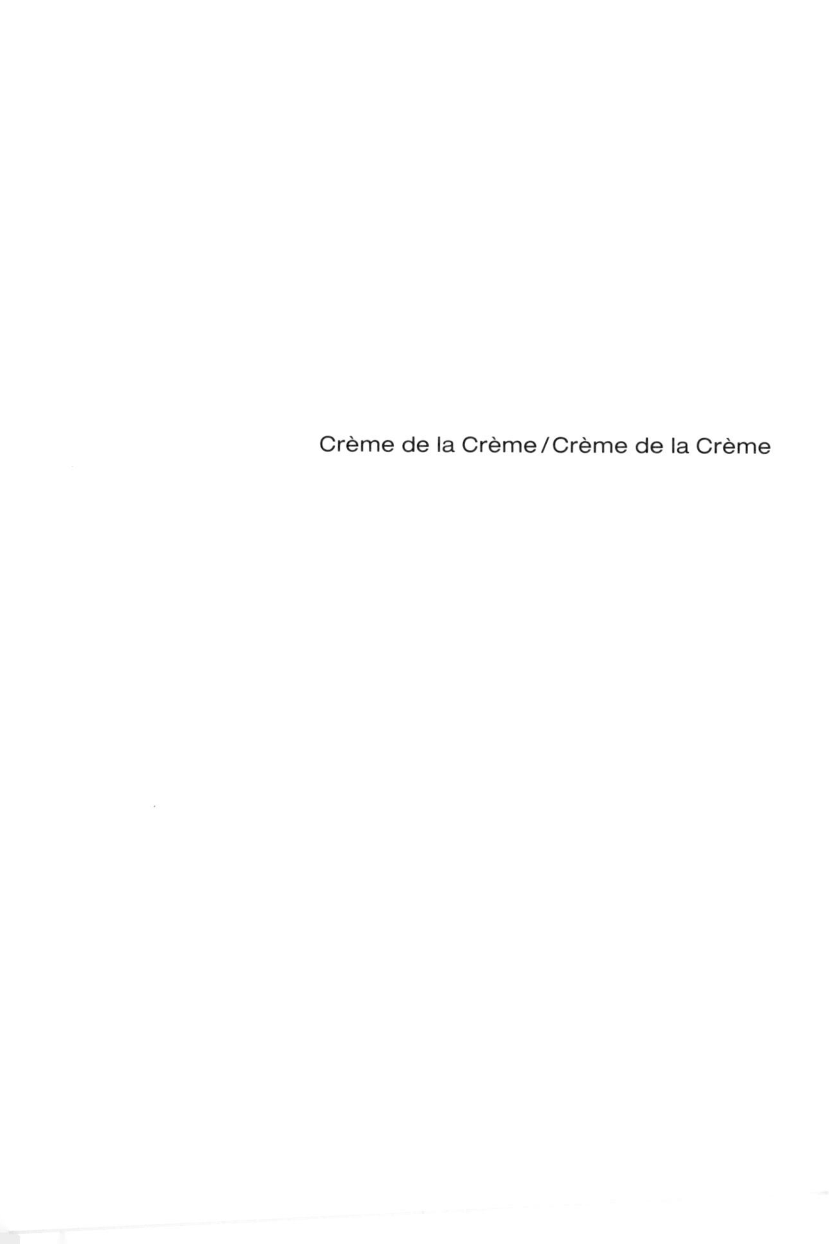

Crème de la Crème / Crème de la Crème

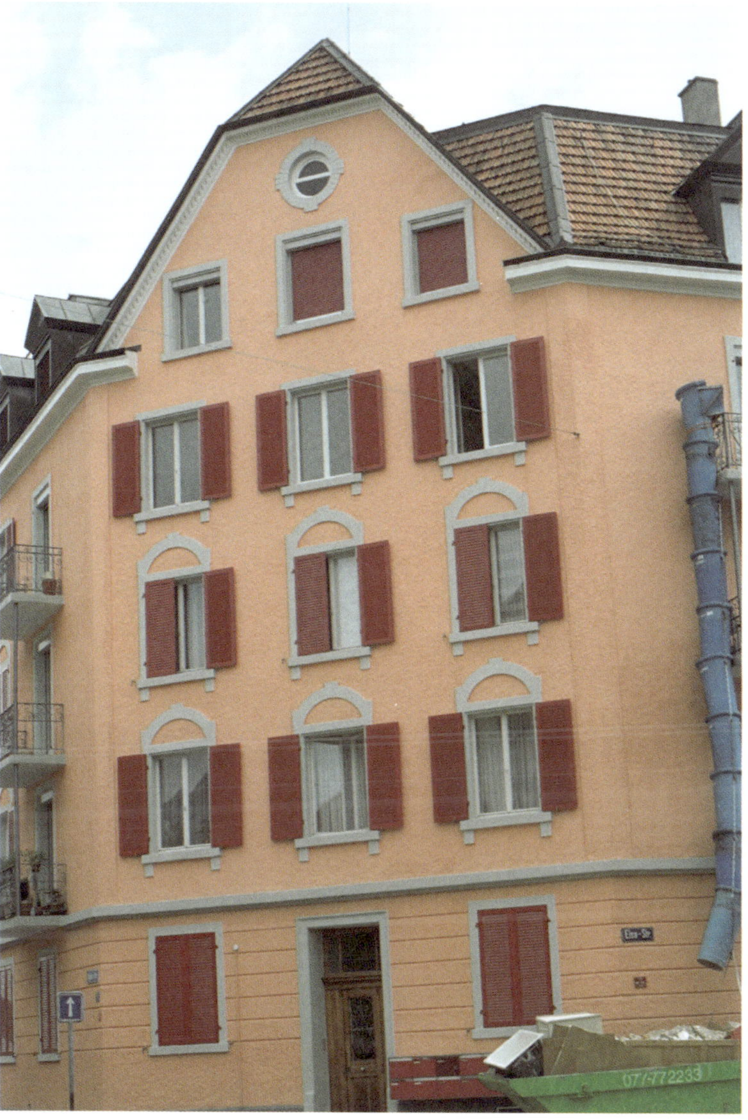

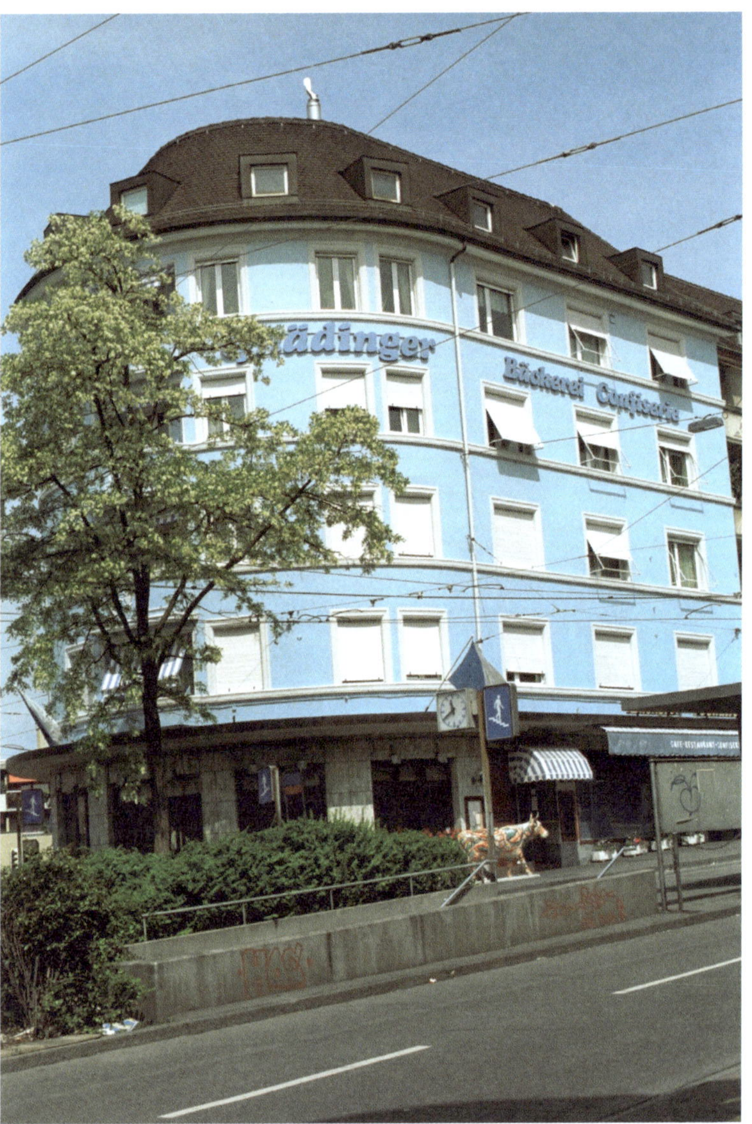

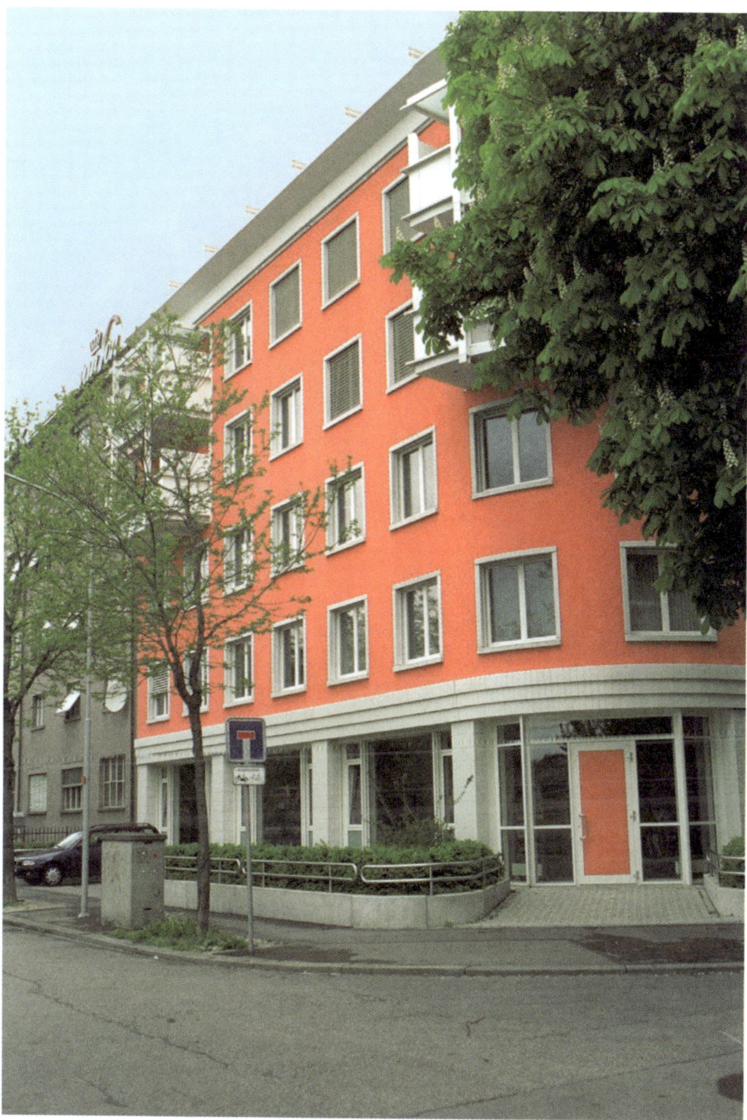

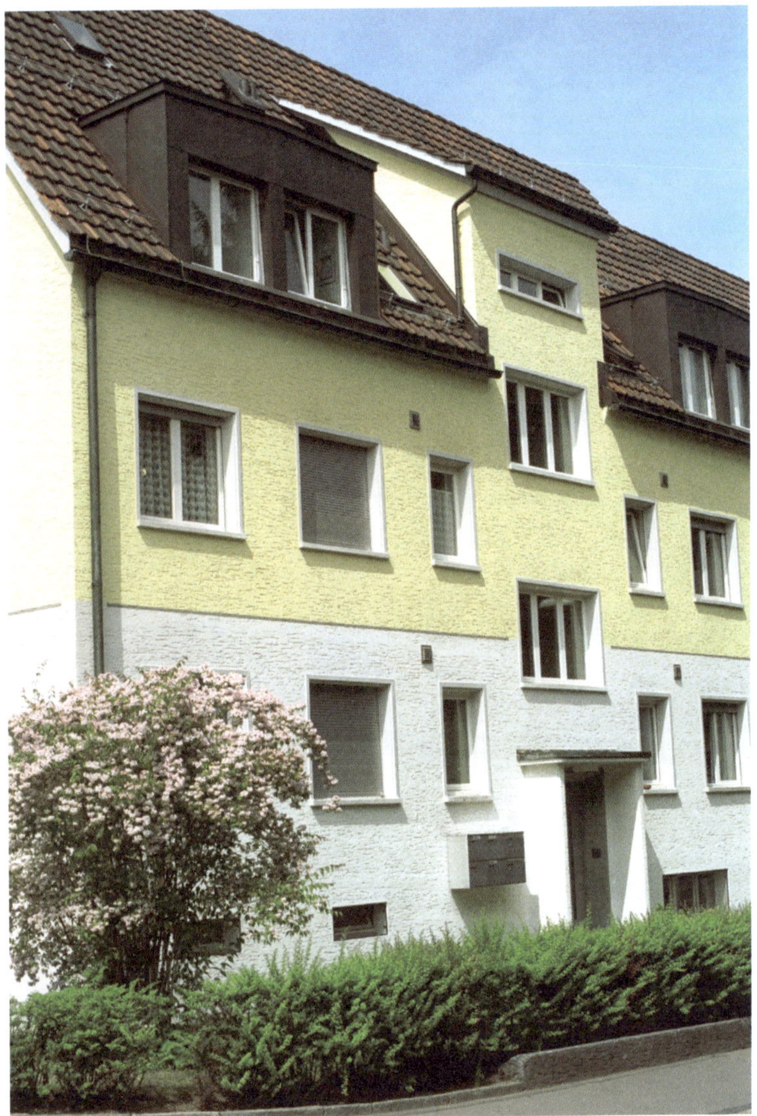

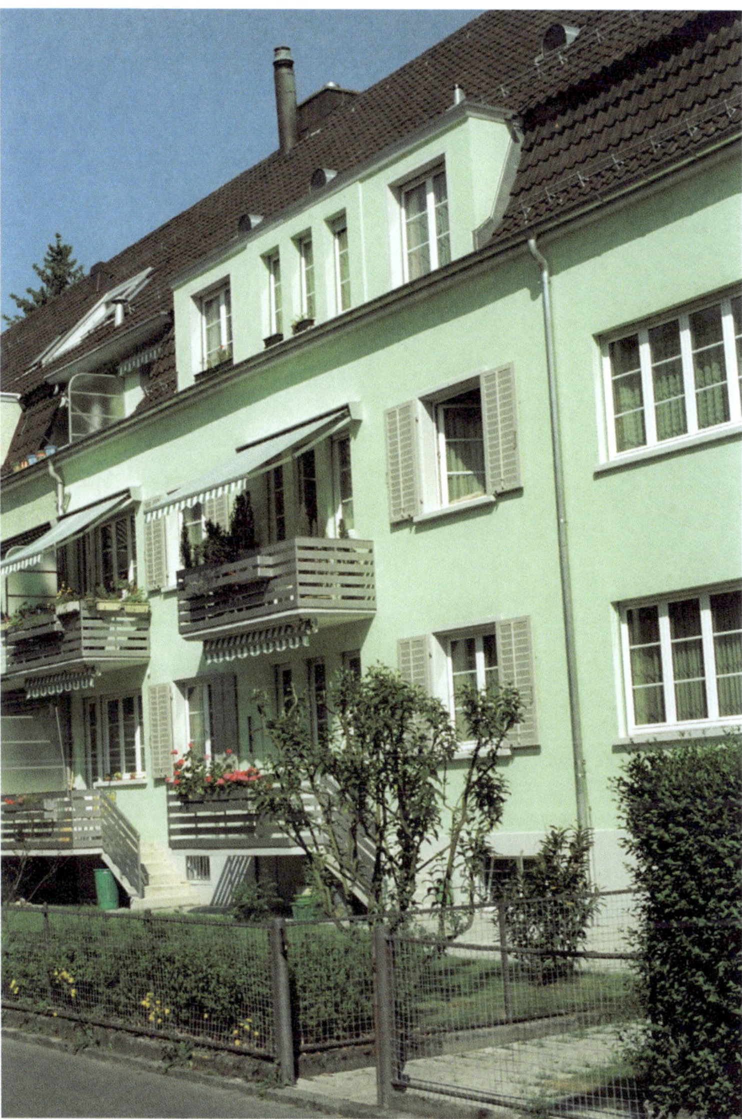

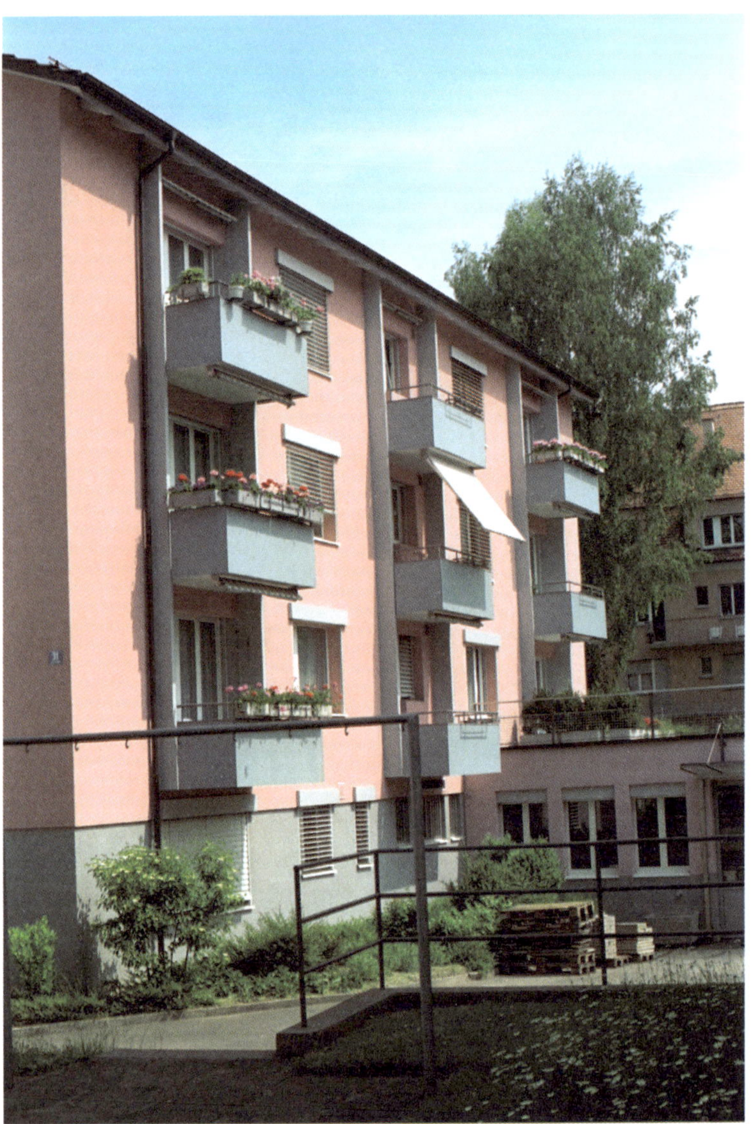

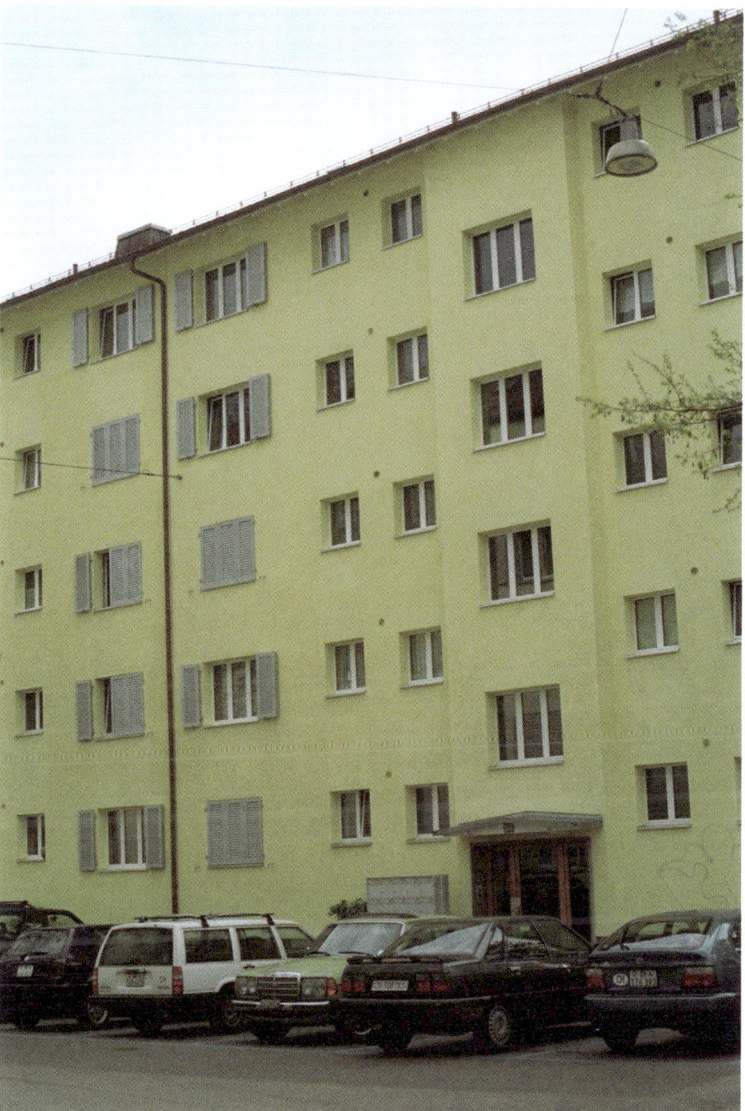

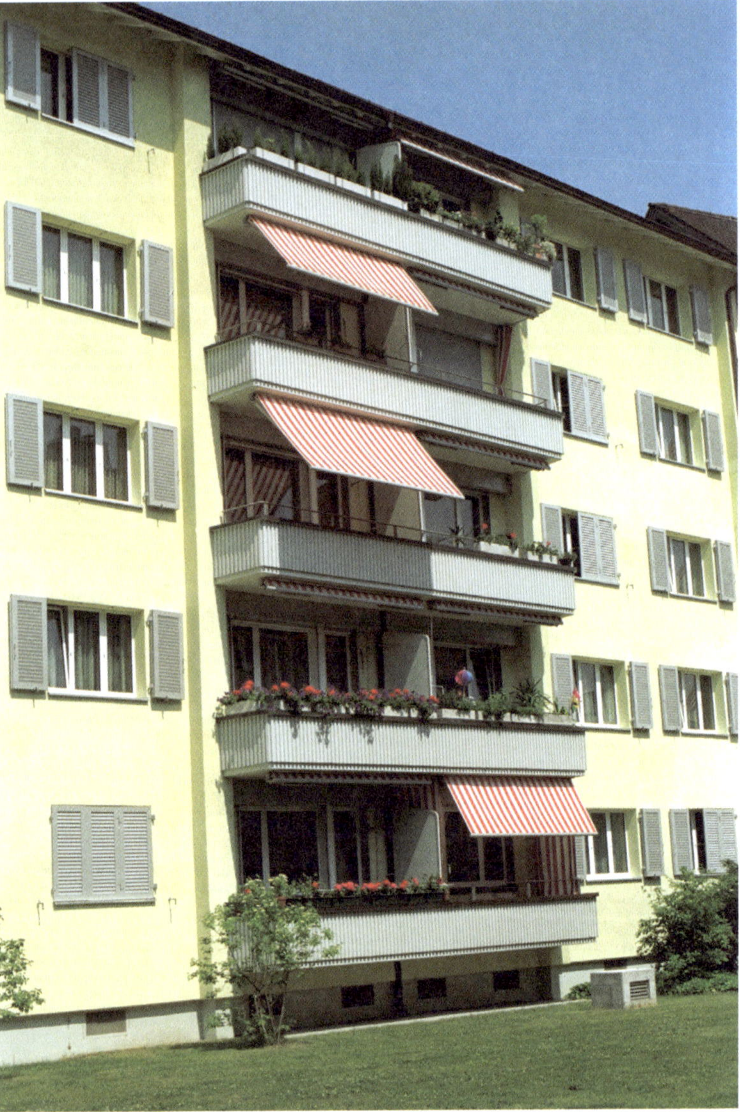

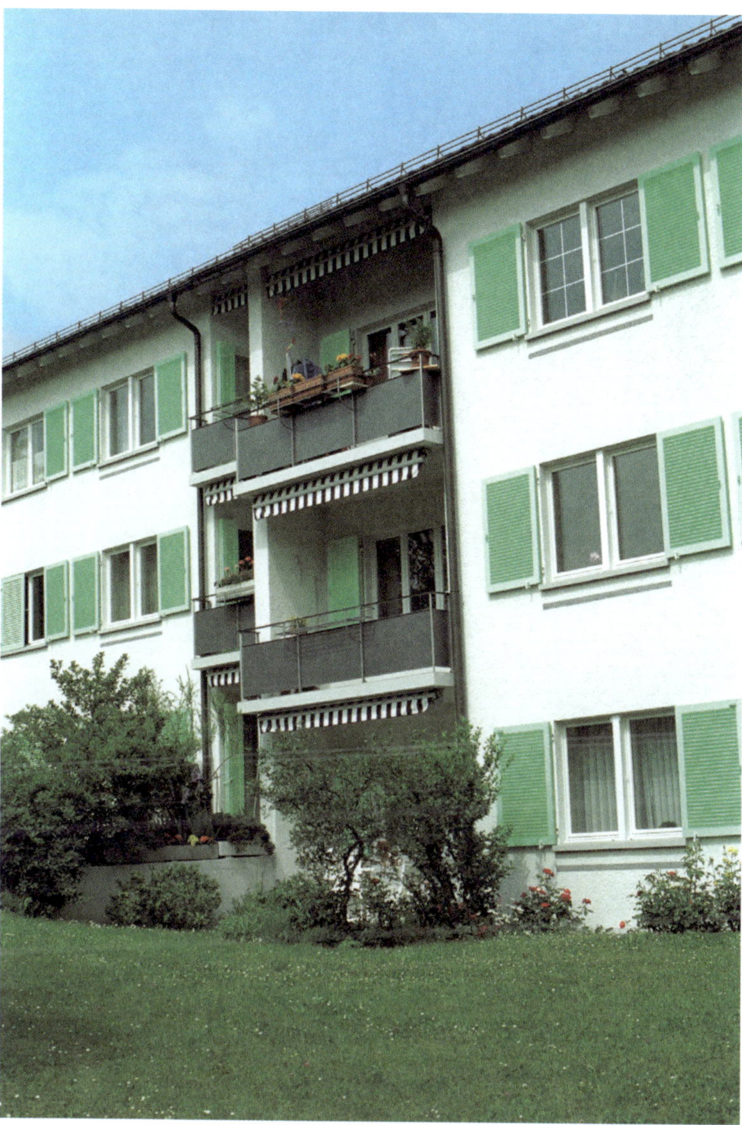

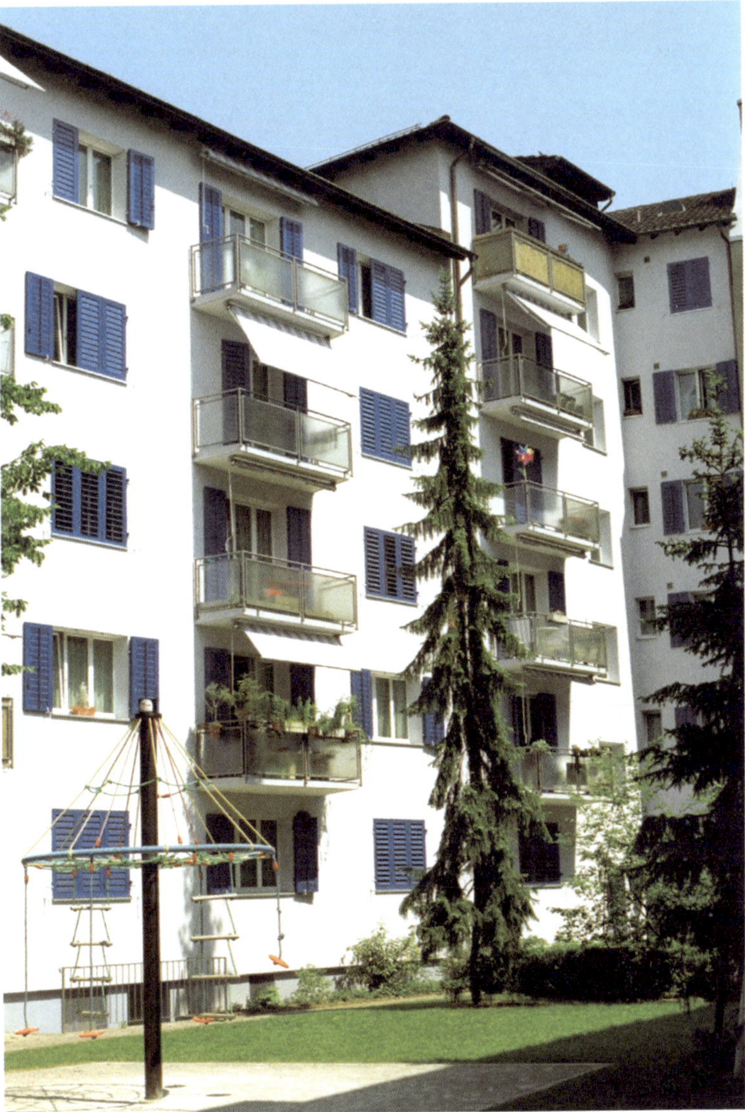

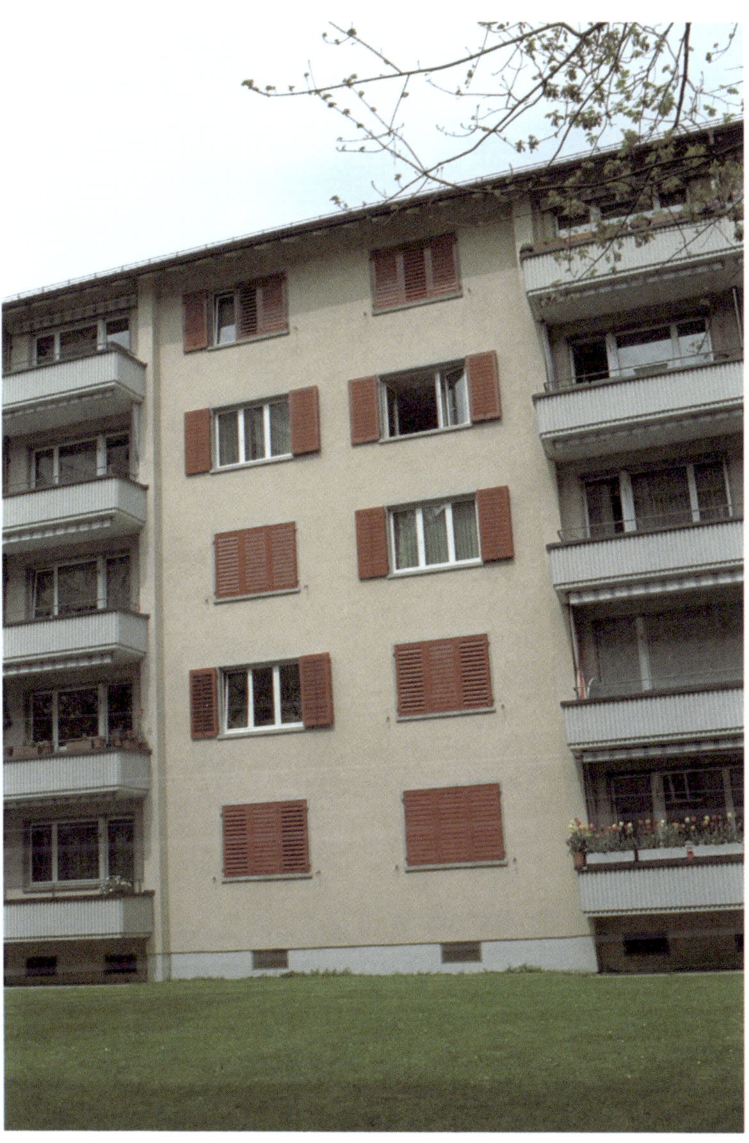

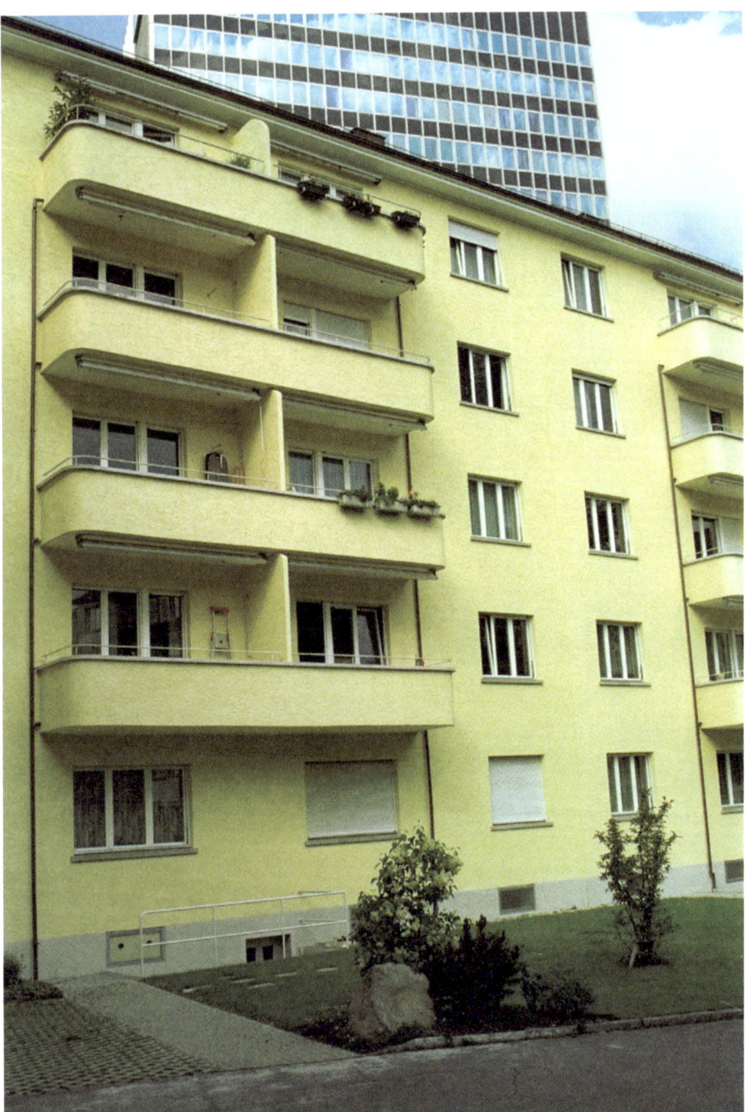

Tête-à-tête / Tête-à-tête

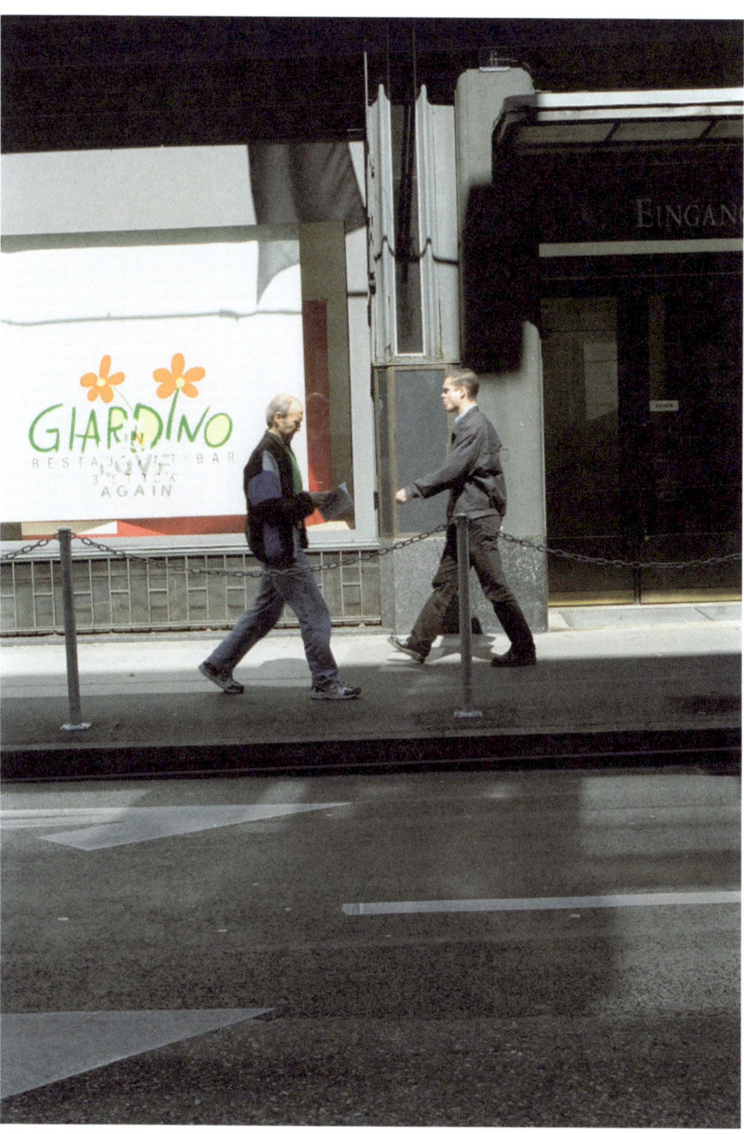
GIARDINO
RESTAURANT BAR
AGAIN
EINGANG

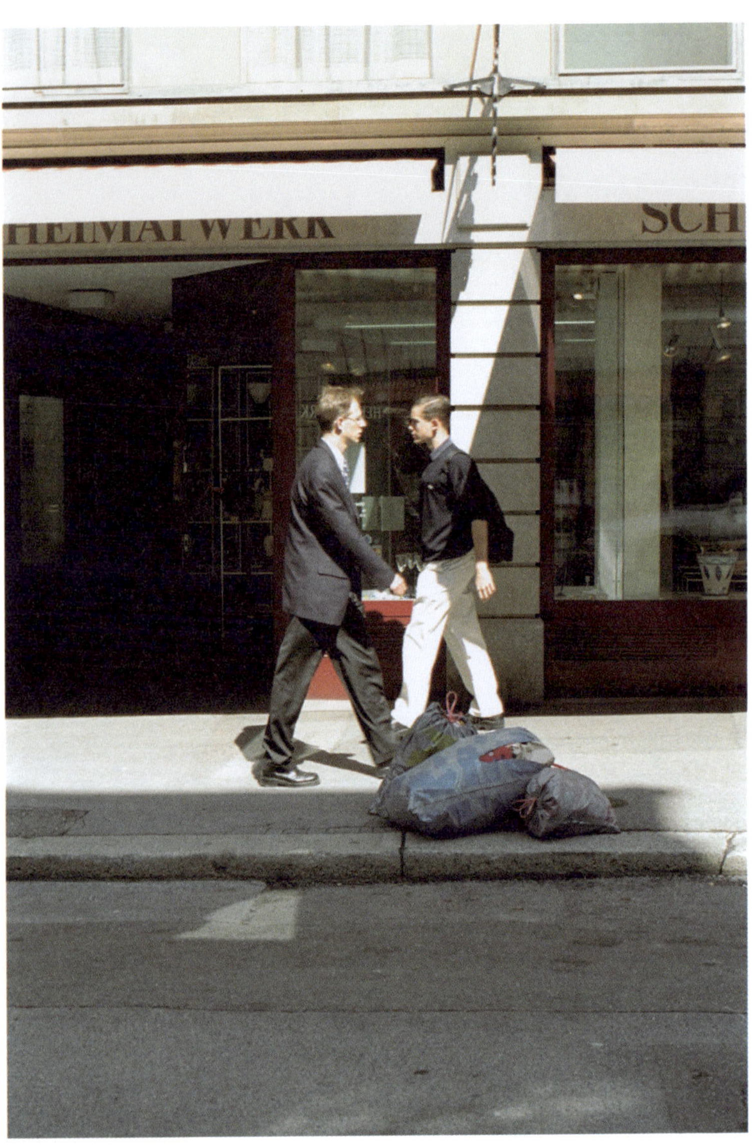
HEIMATWERK
SCH

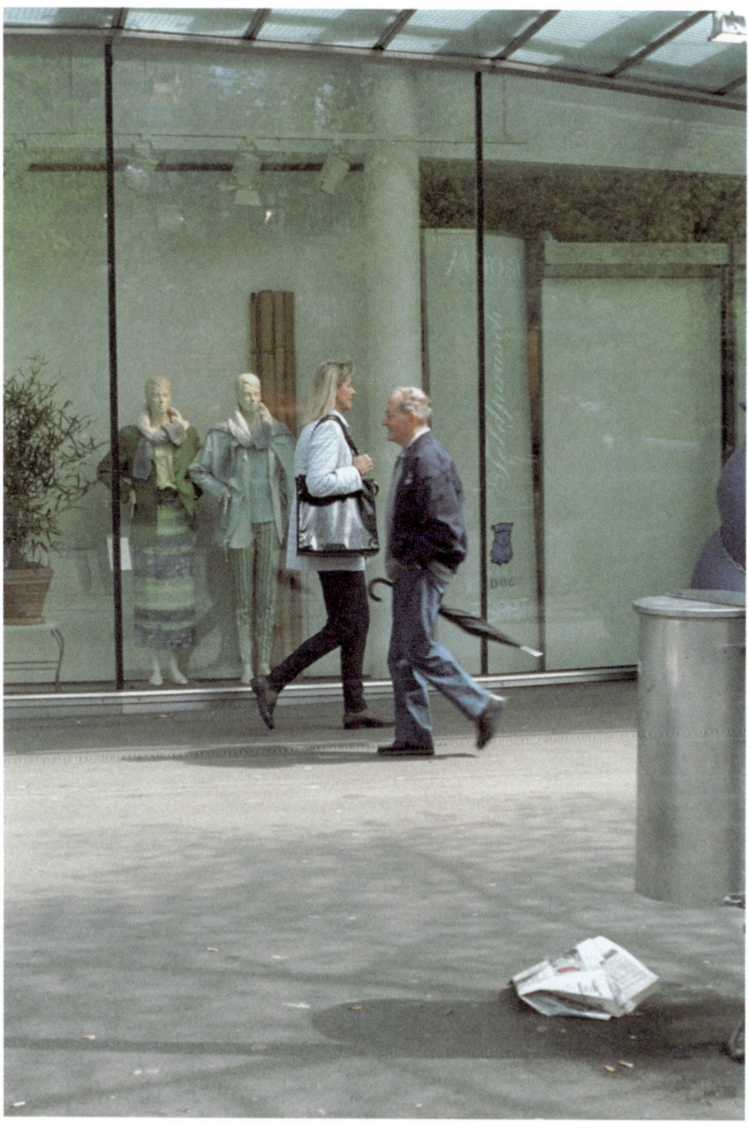

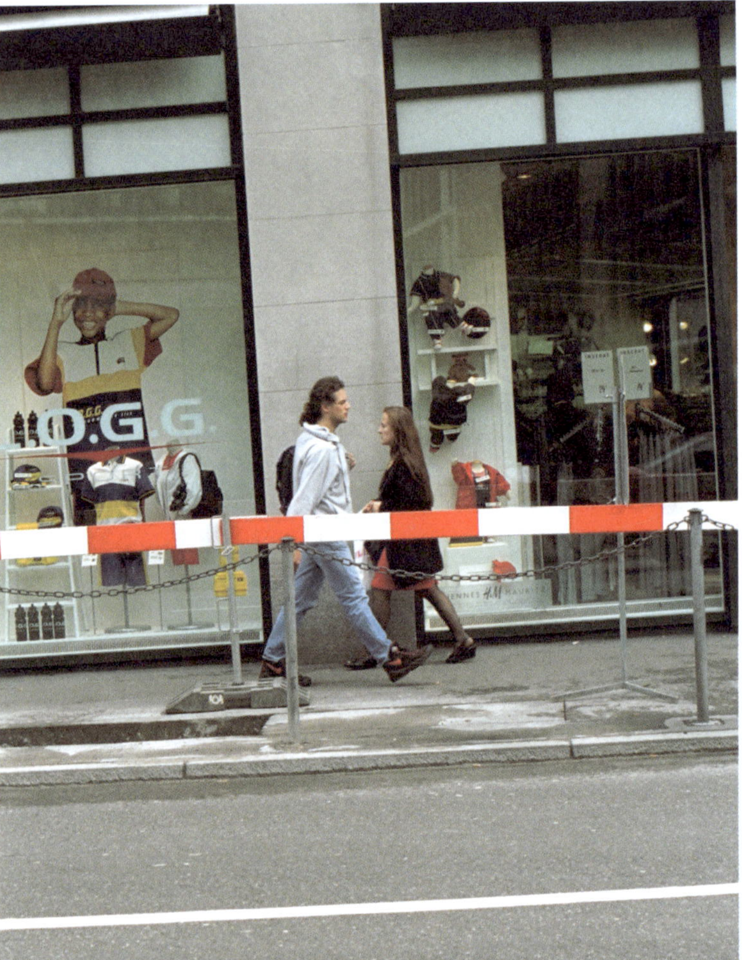
O.G.G.
H&M

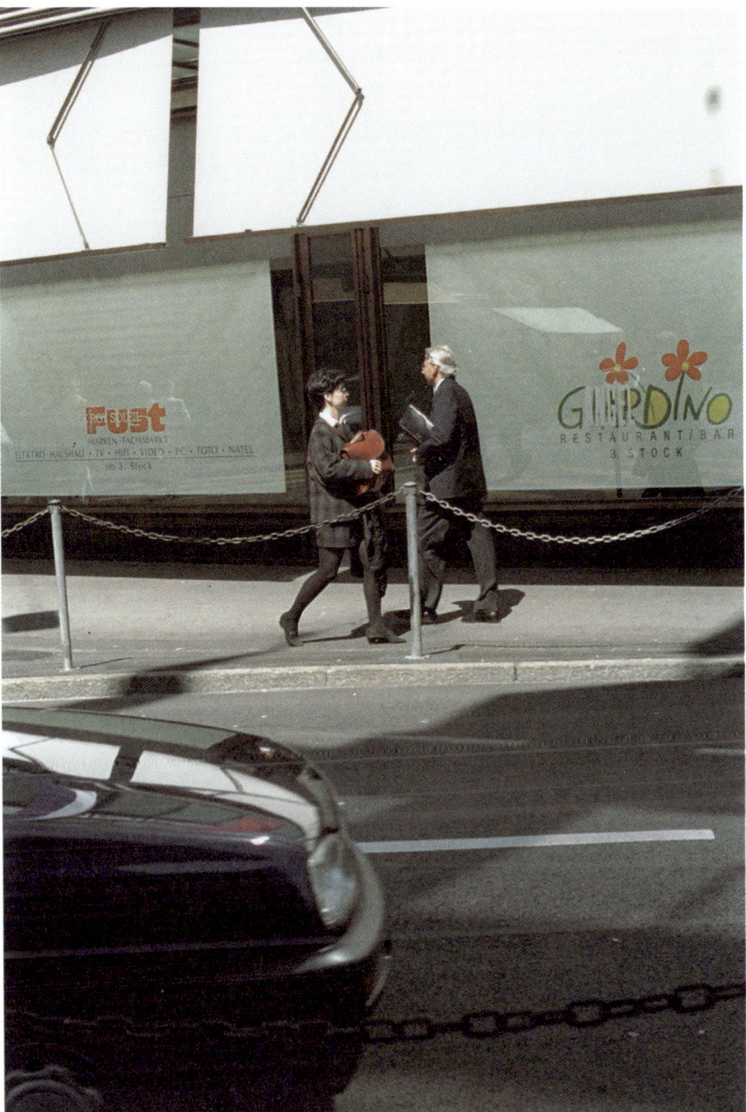
Rex SOLEIL
fust
MARKEN-FACHMARKT
ELEKTRO-HAUSHALT · TV · HIFI · VIDEO · PC · FOTO · NATEL
im 3. Stock
GIARDINO
RESTAURANT/BAR
3. STOCK

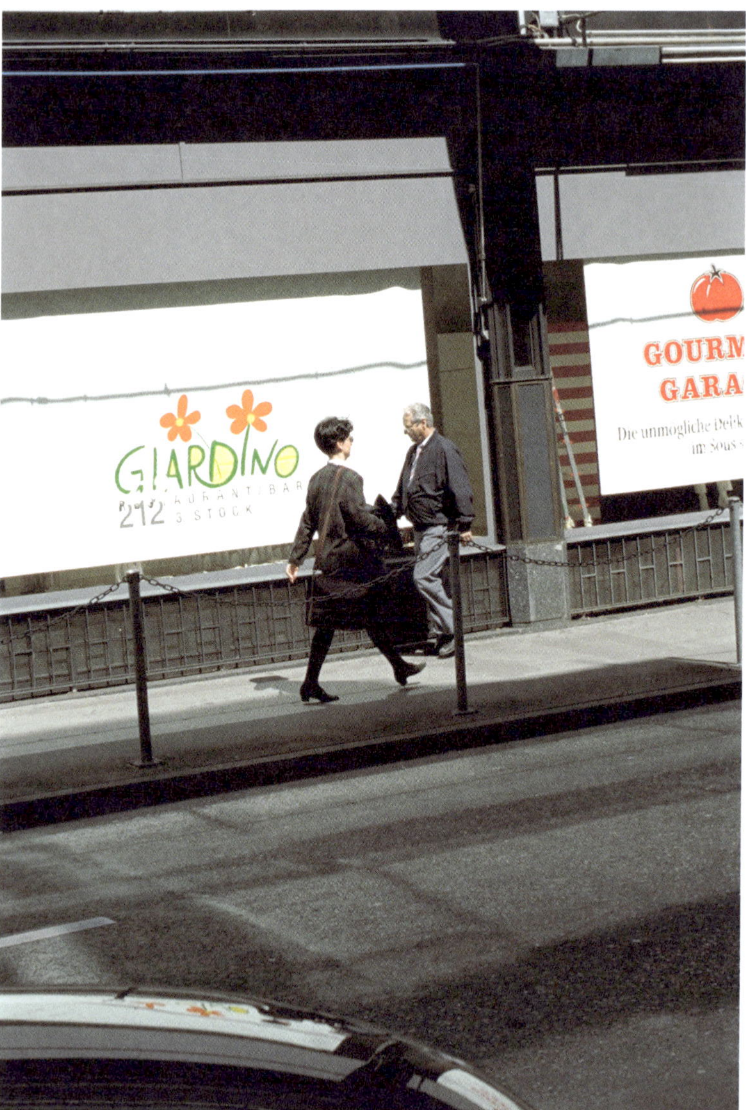

GIARDINO
RISTORANTE BAR
3. STOCK
212
GOURM
GARA
Die unmogliche Delik
im Sous

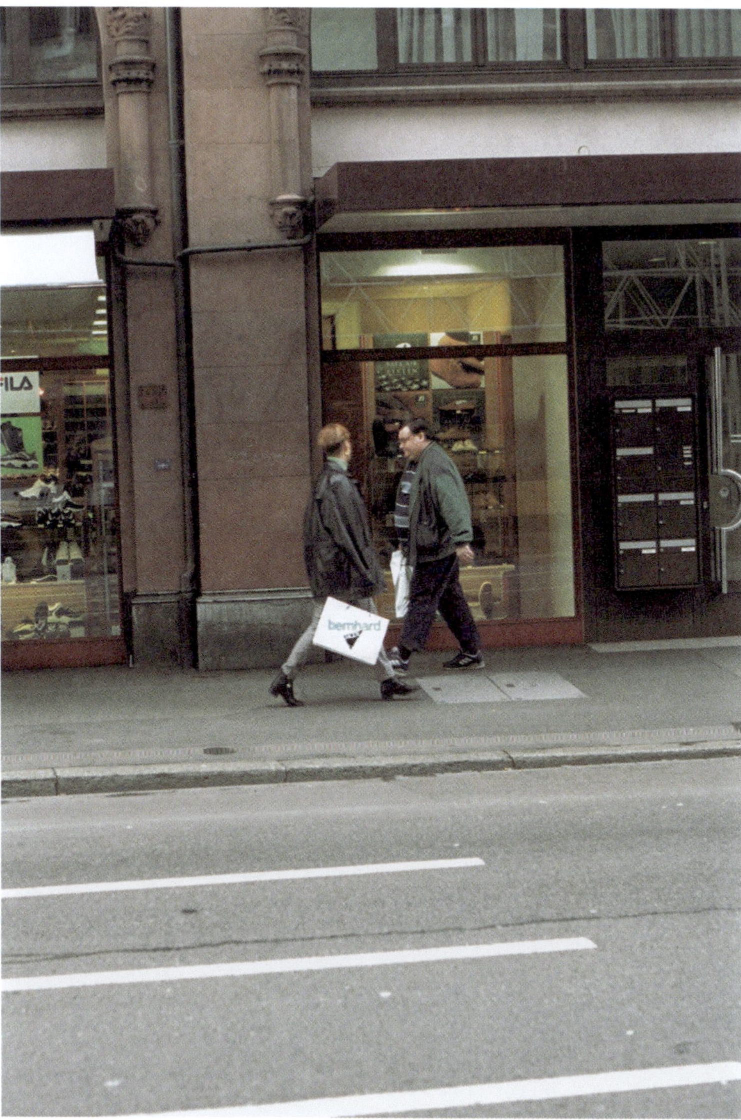

FILA
bernhard

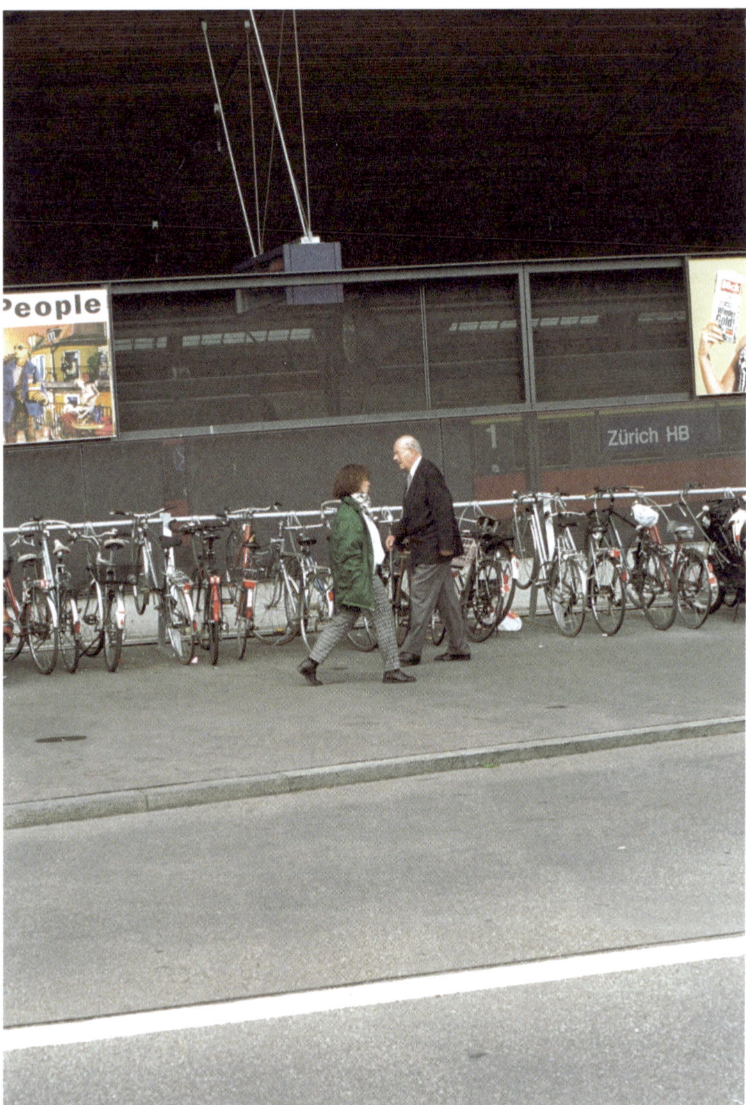
People
Bild
Wieder
Gold!
1
Zürich HB

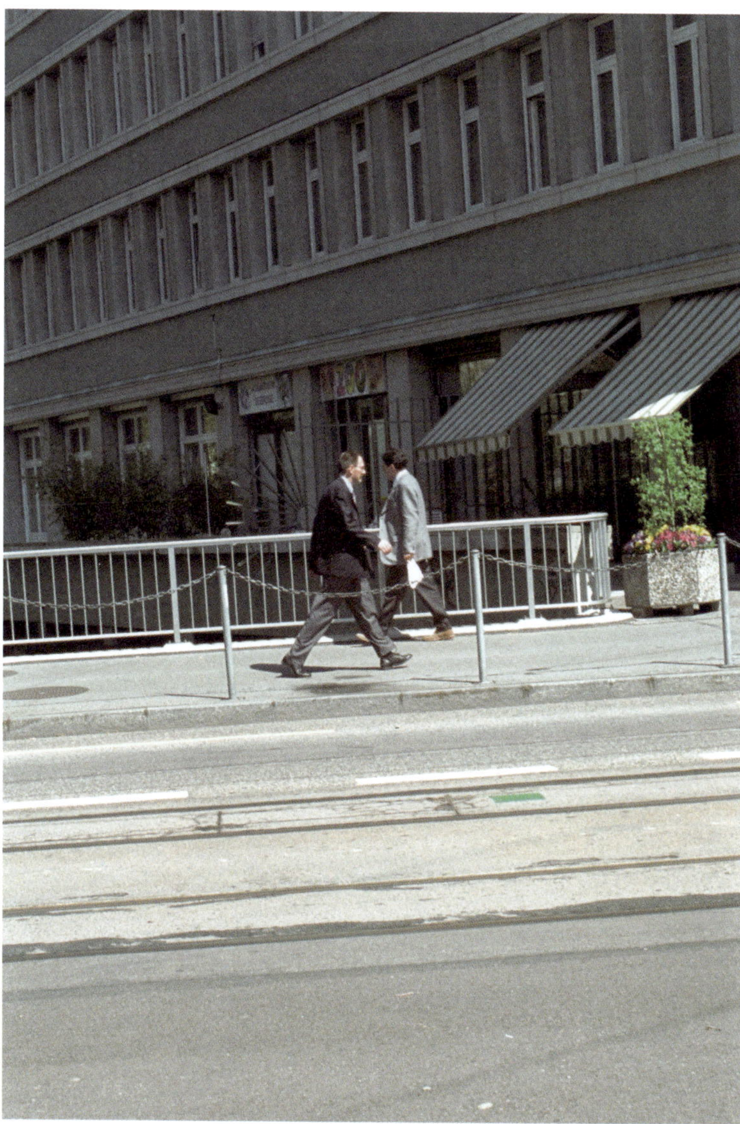

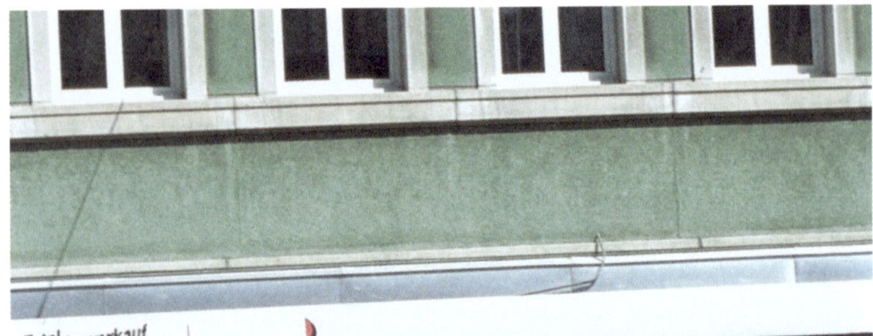

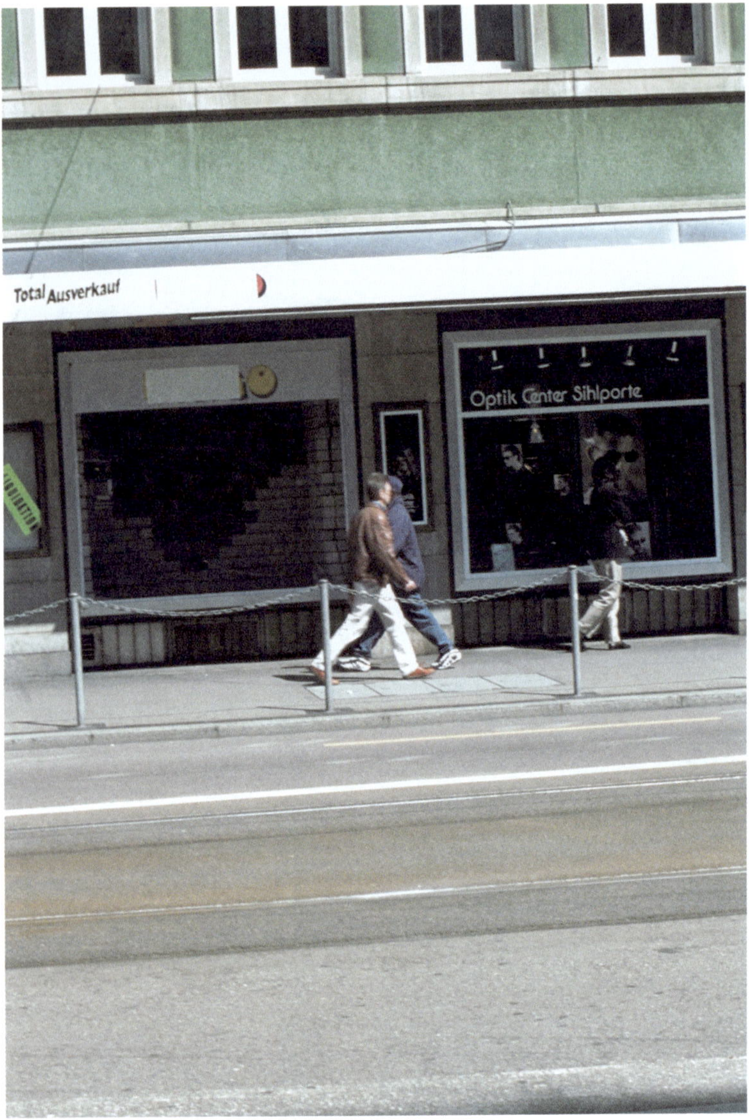

Total Ausverkauf
Optik Center Sihlporte

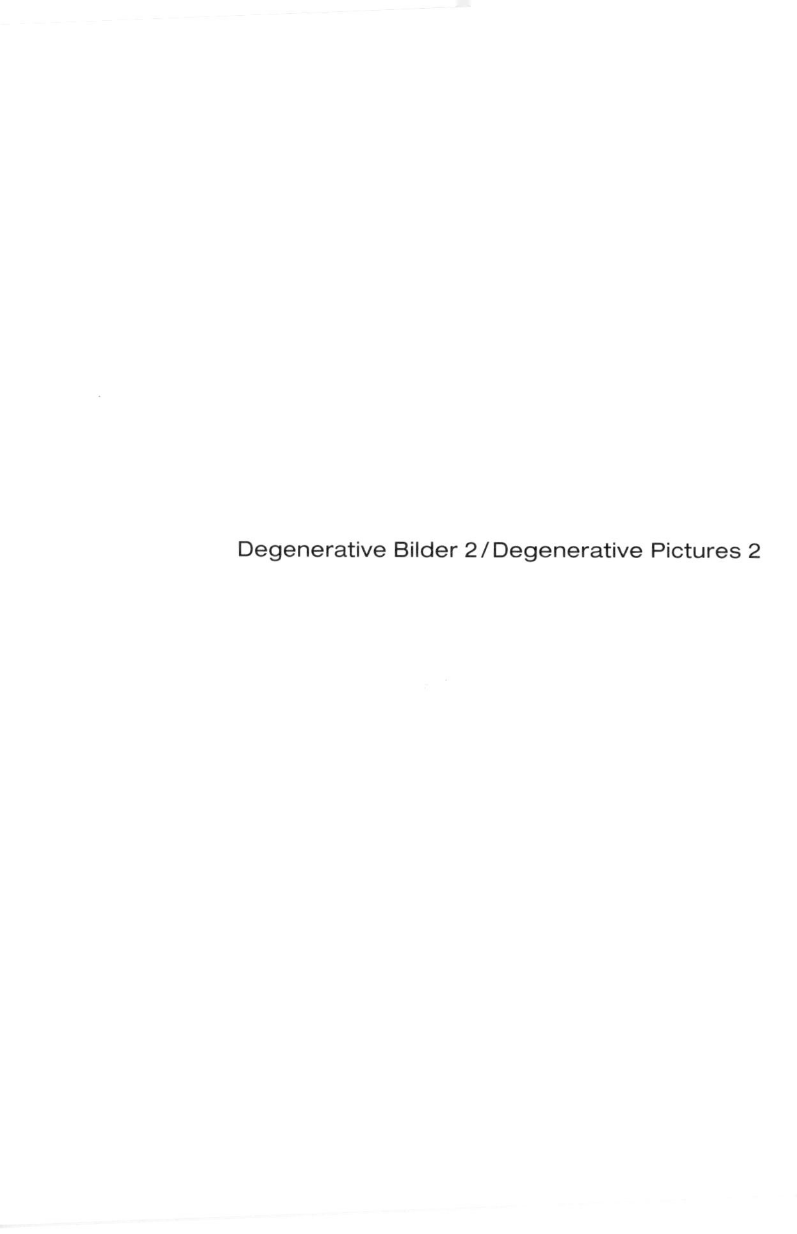

Degenerative Bilder 2 / Degenerative Pictures 2

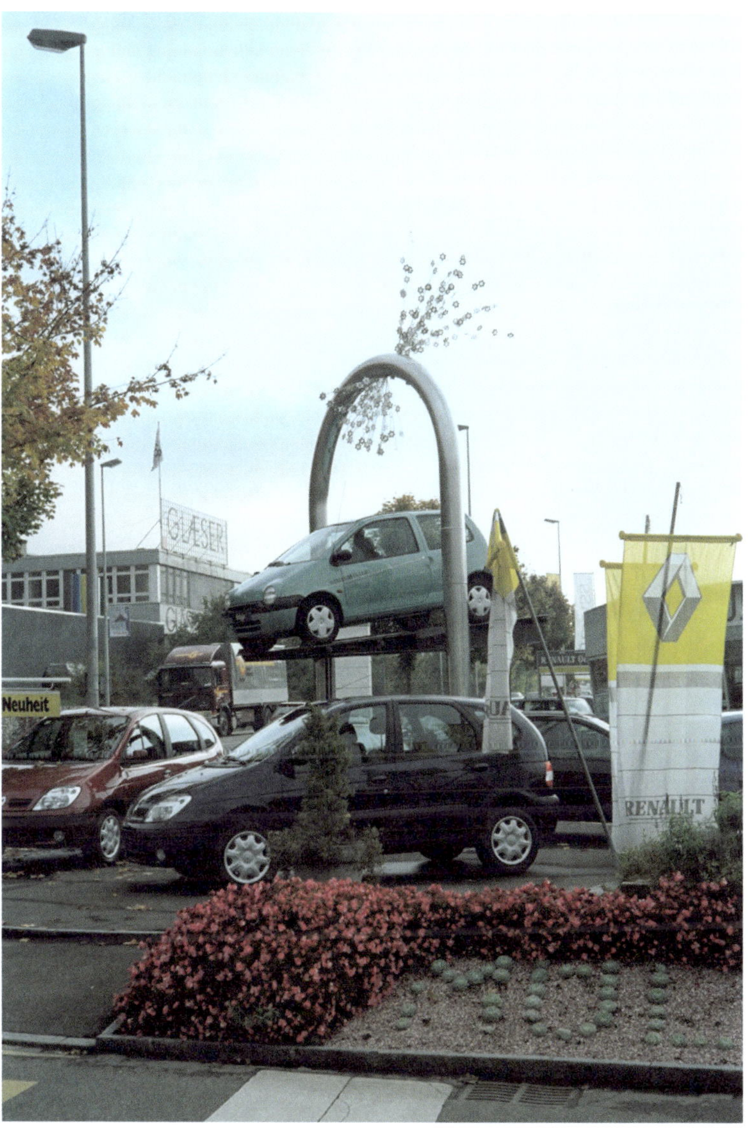

GLÆSER
Neuheit
RENAULT

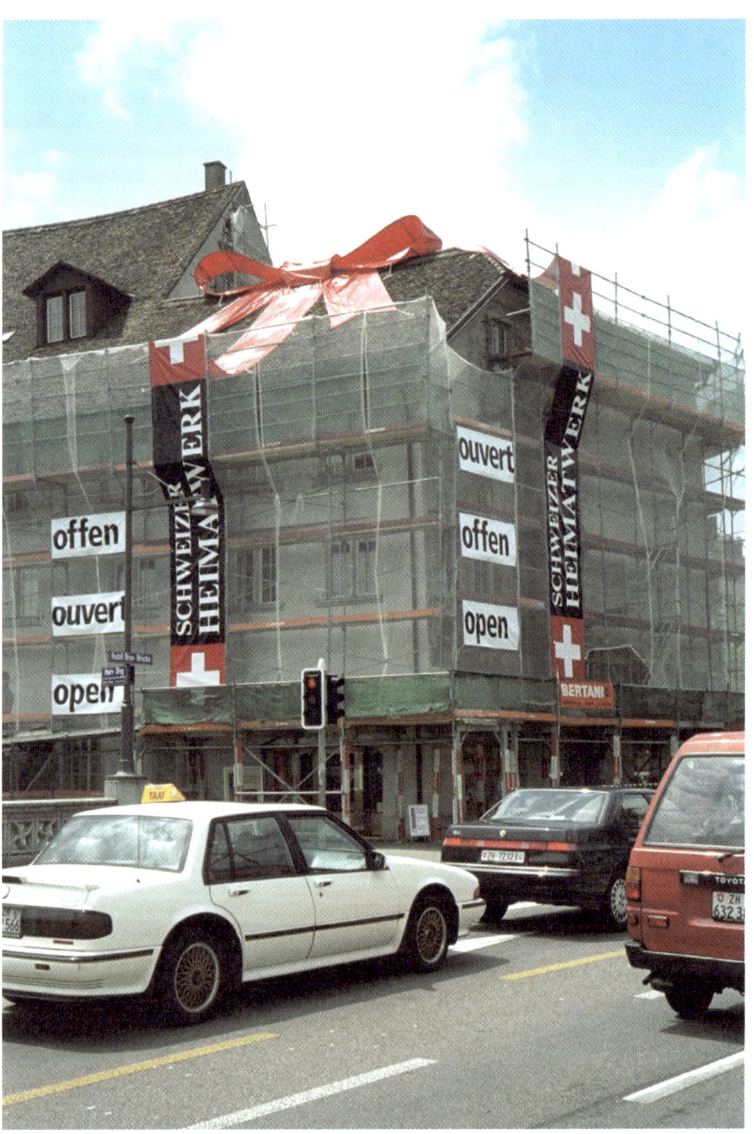

offen
ouvert
open
SCHWEIZER HEIMATWERK
ouvert
offen
open
SCHWEIZER HEIMATWERK
BERTANI
TAXI
ZH 773234
TOYOTA
ZH 6323

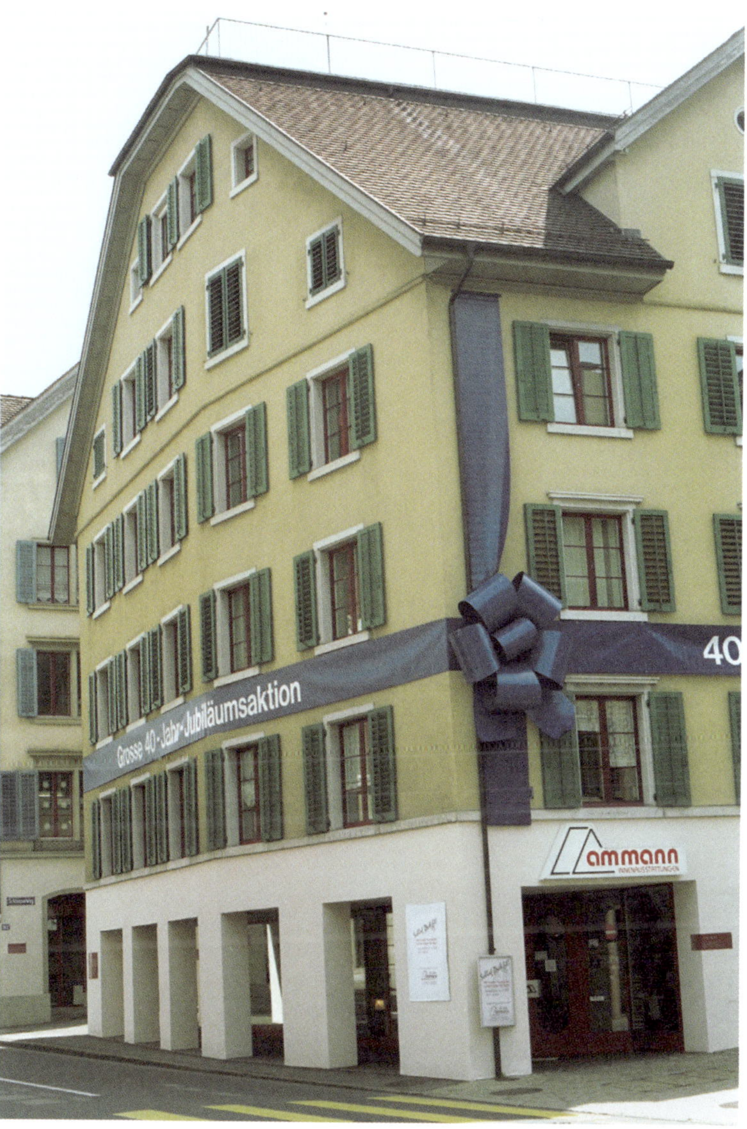

Grosse 40-Jahr-Jubiläumsaktion
40
ammann
INNENAUSSTATTUNGEN

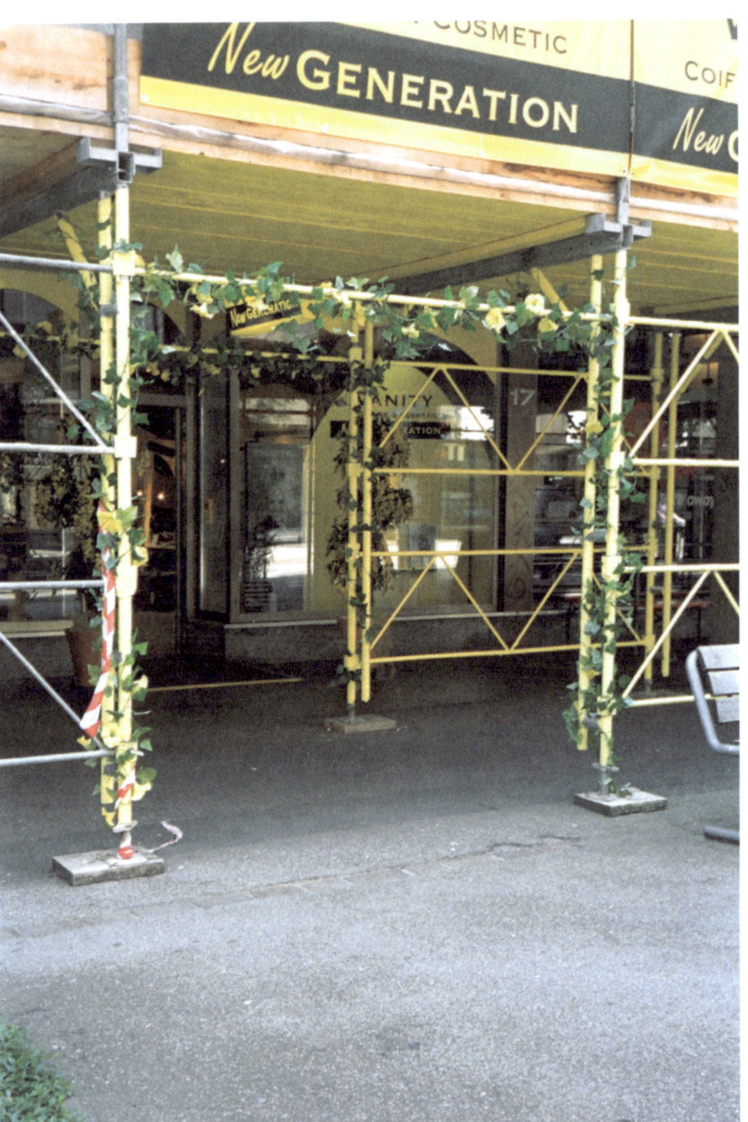
COSMETIC
New GENERATION
COIF
New G
VANITY
17

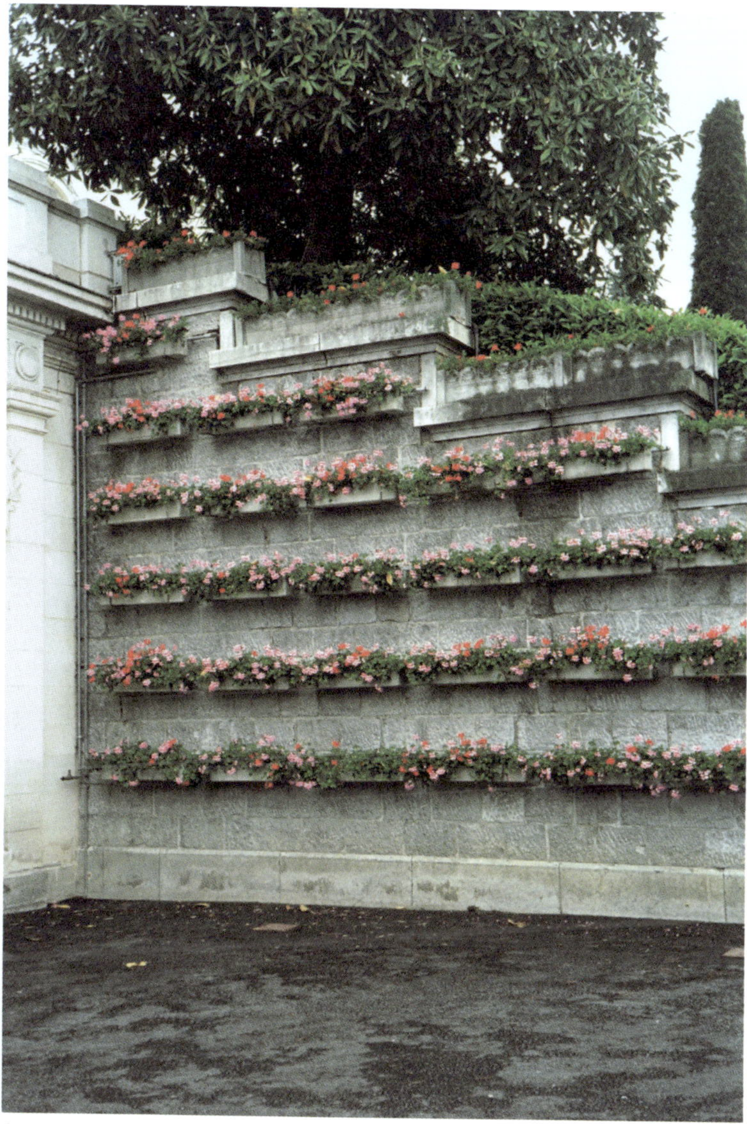

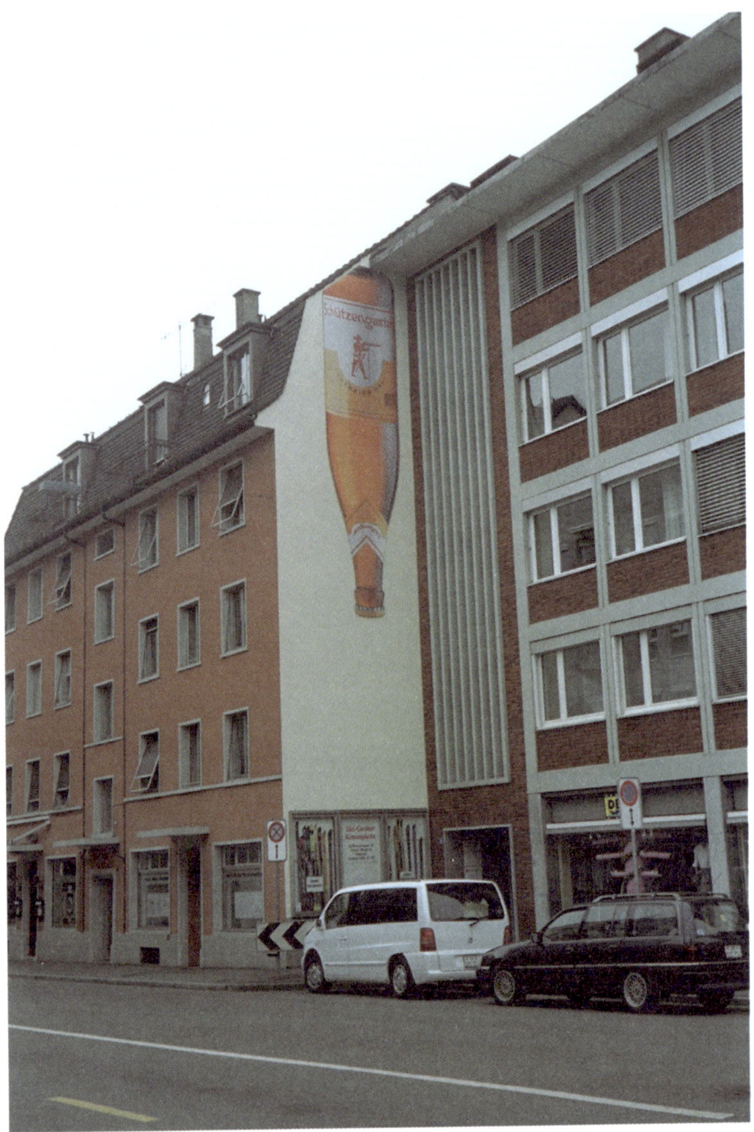

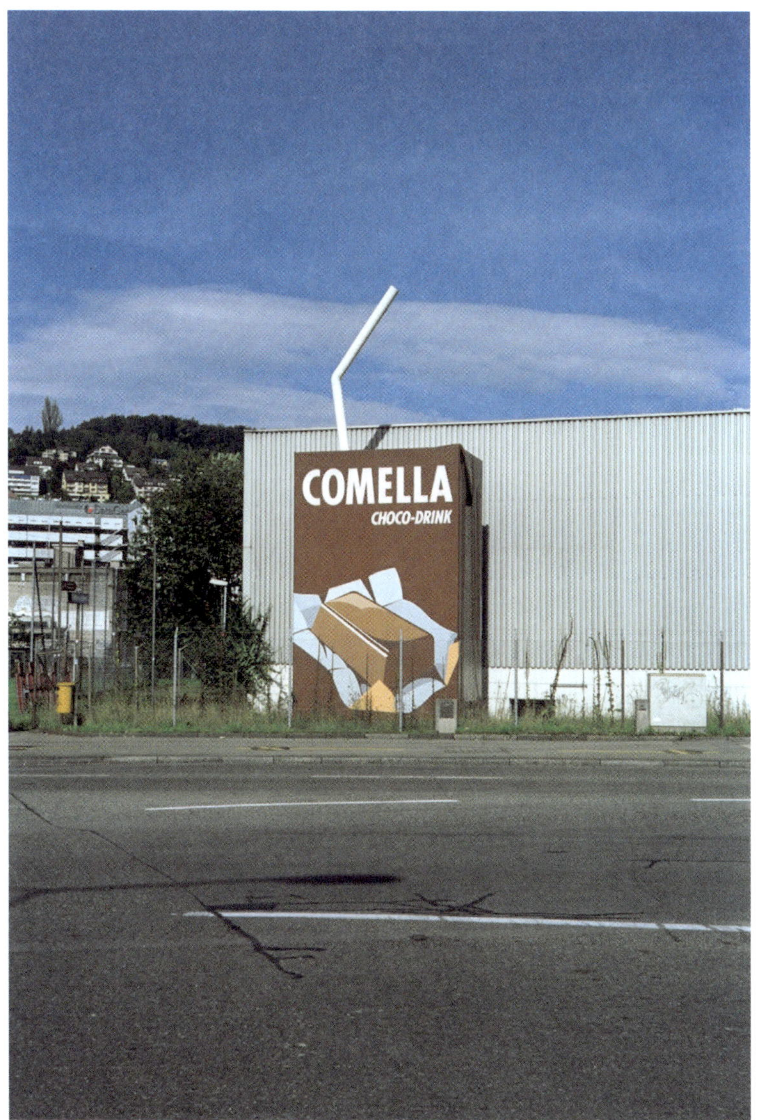

COMELLA
CHOCO-DRINK

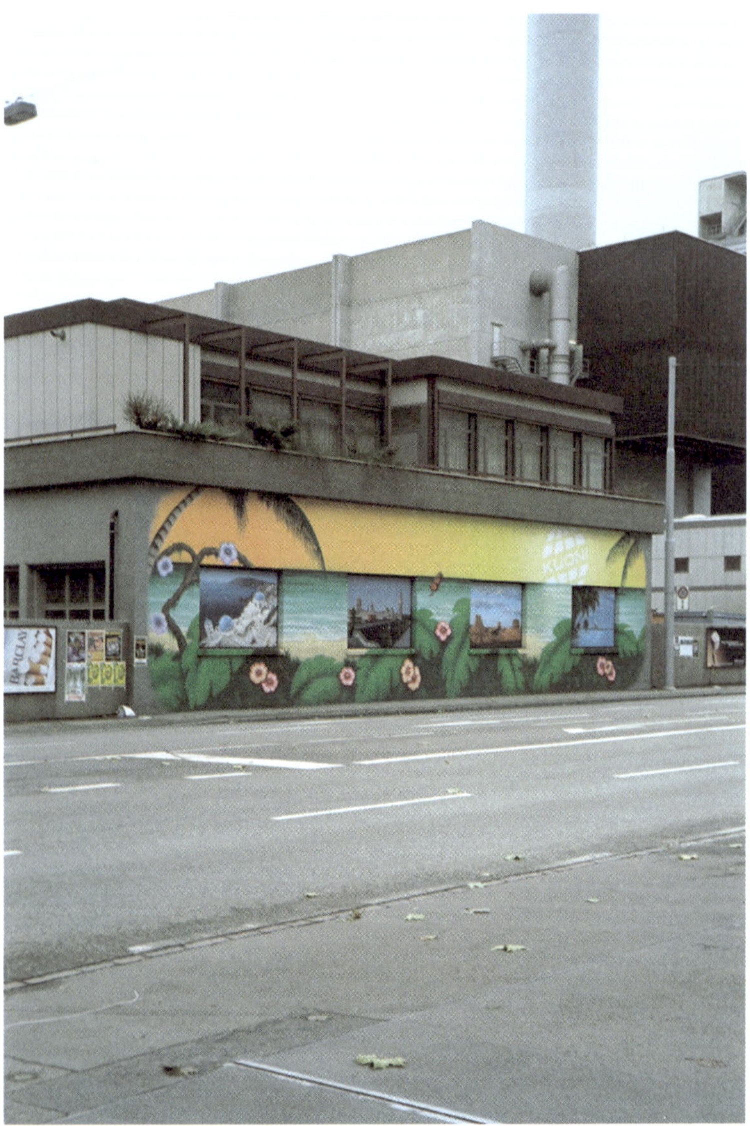

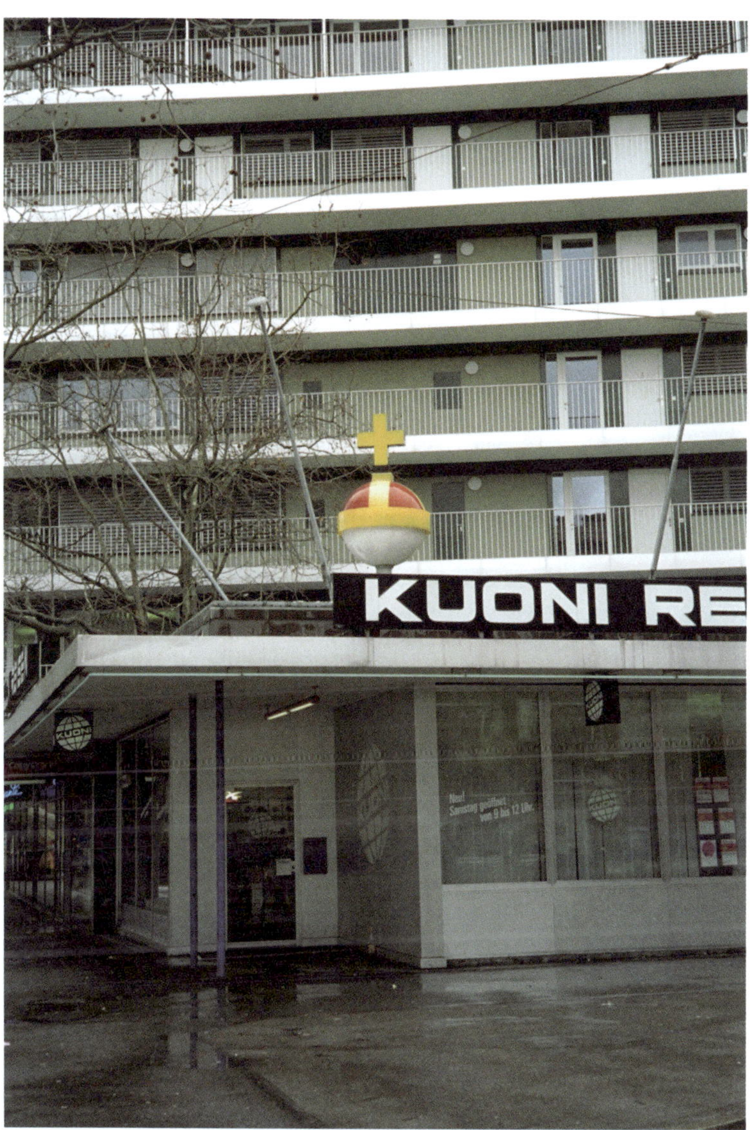

KUONI RE
KUONI
Neu!
Samstag geöffnet
von 9 bis 12 Uhr.

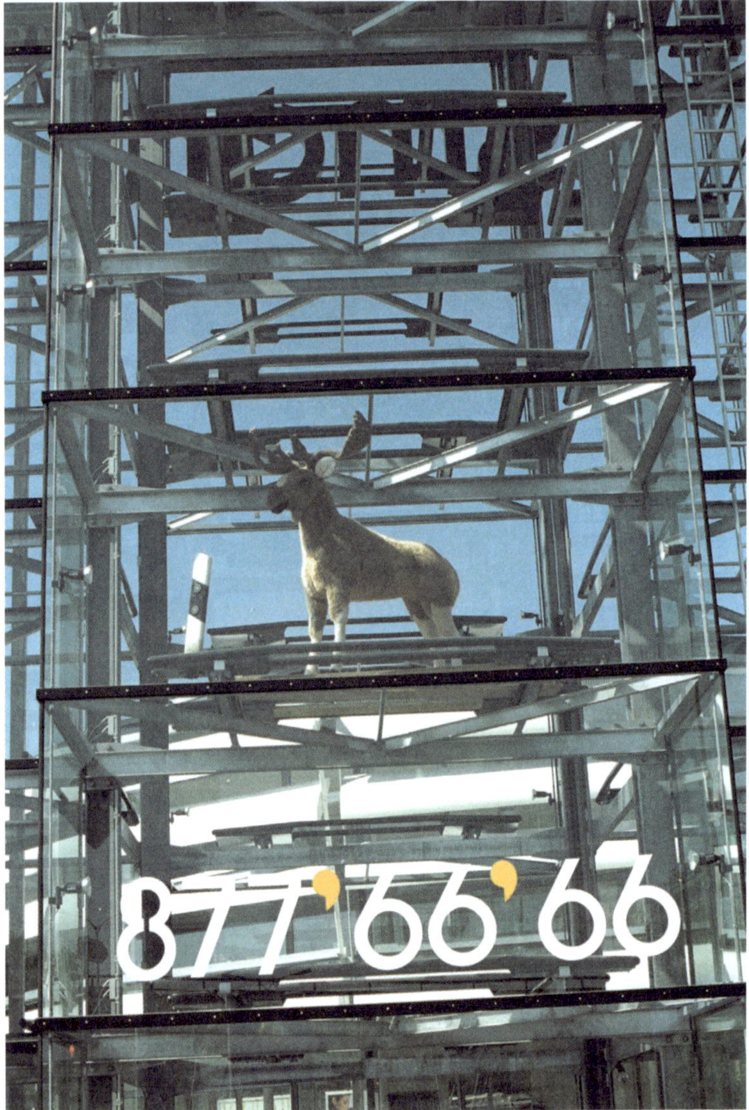

877'66'66

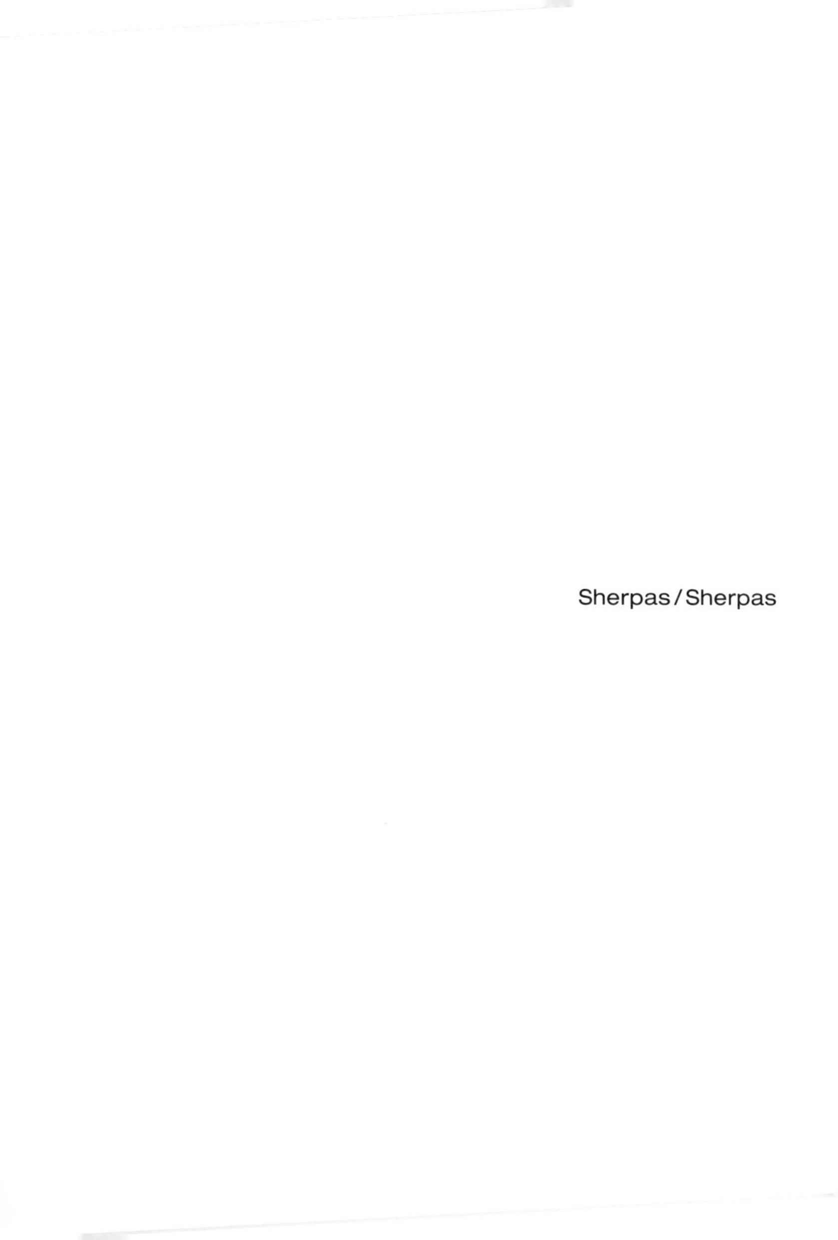

Sherpas / Sherpas

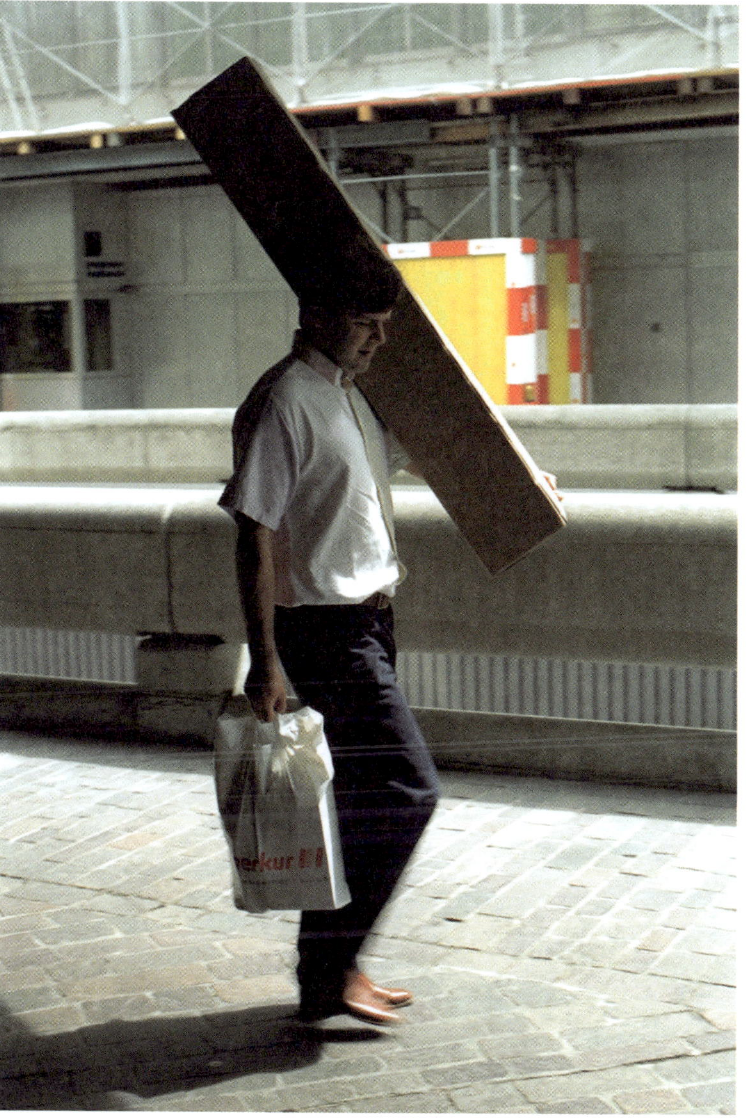

erkur

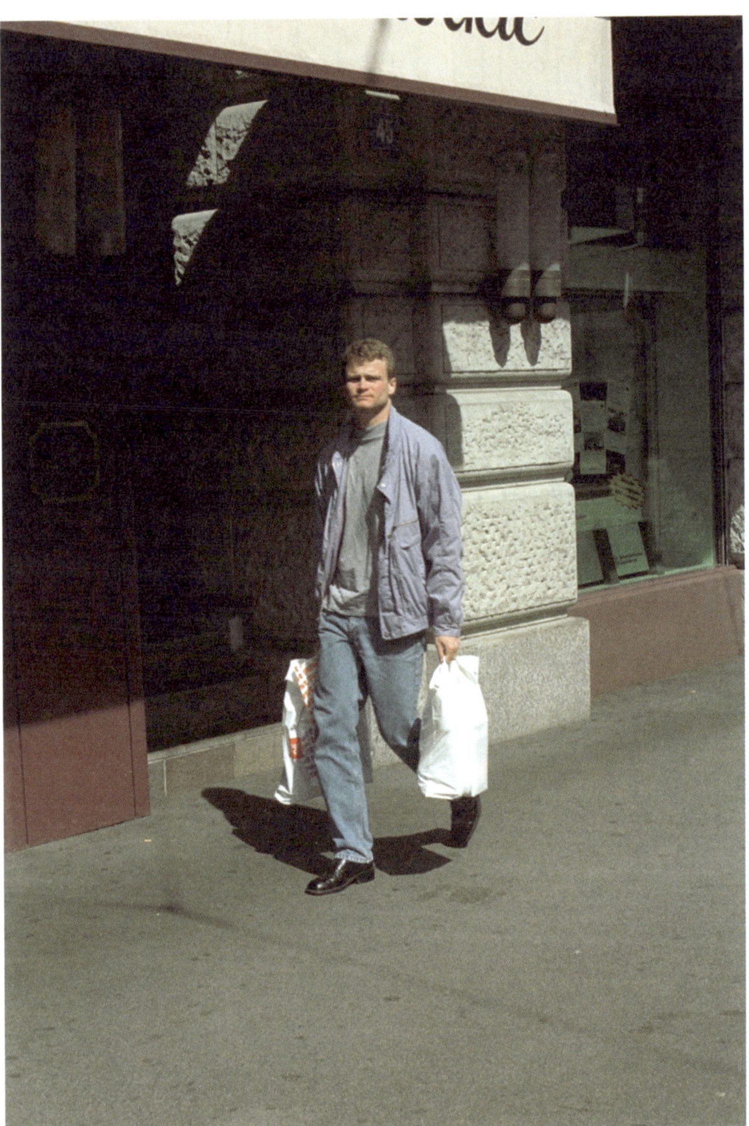

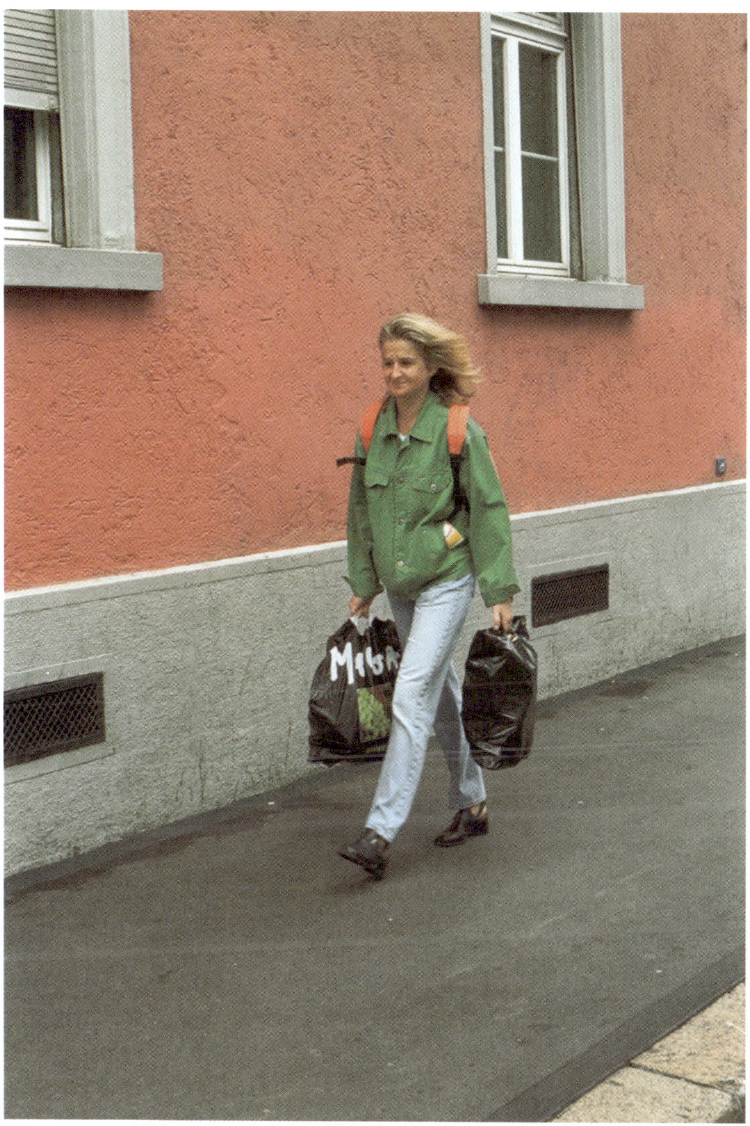

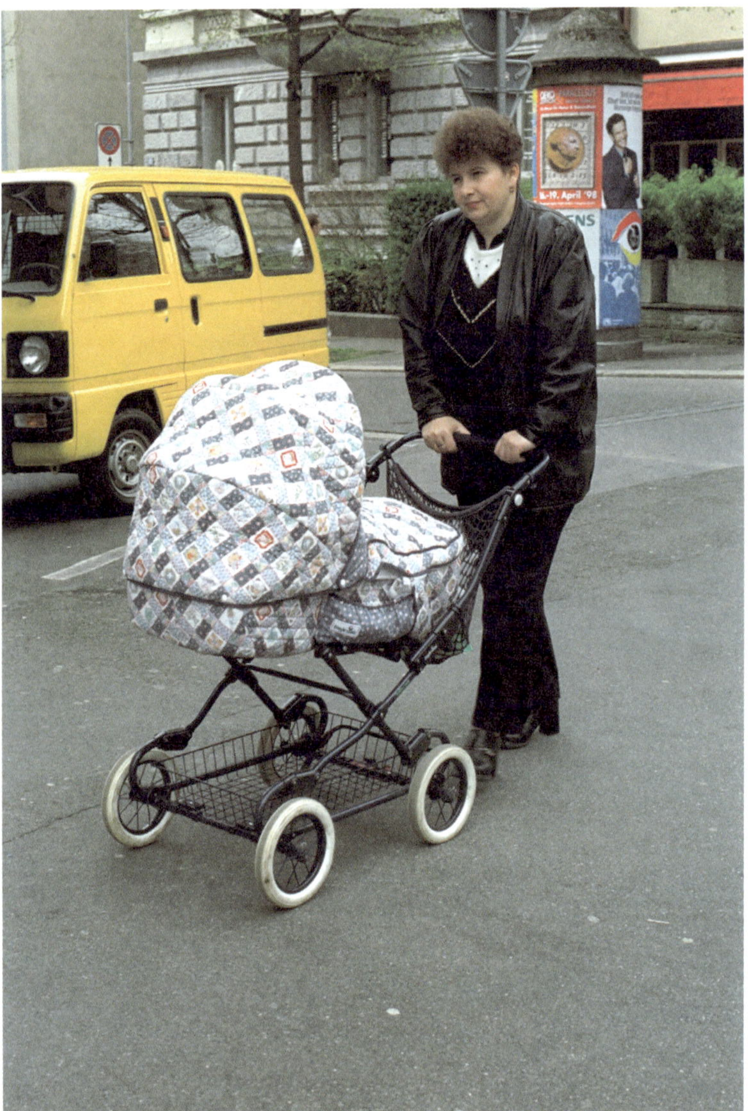
16.-19. April '98
NS

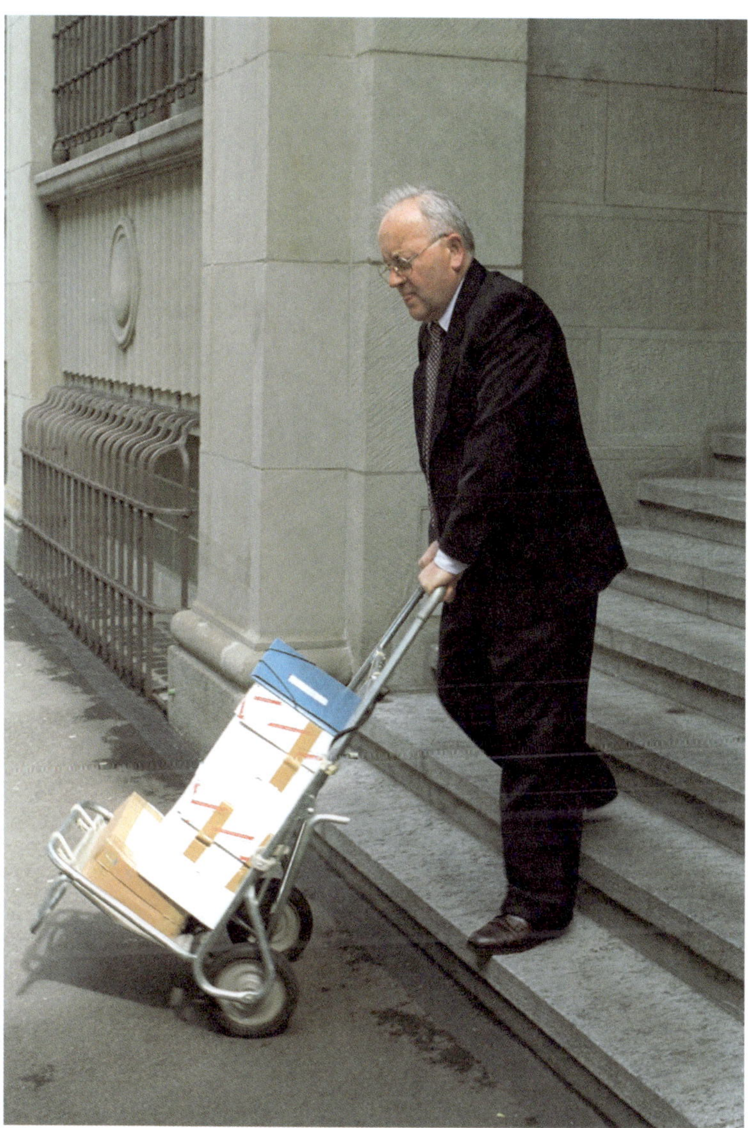

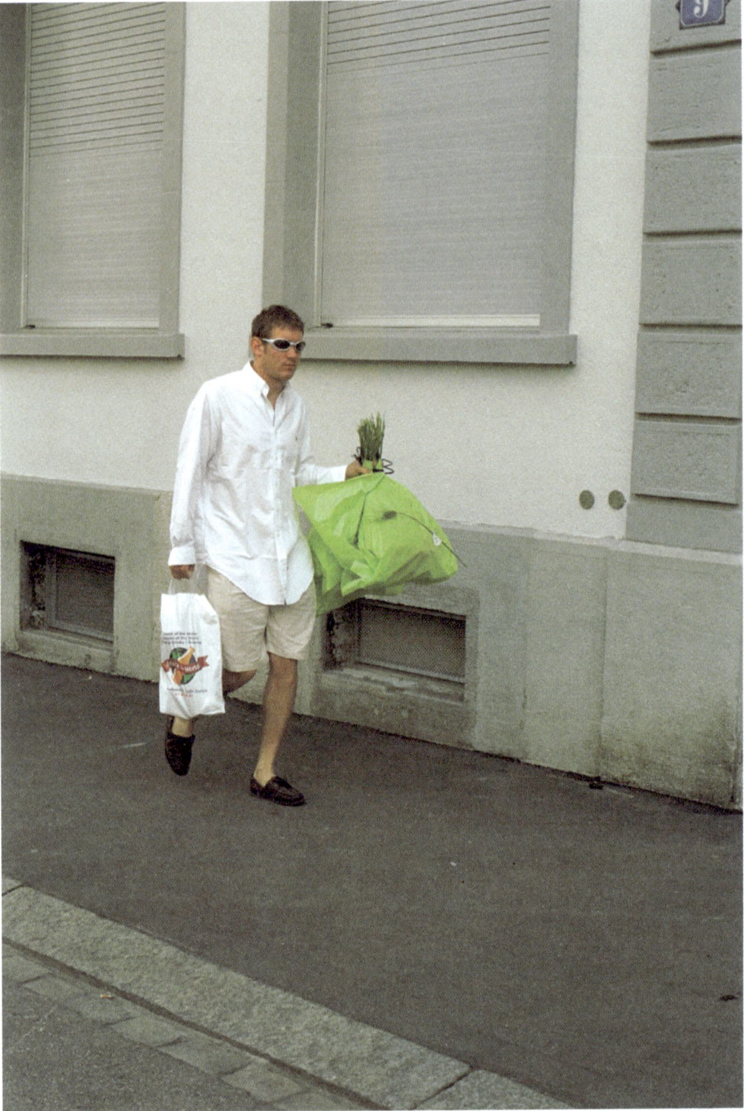

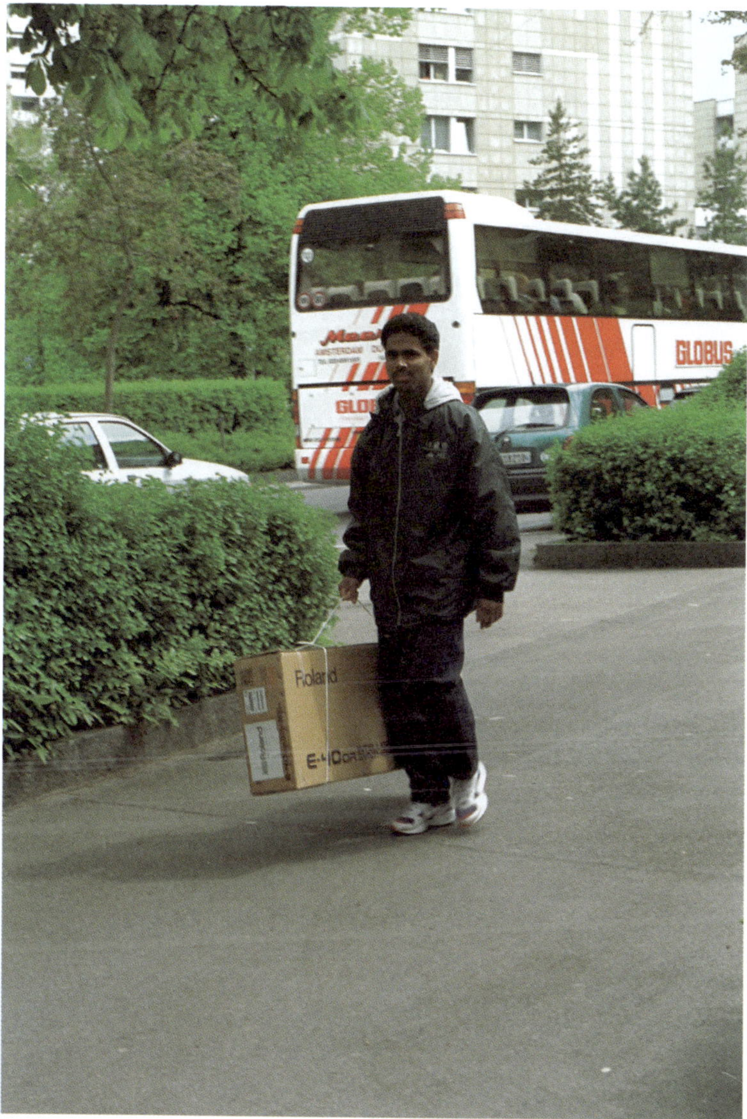

GLOBUS
Roland
E-40

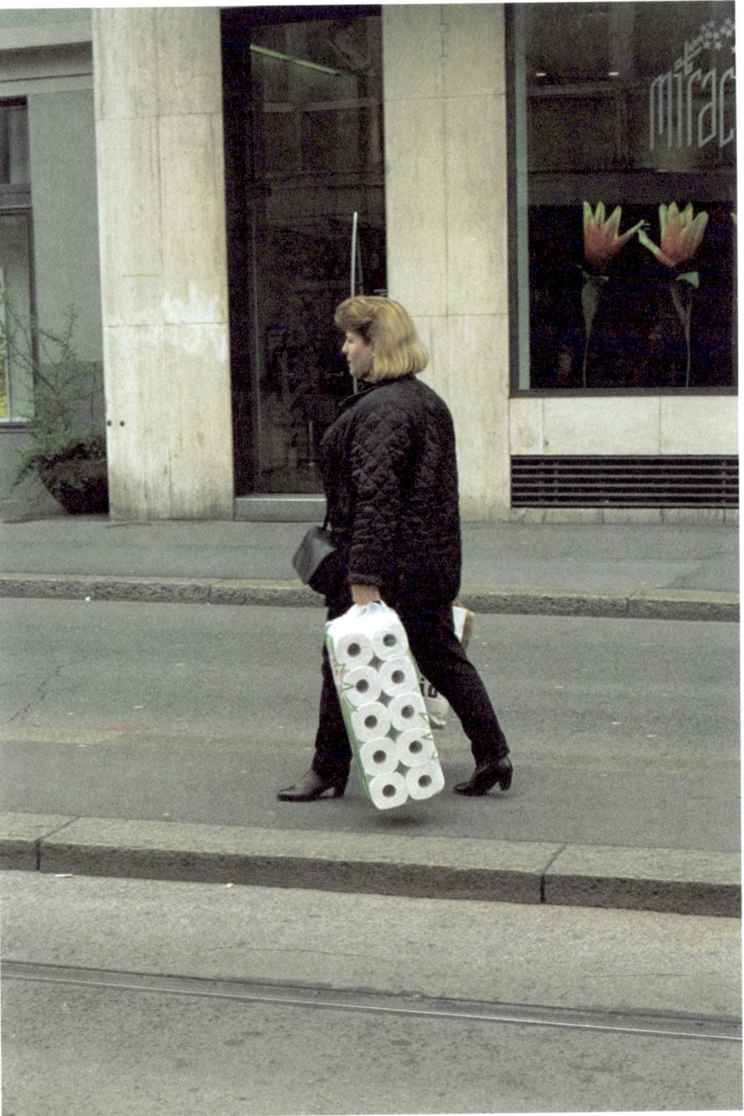
mirac

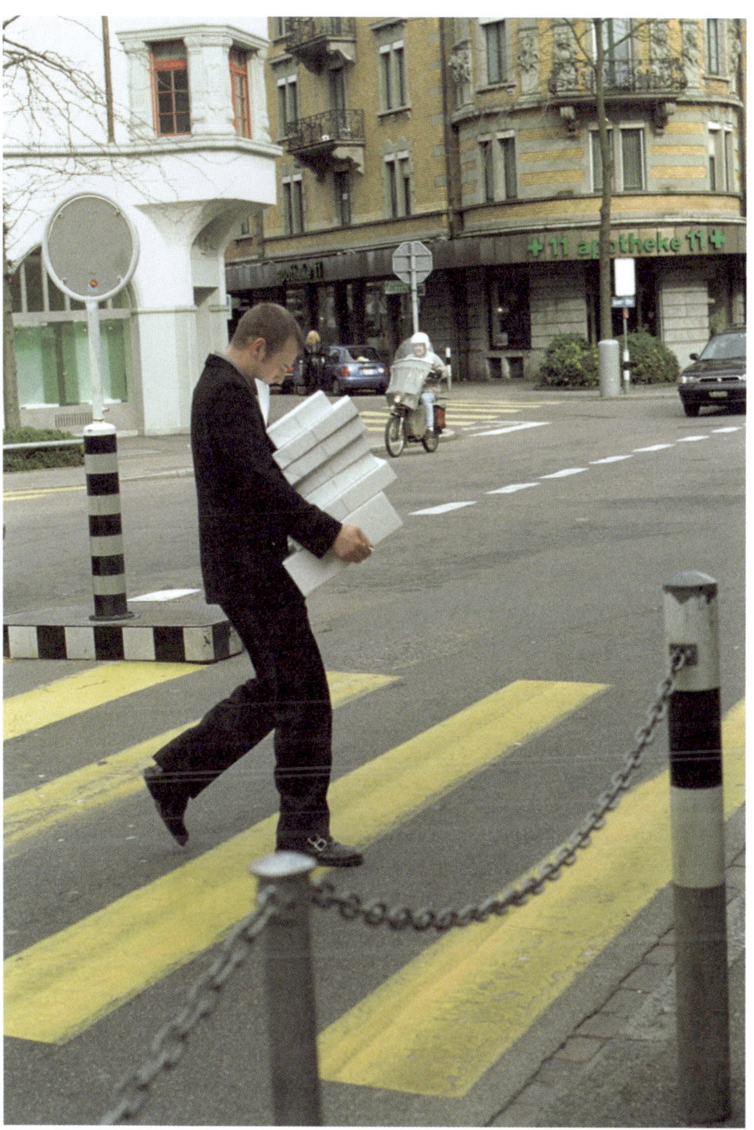

+ 11 apotheke 11 +

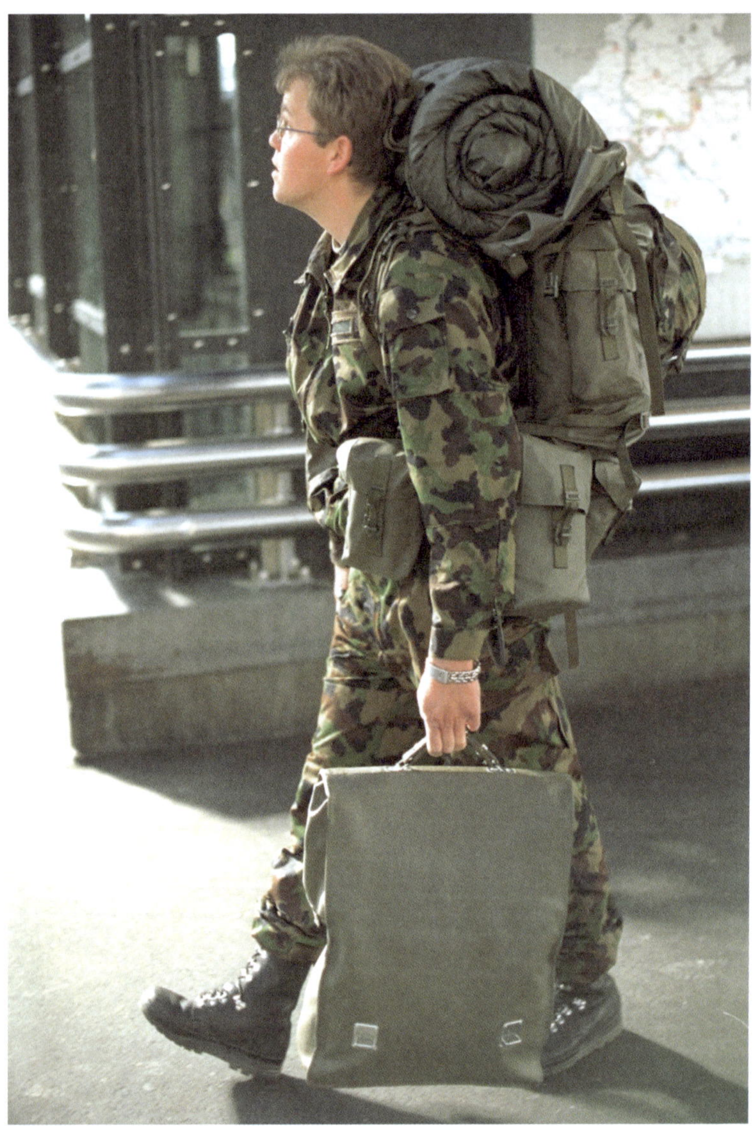

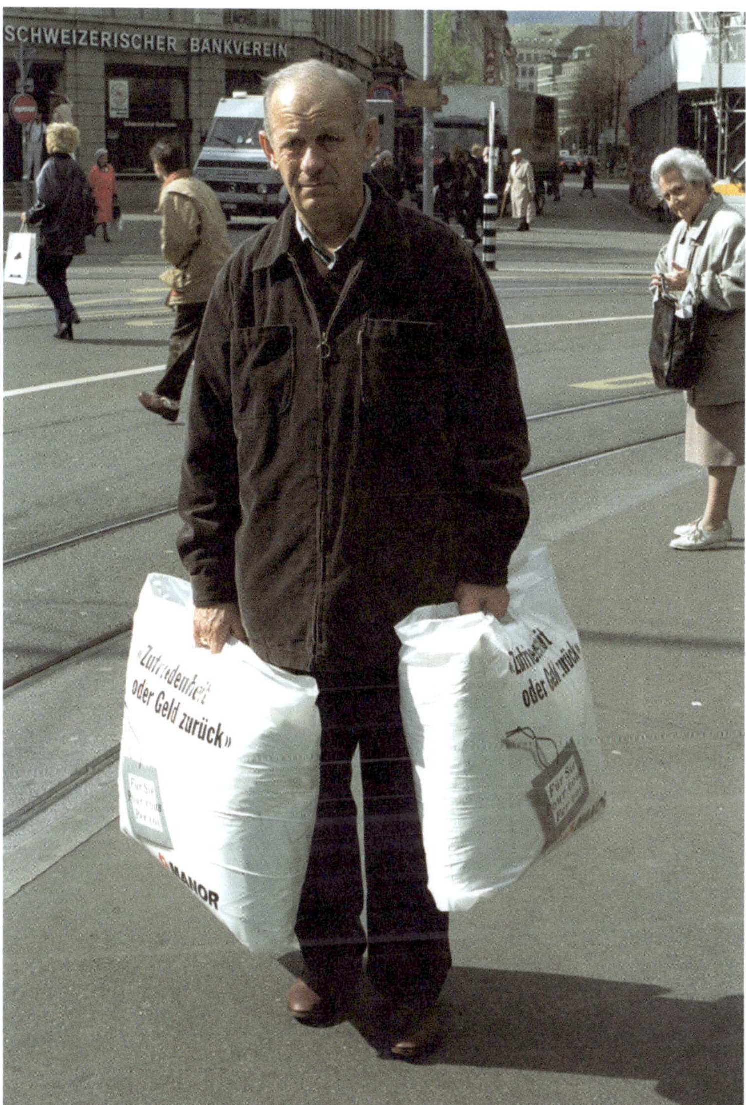
SCHWEIZERISCHER BANKVEREIN
«Zufriedenheit oder Geld zurück»
«Zufriedenheit oder Geld zurück»
MANOR

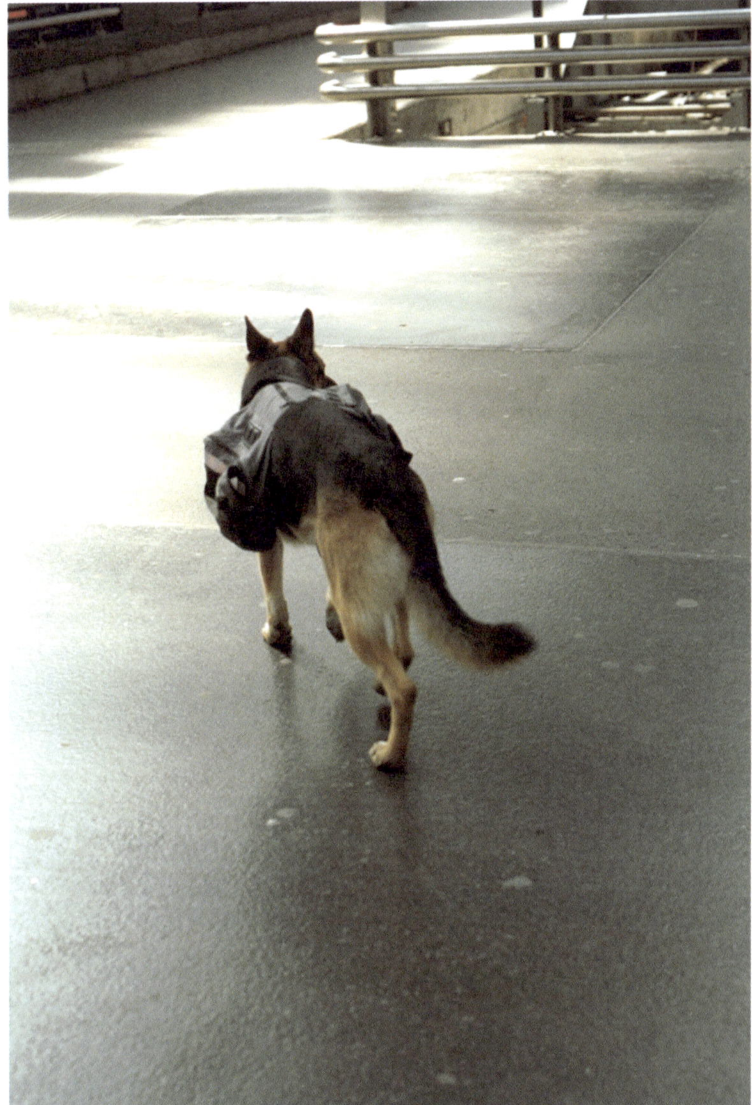

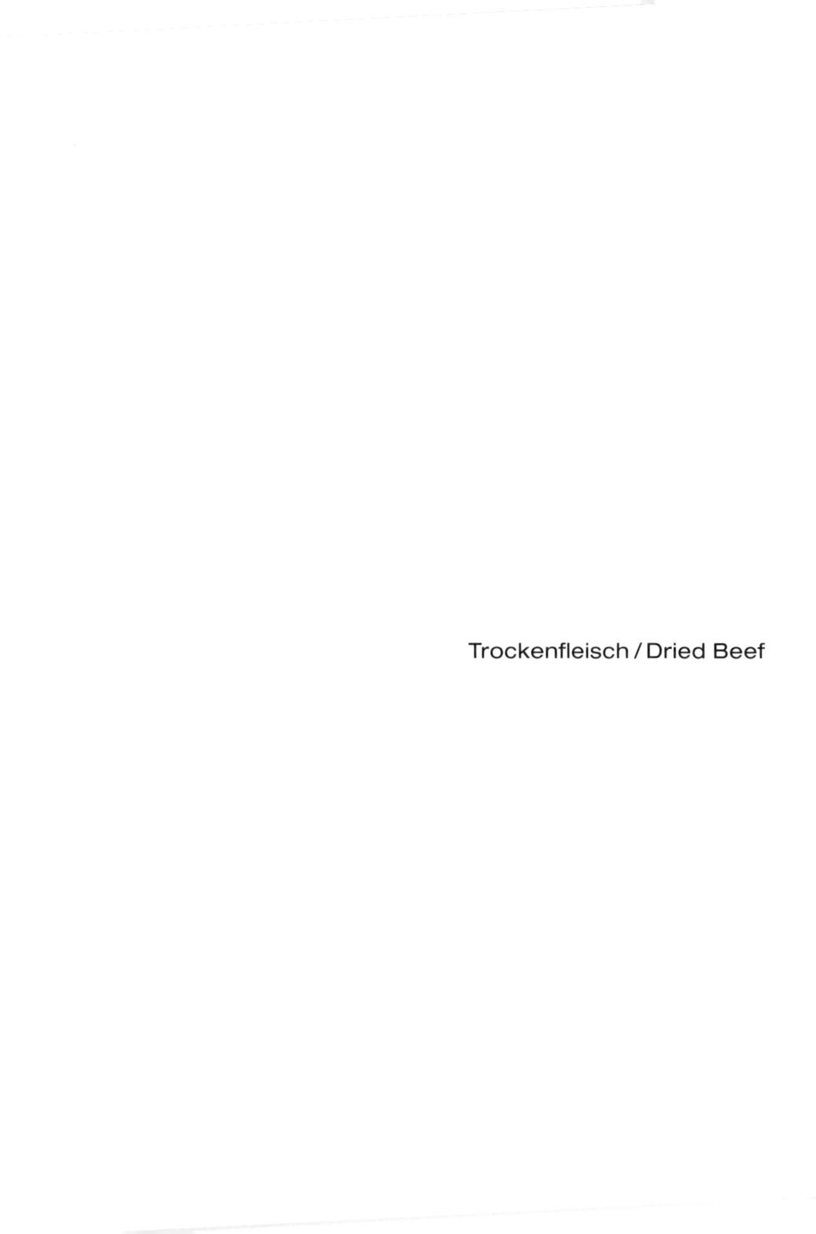

Trockenfleisch / Dried Beef

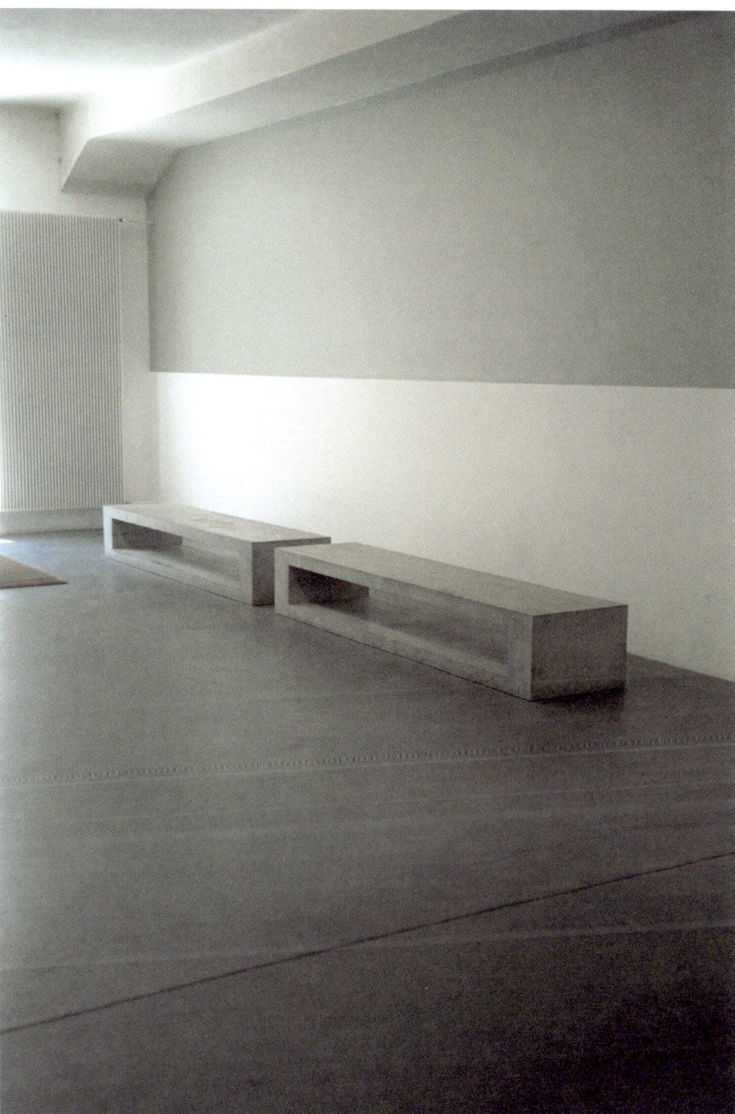

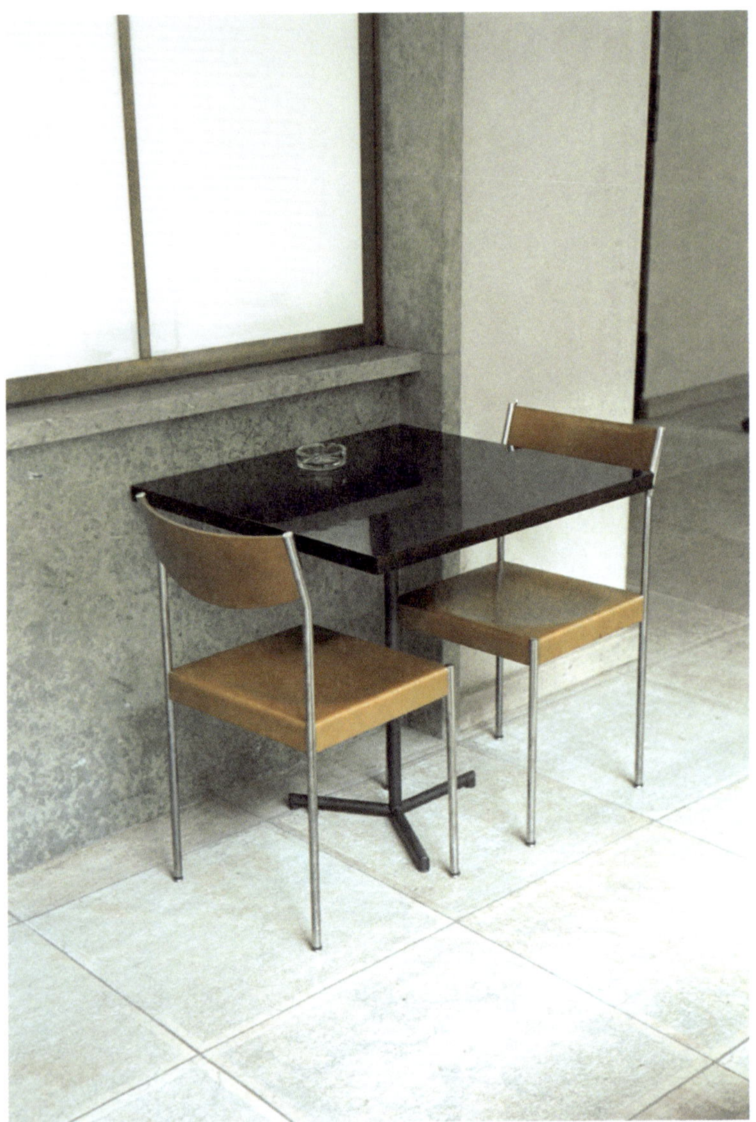

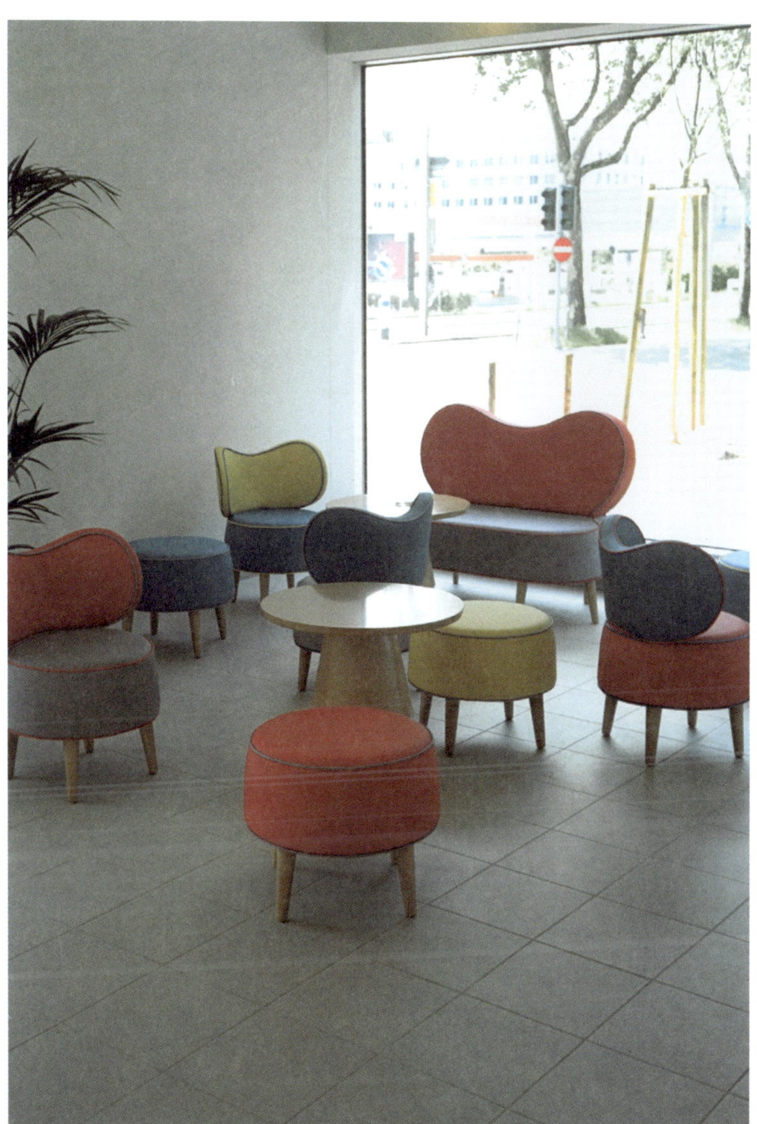

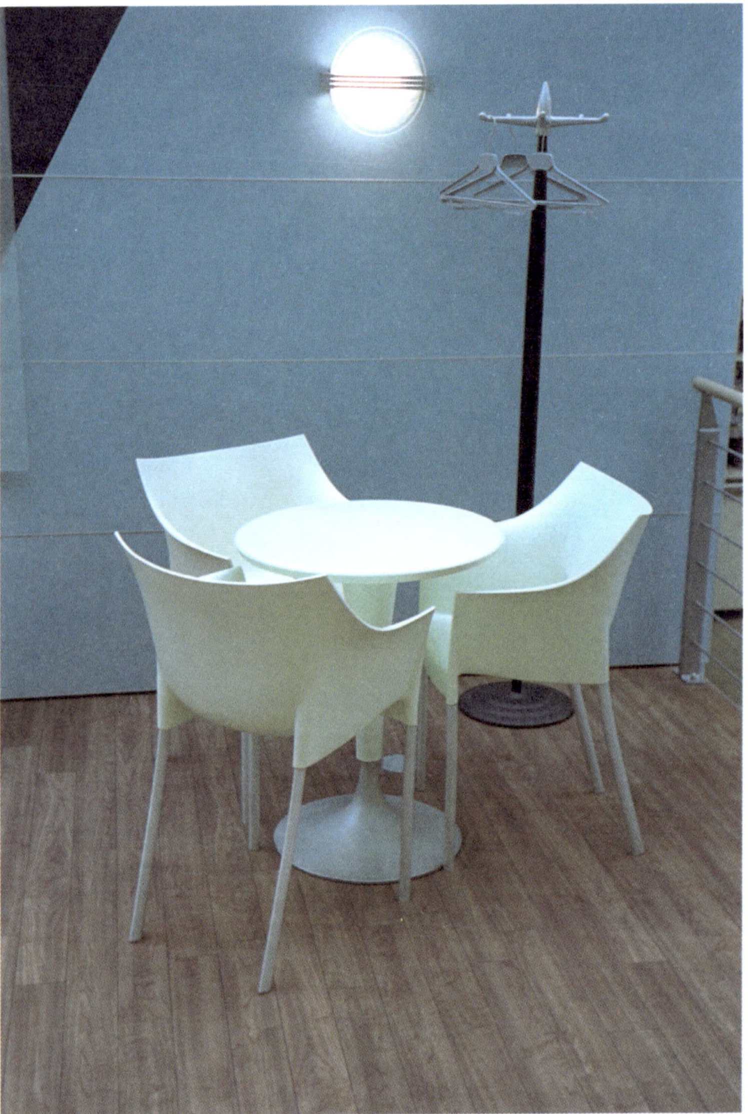

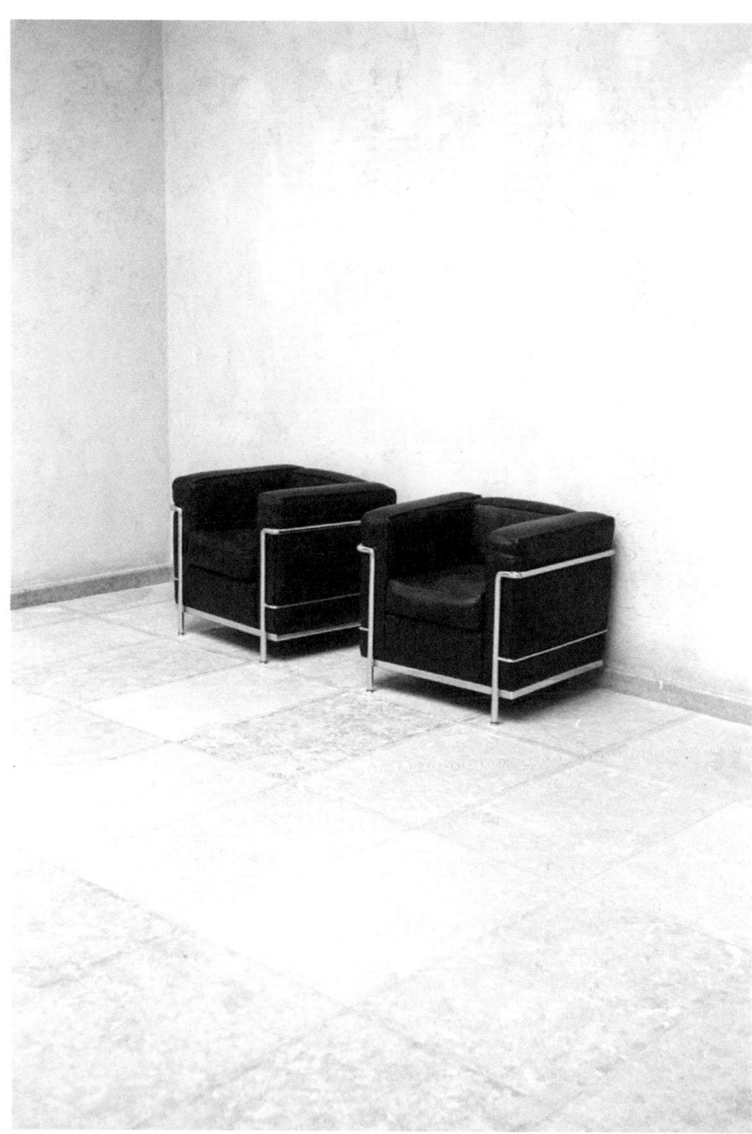

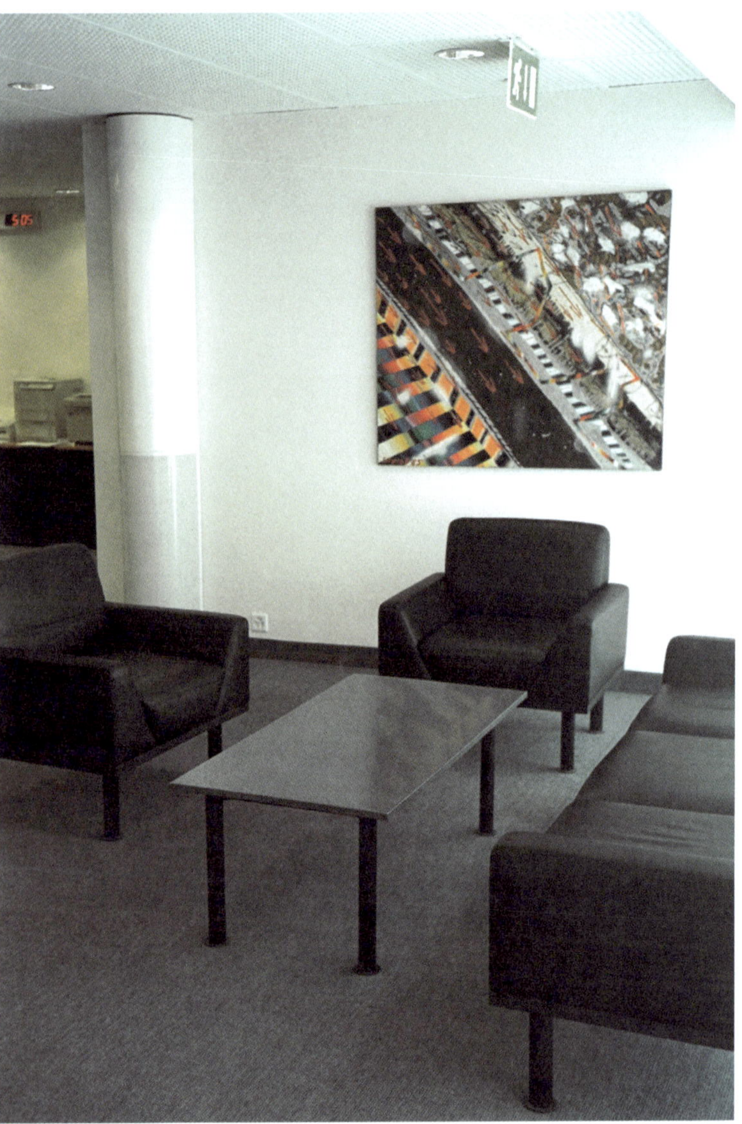

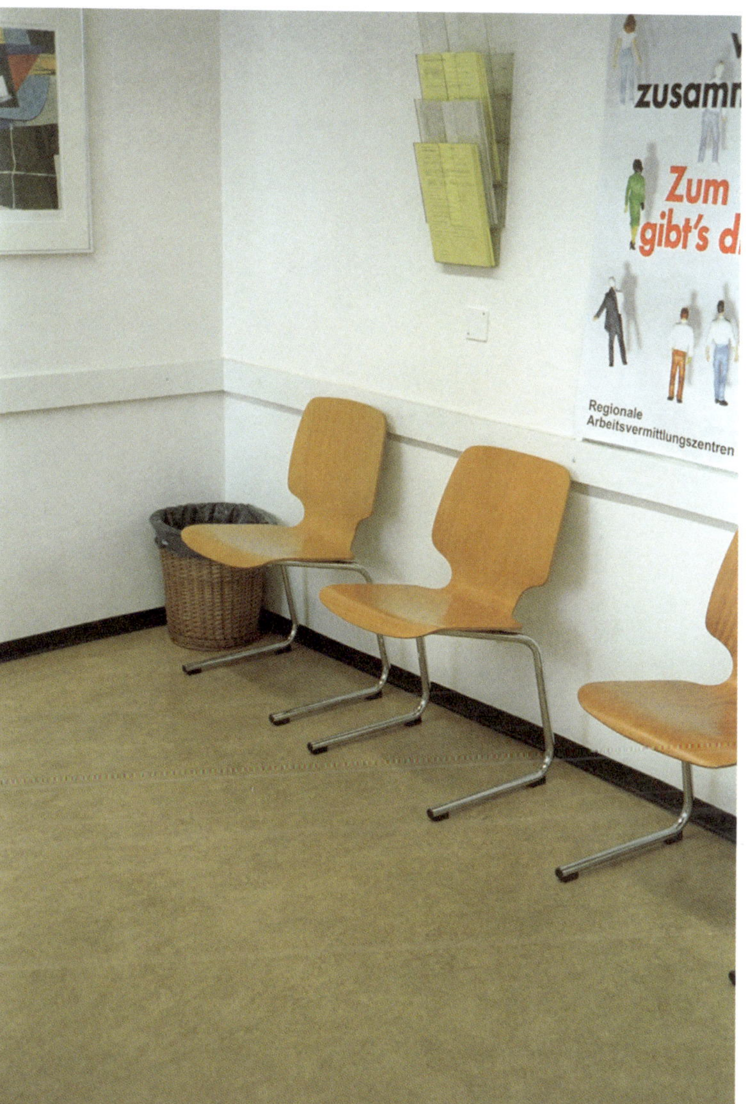
zusamm
Zum
gibt's d
Regionale
Arbeitsvermittlungszentren

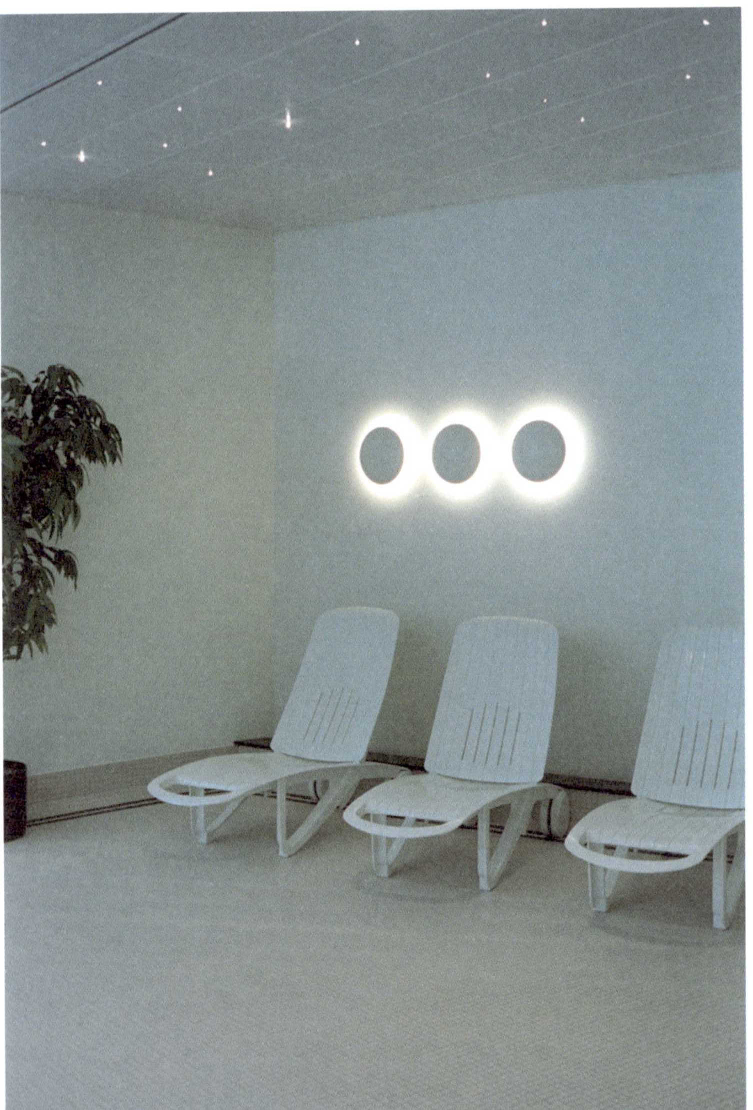

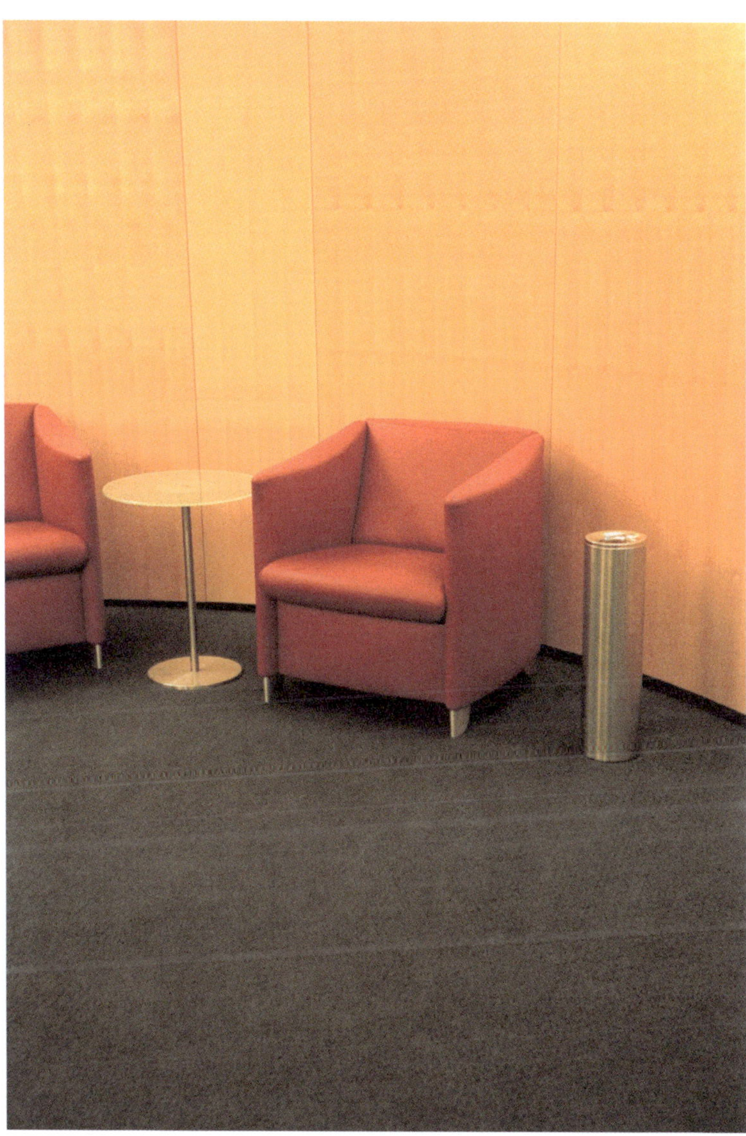

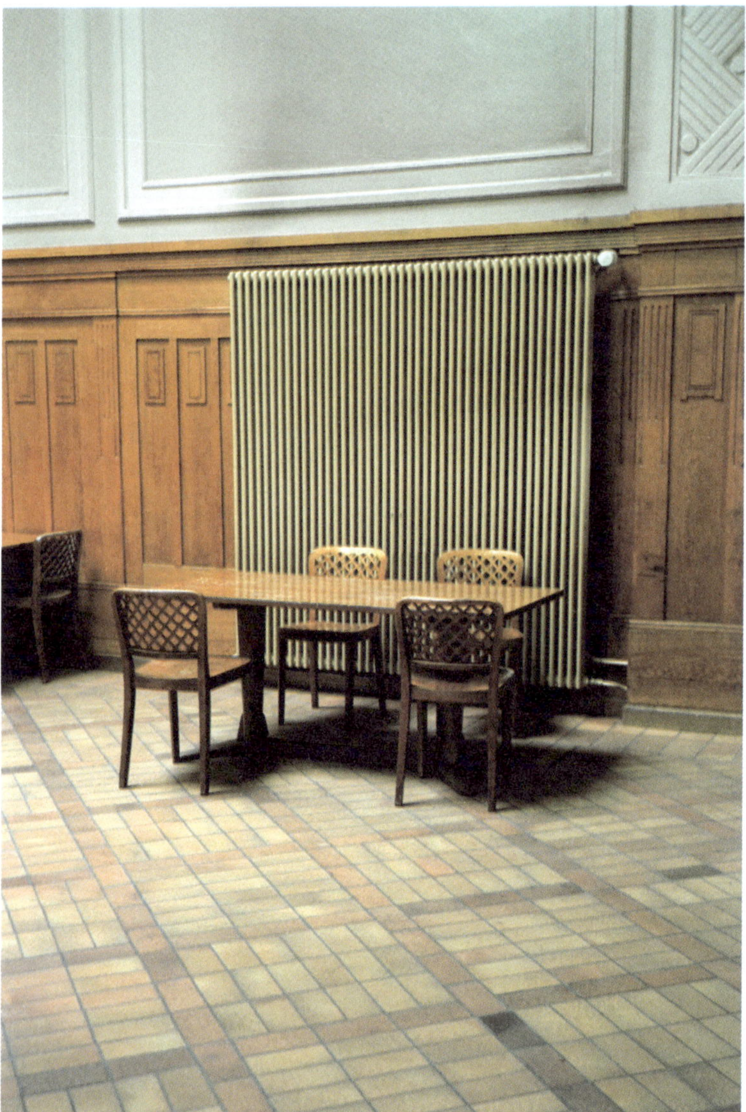

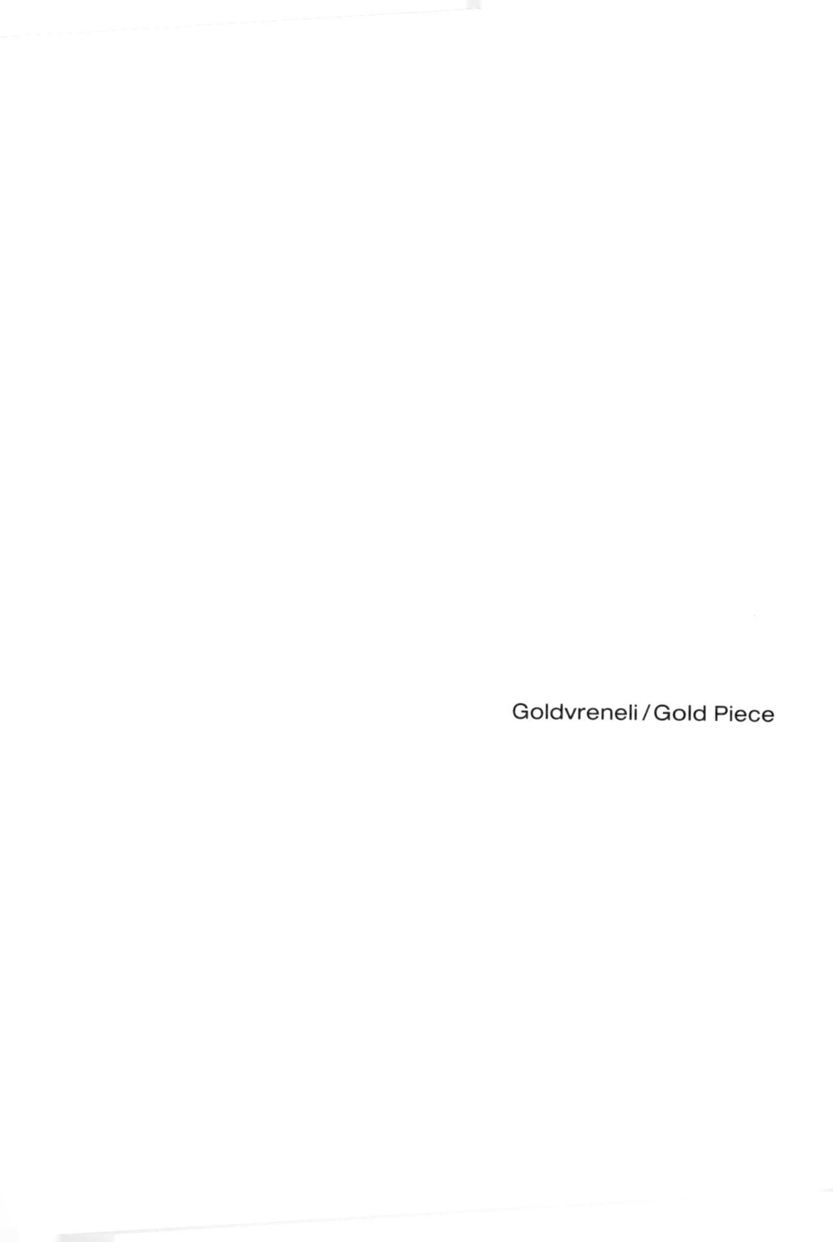

Goldvreneli / Gold Piece

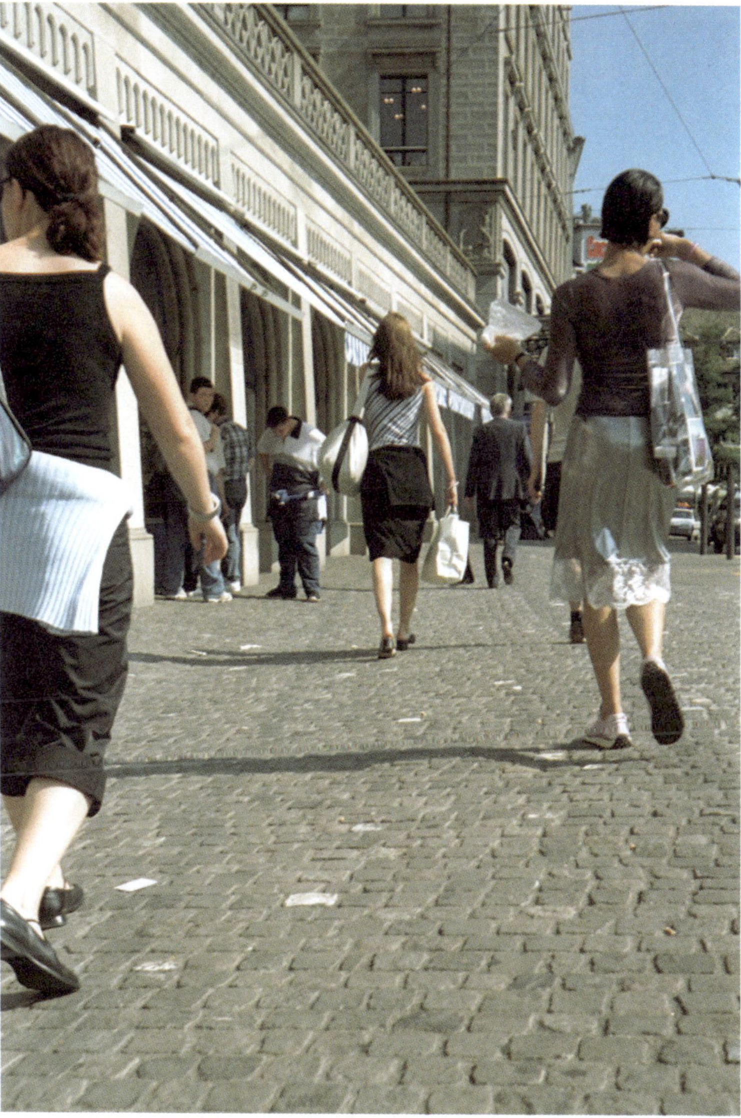

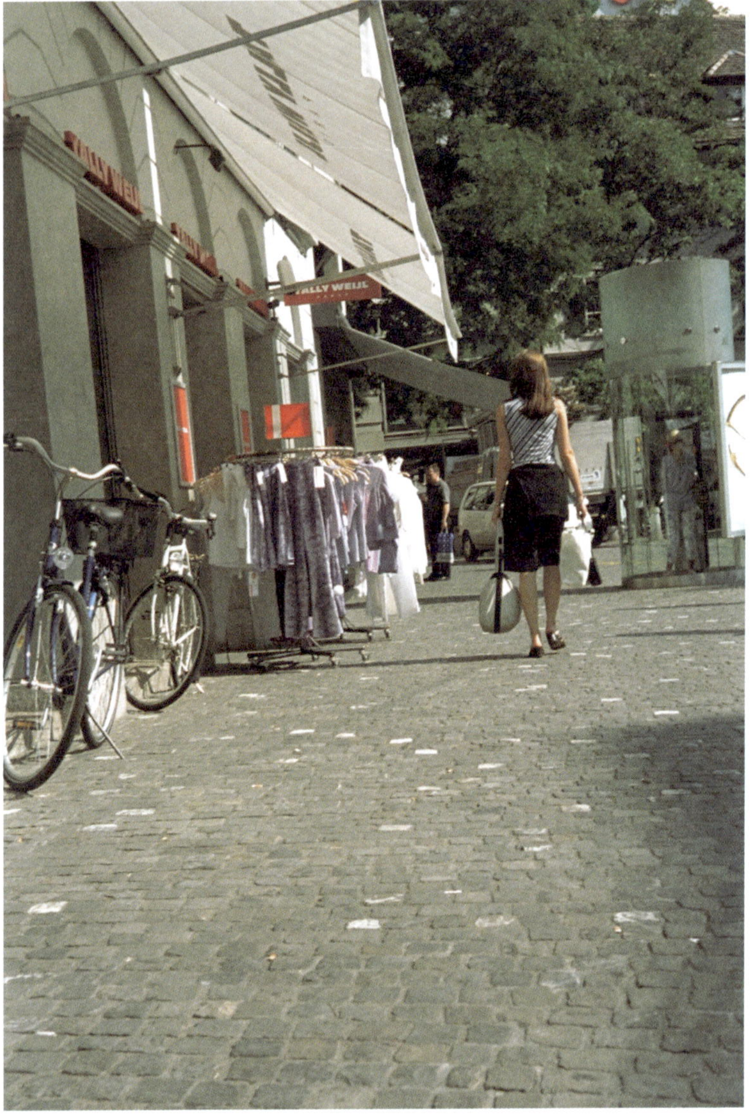

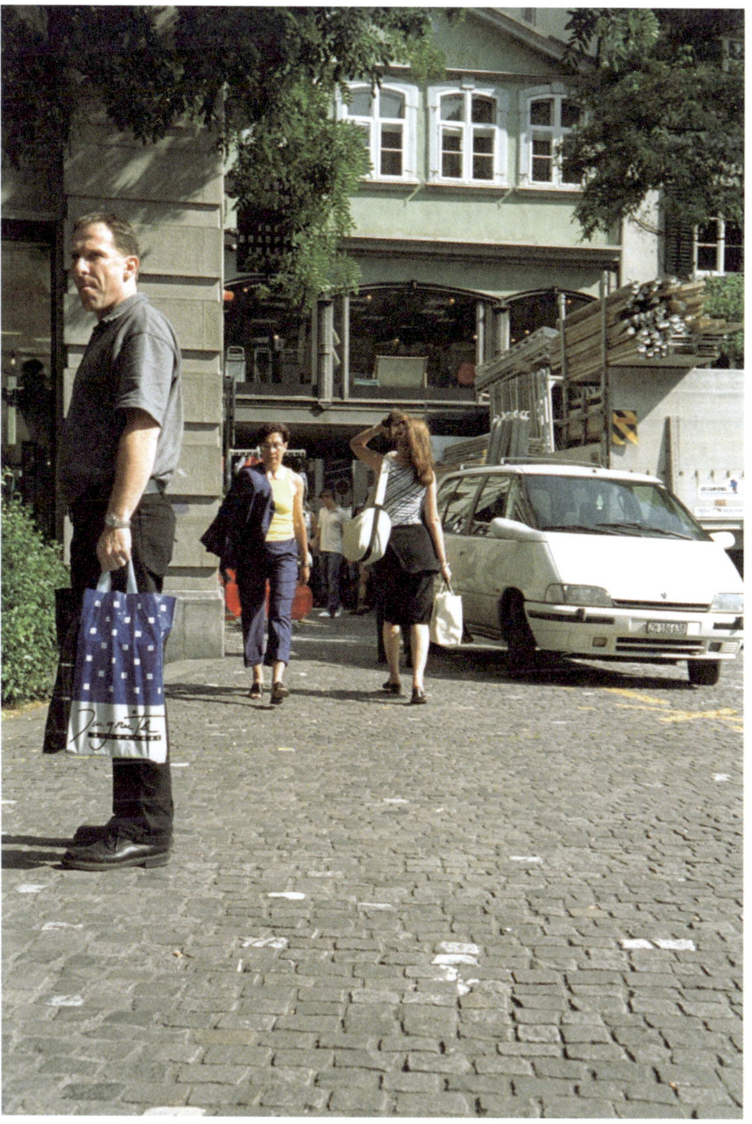

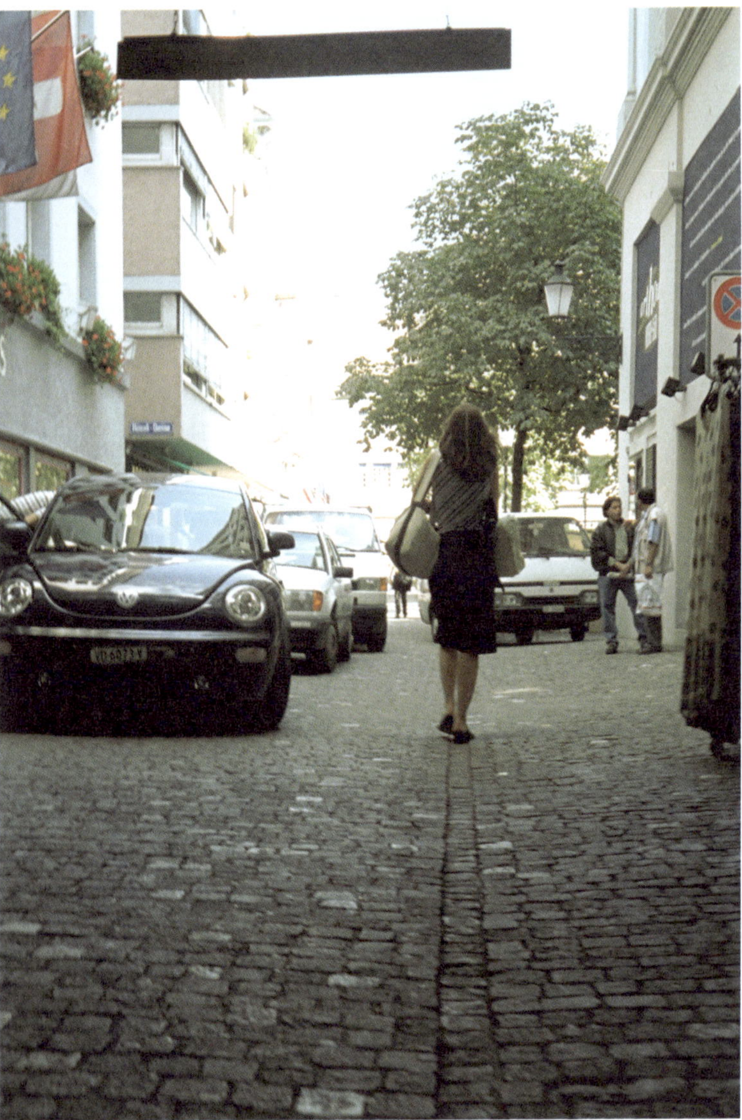

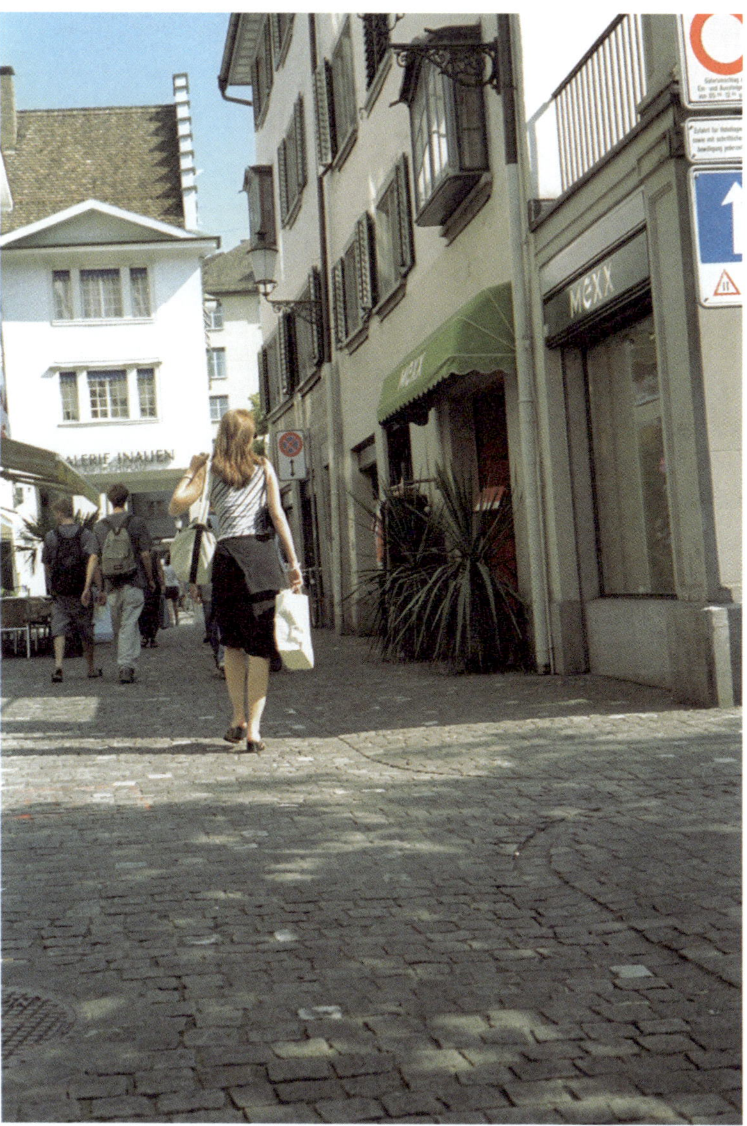

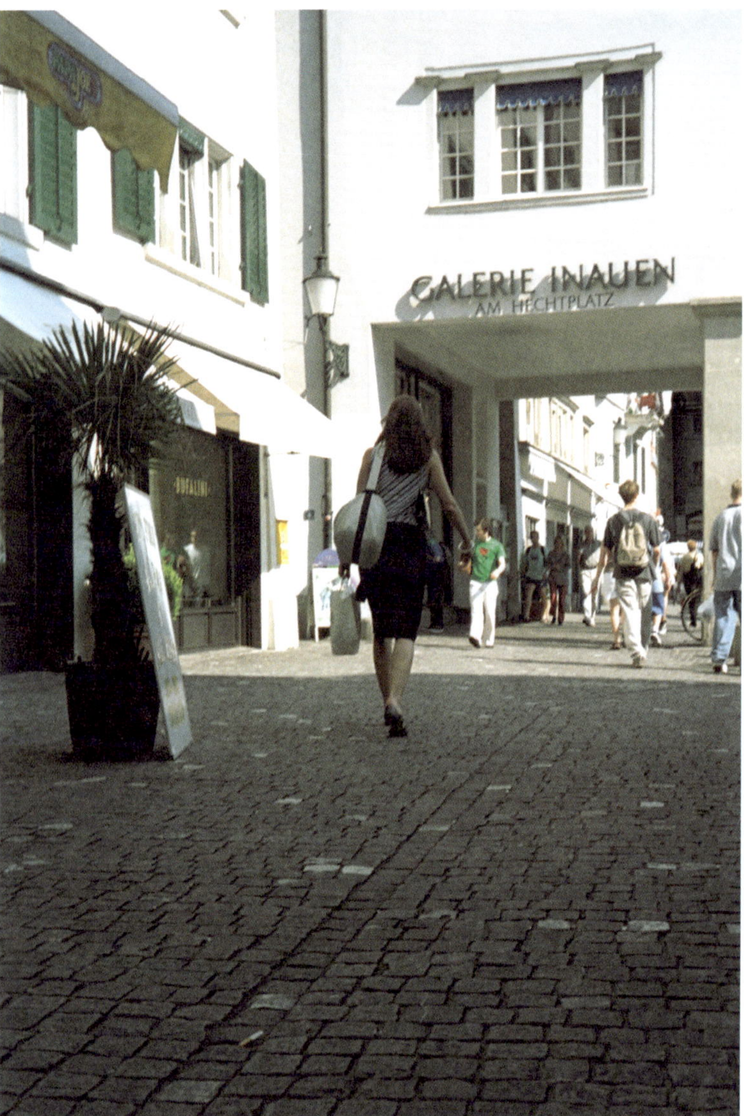

GALERIE INAUEN
AM HECHTPLATZ

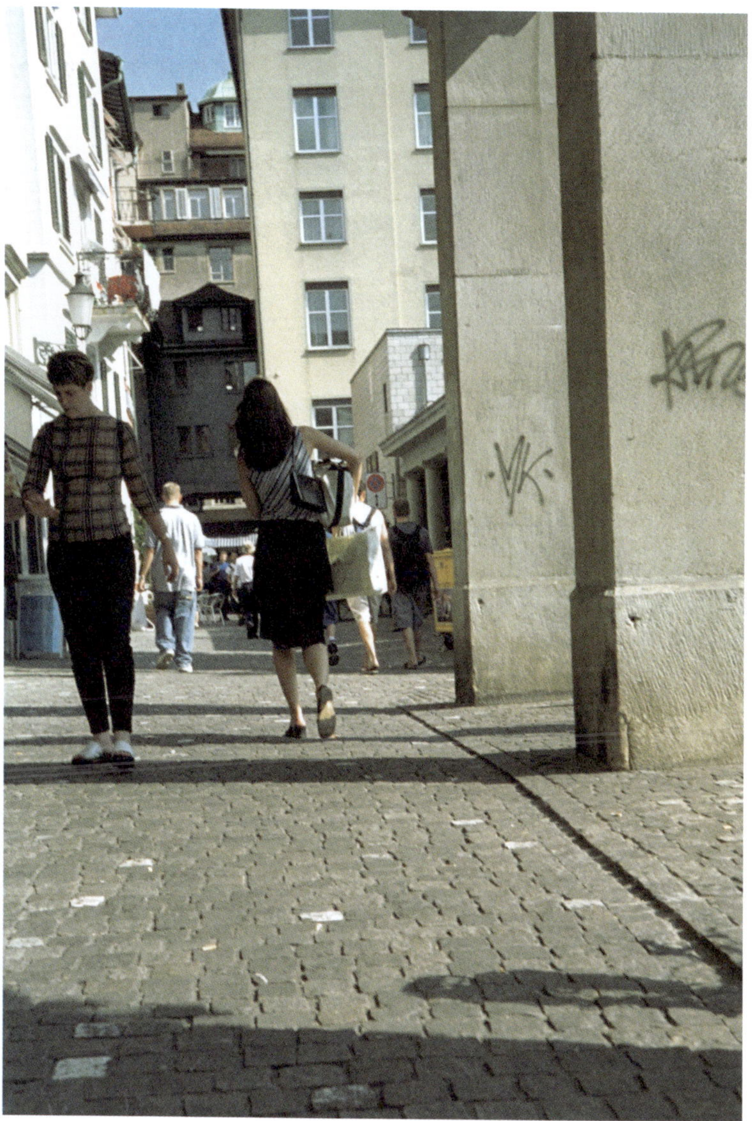

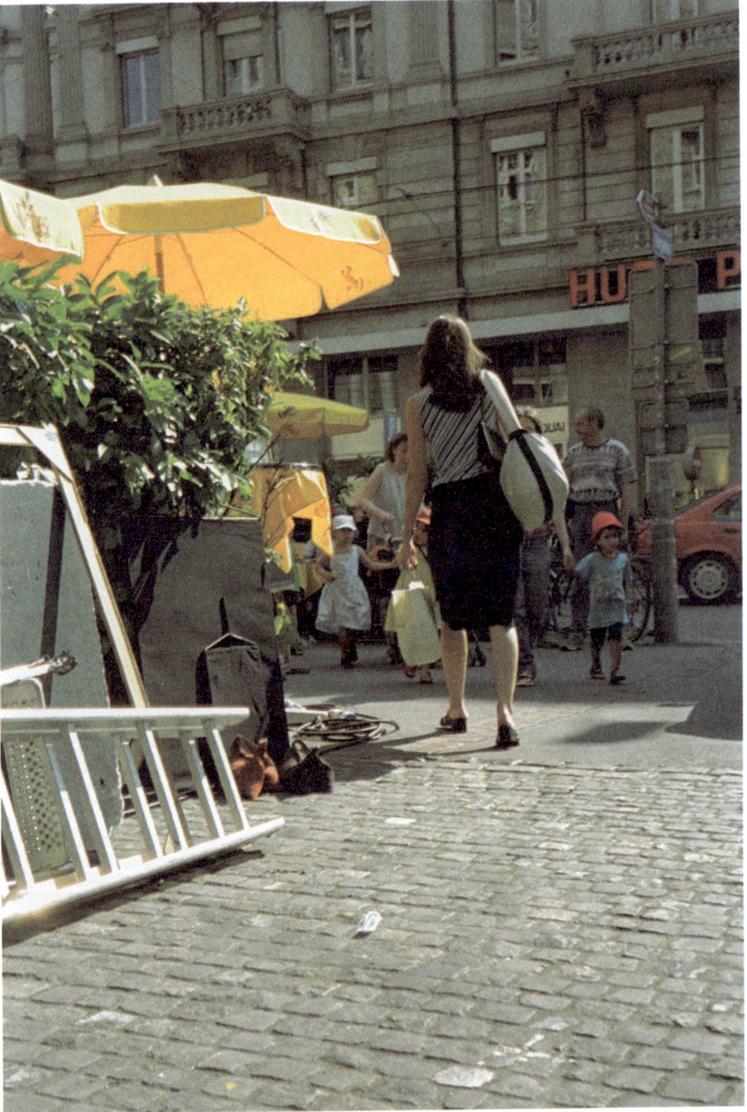

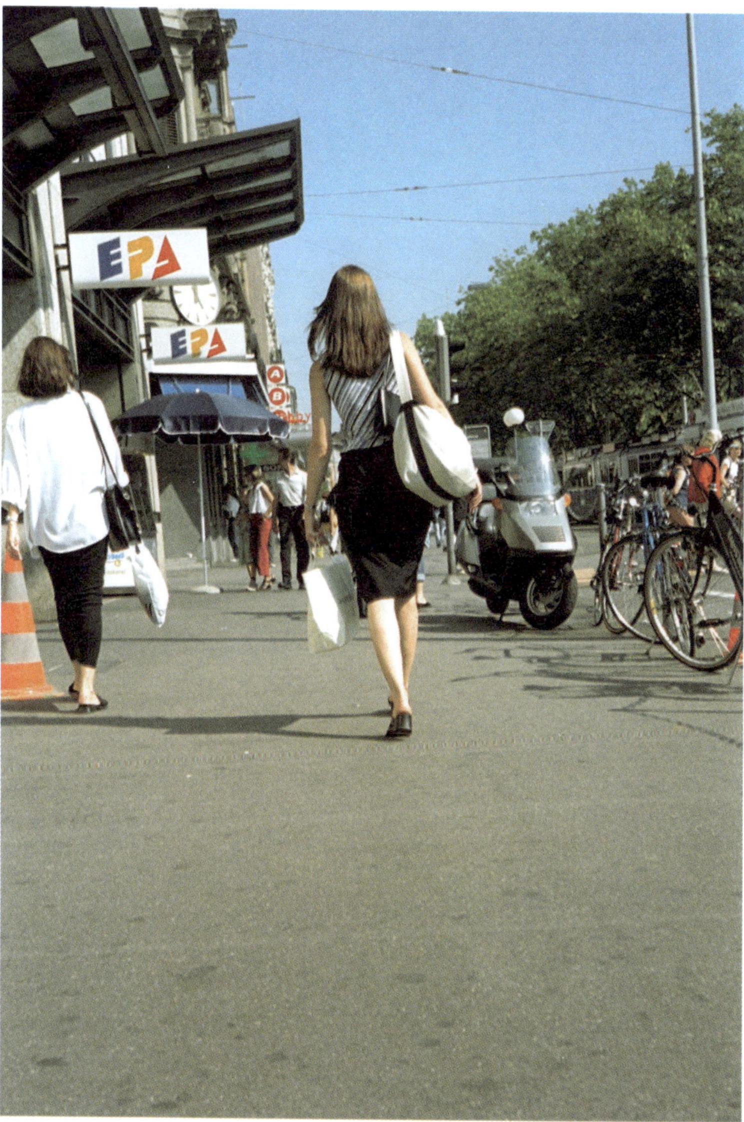

EPA
EPA

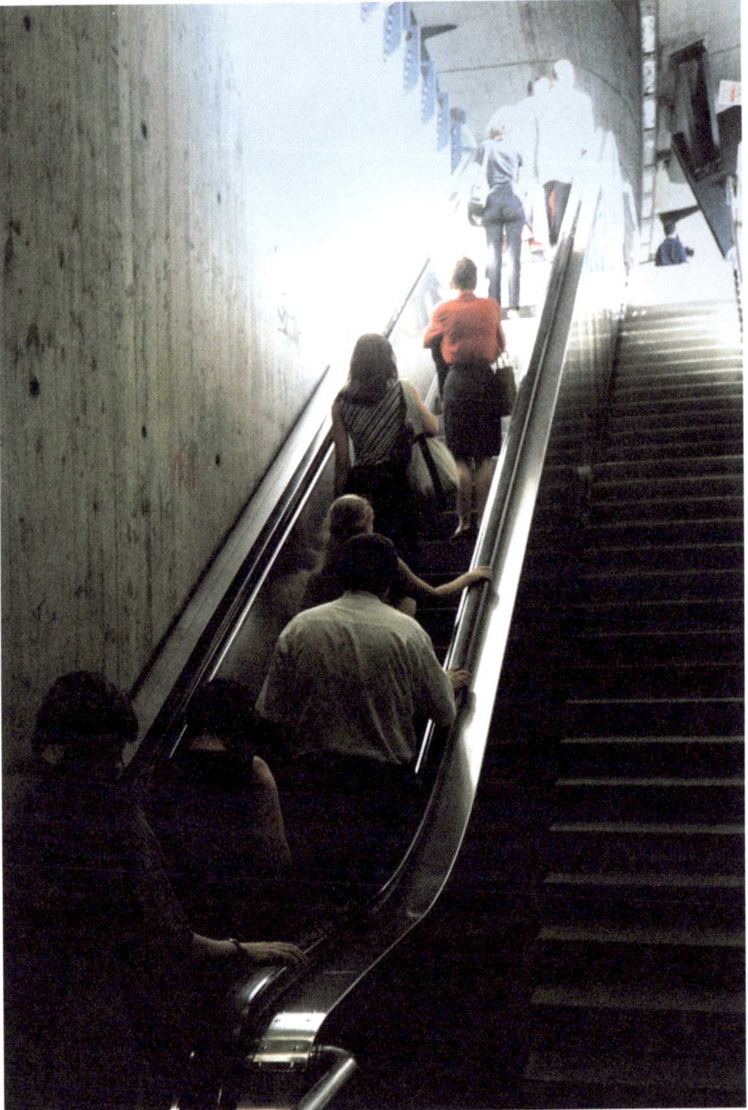

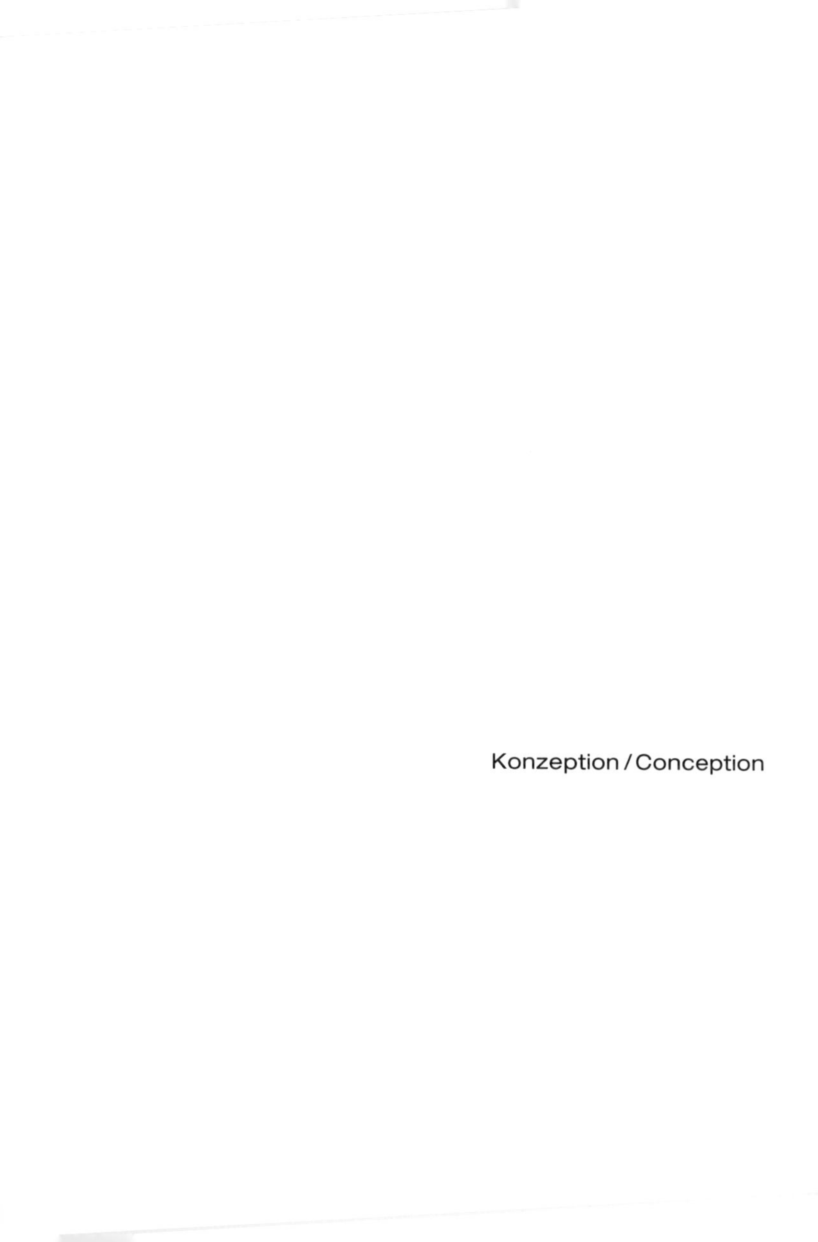
Konzeption / Conception

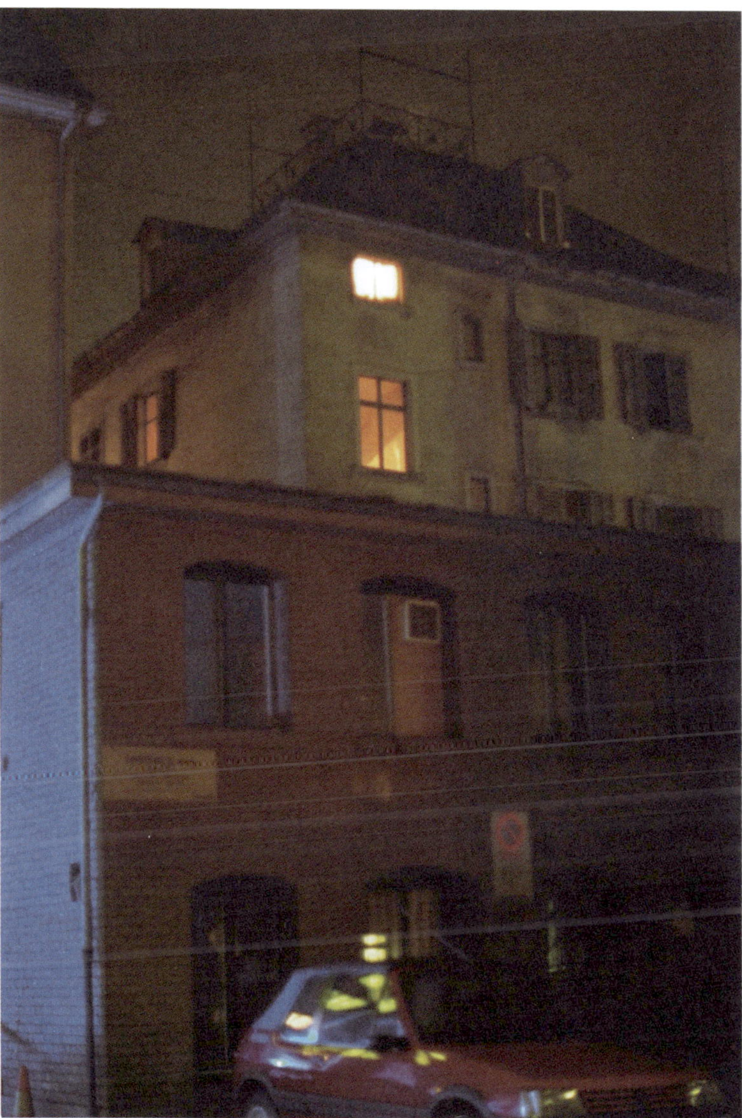

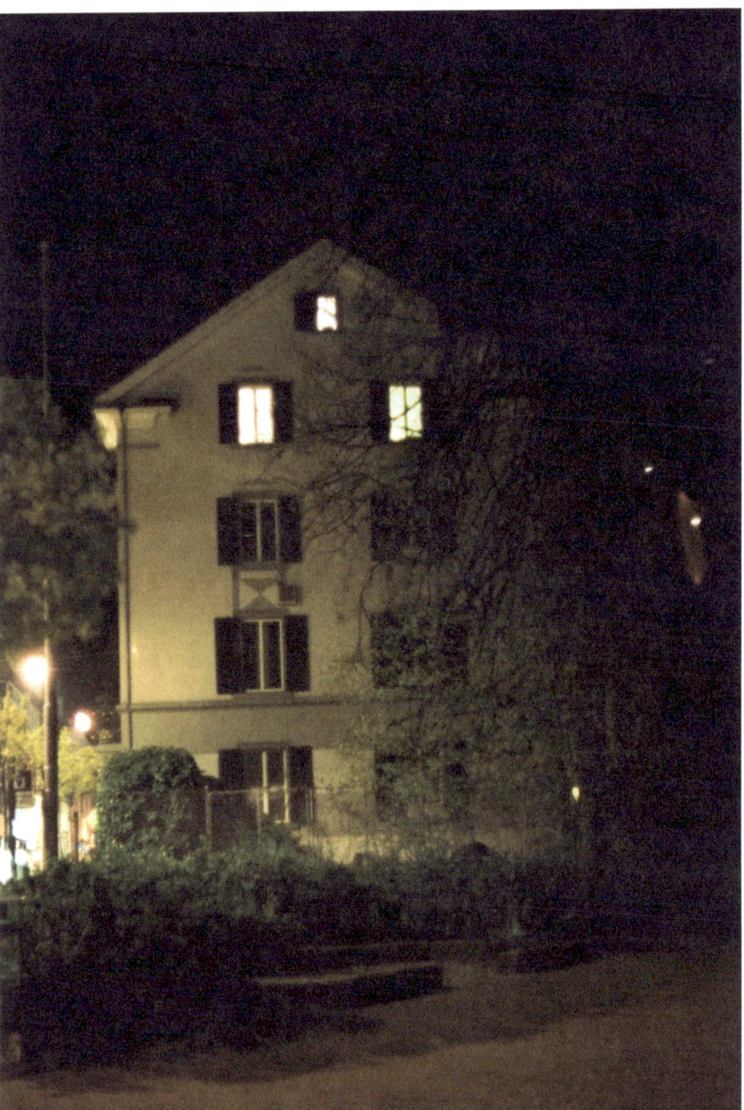

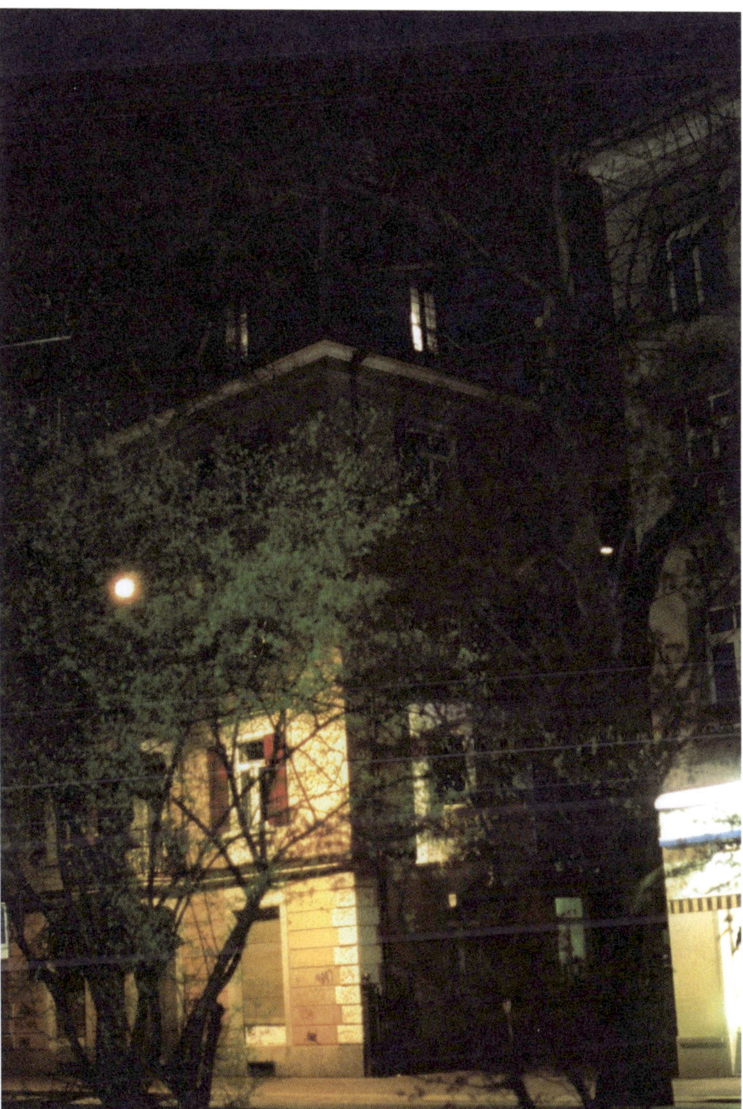

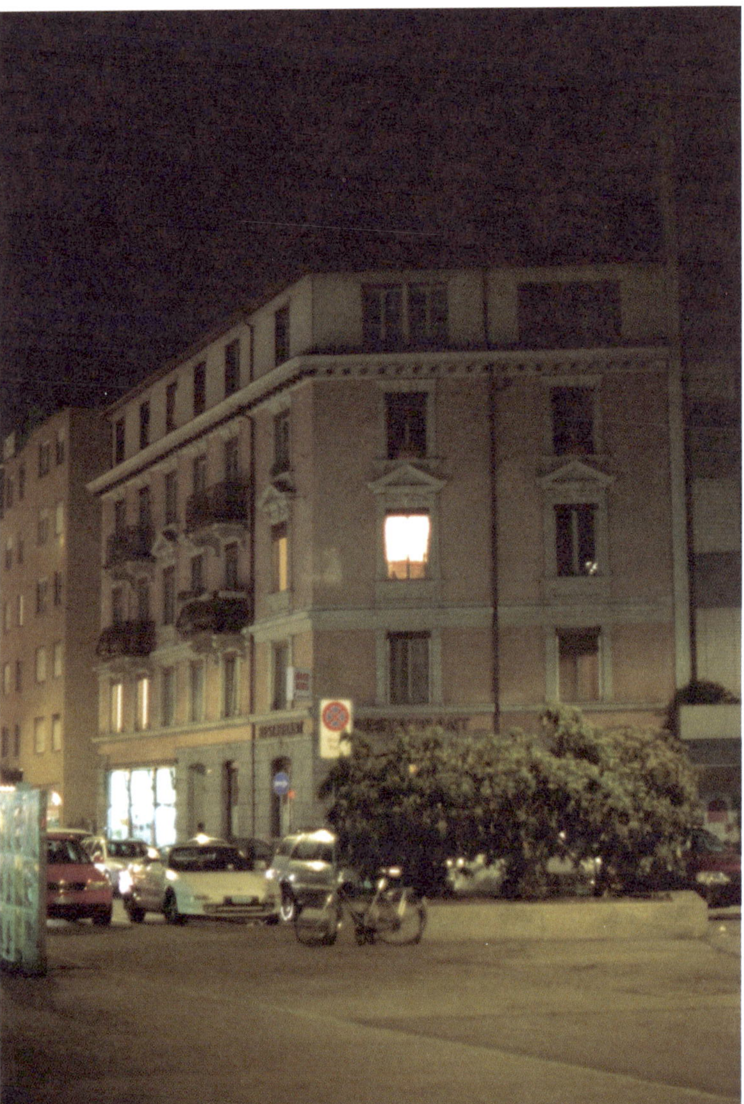

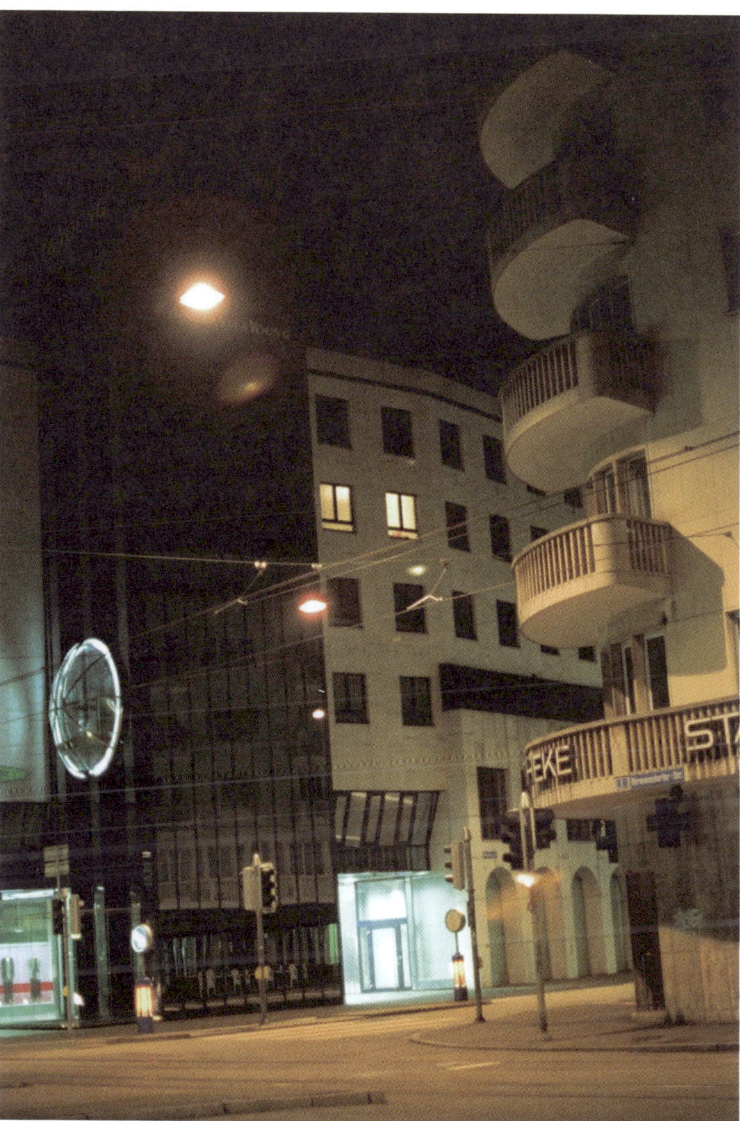

EKE
STA
Braunsberger Str.

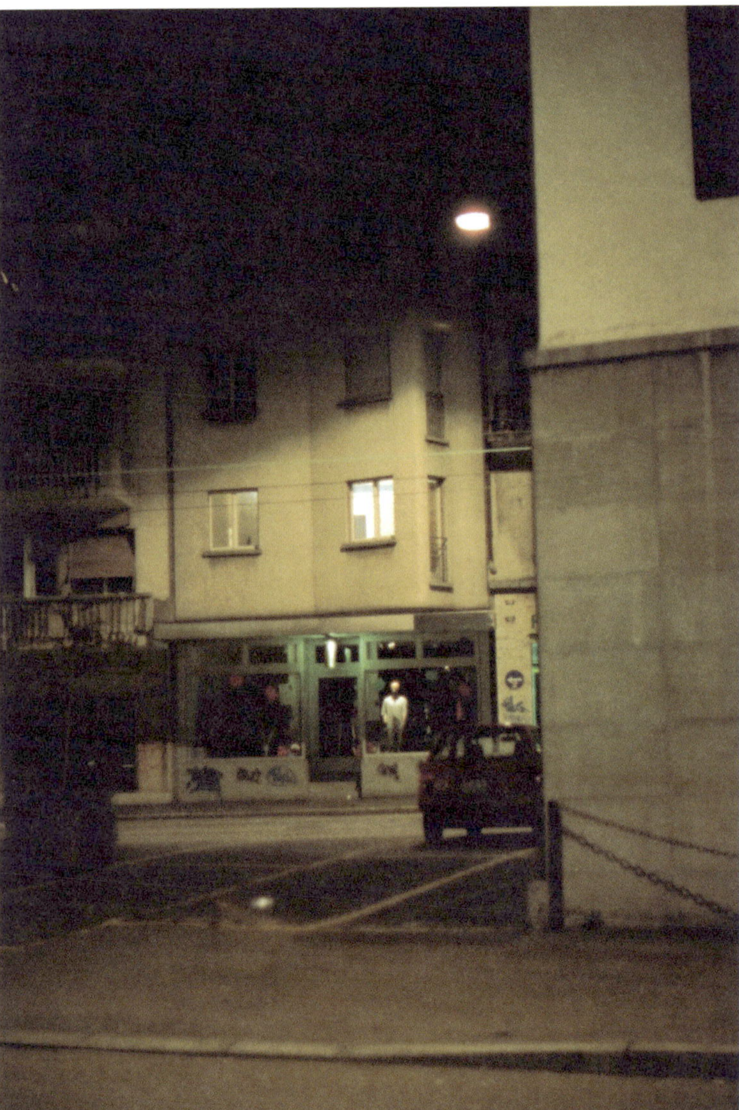

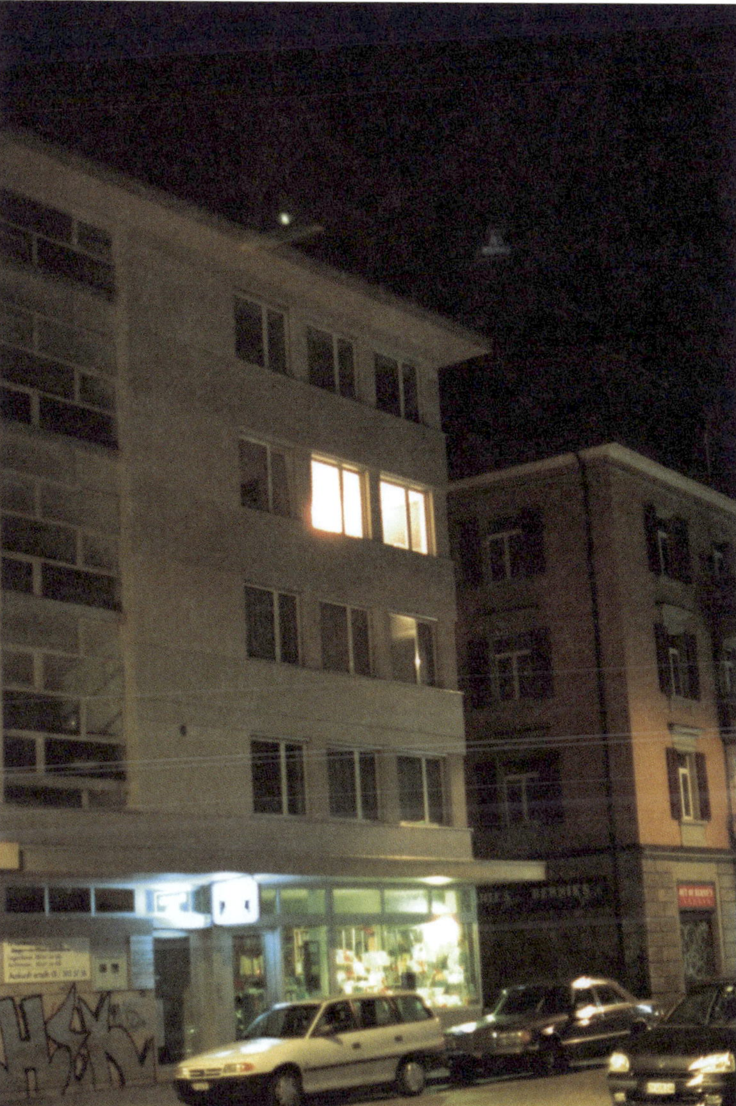

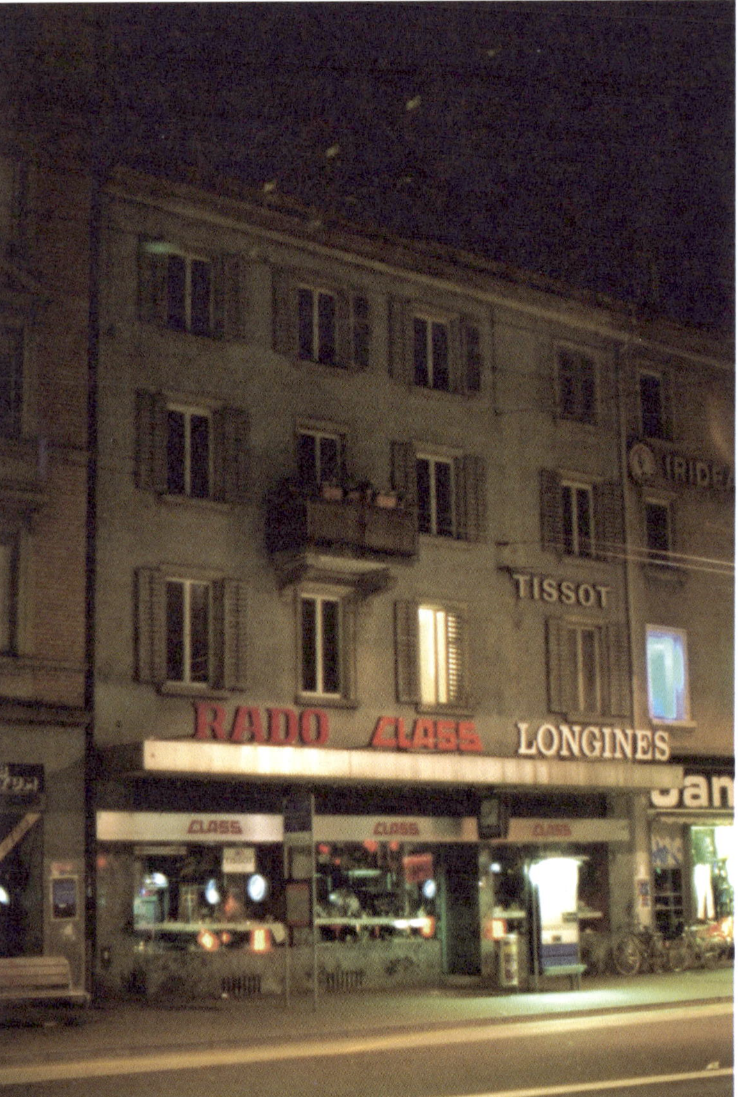

TISSOT
RADO CLASS LONGINES
CLASS
CLASS
CLASS

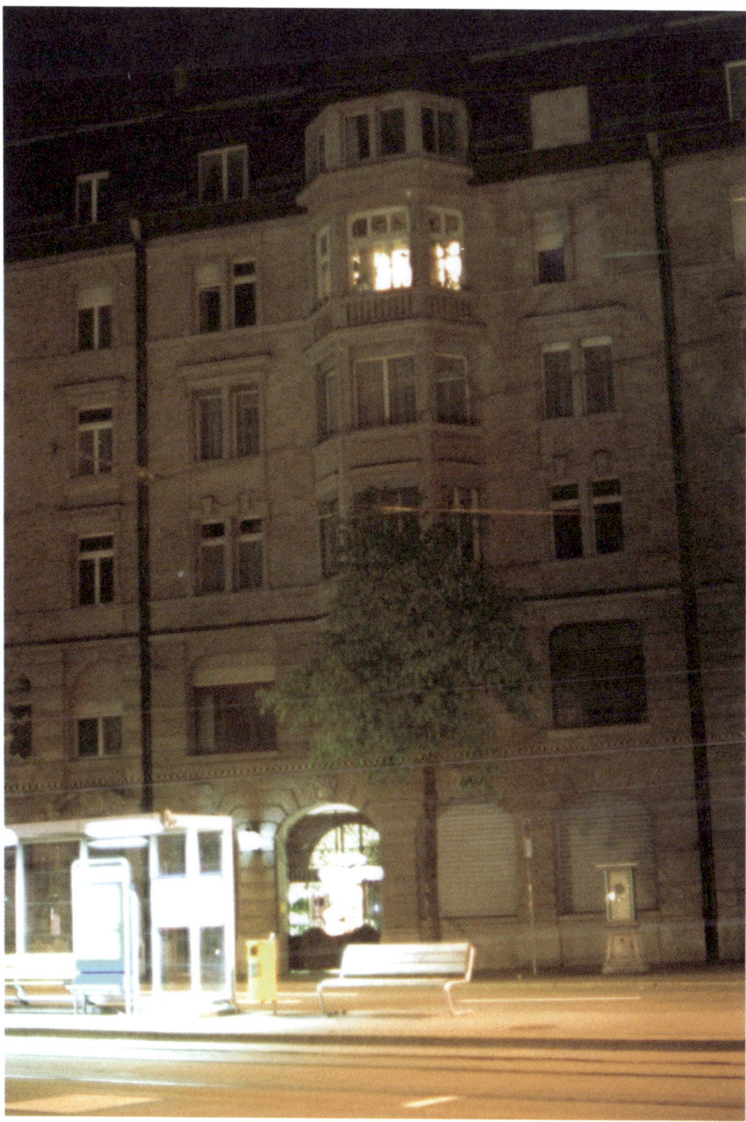

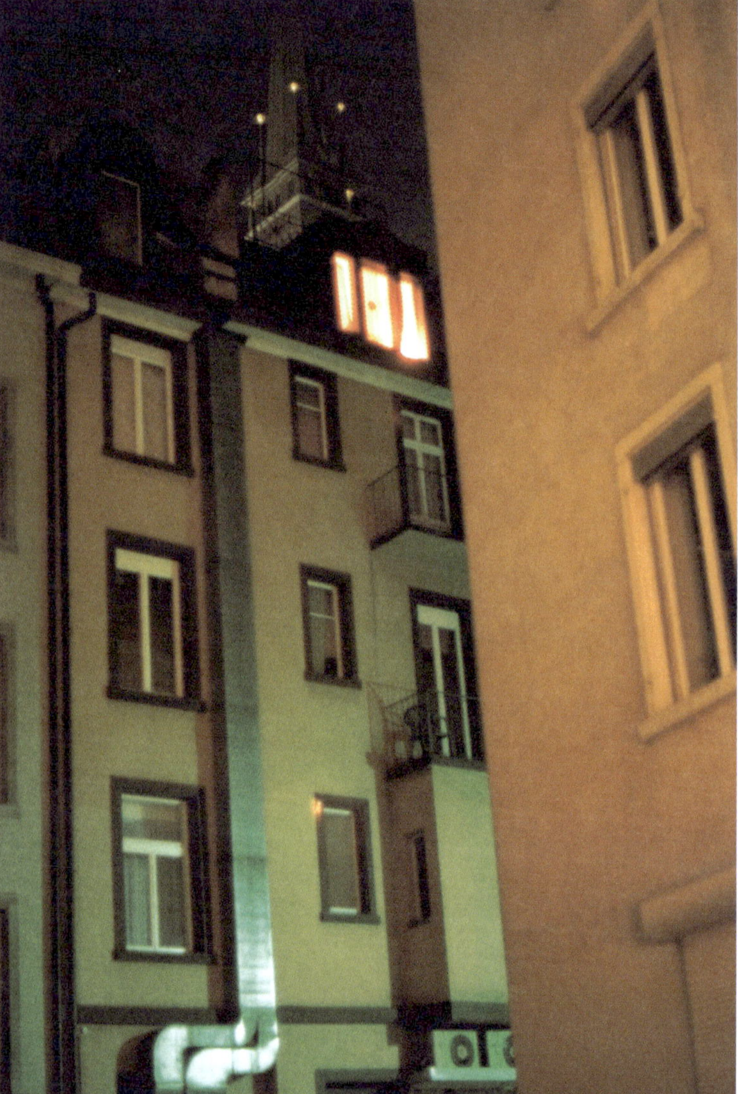

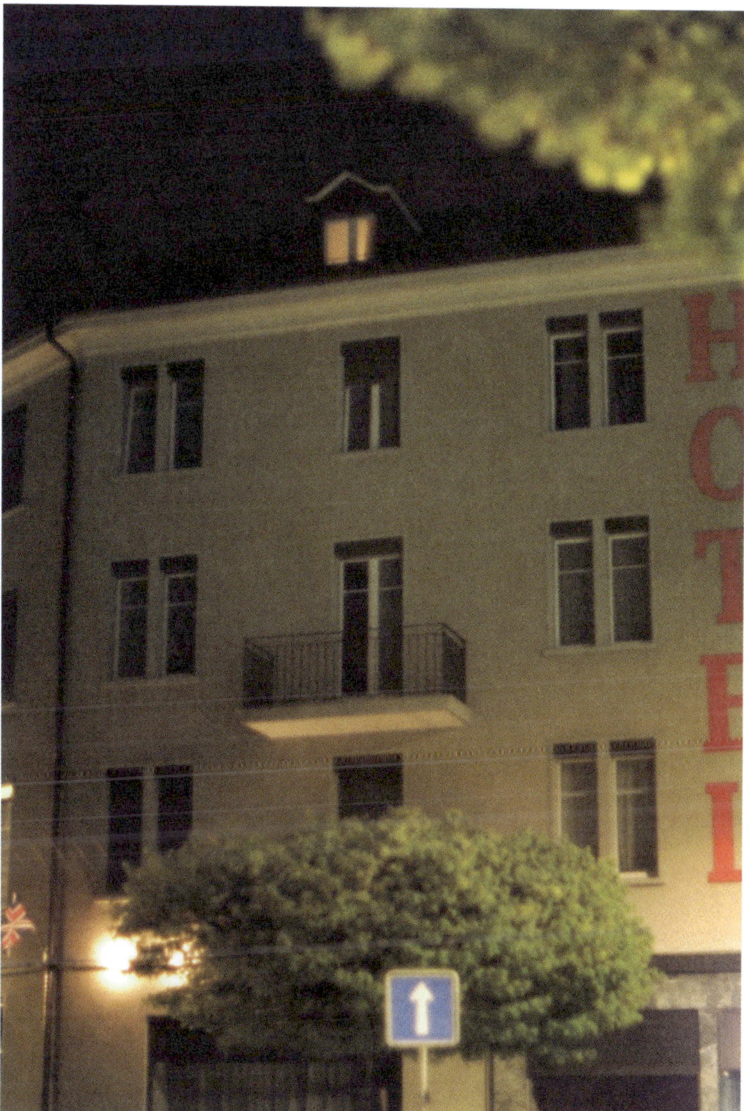

H
O
T
E
L

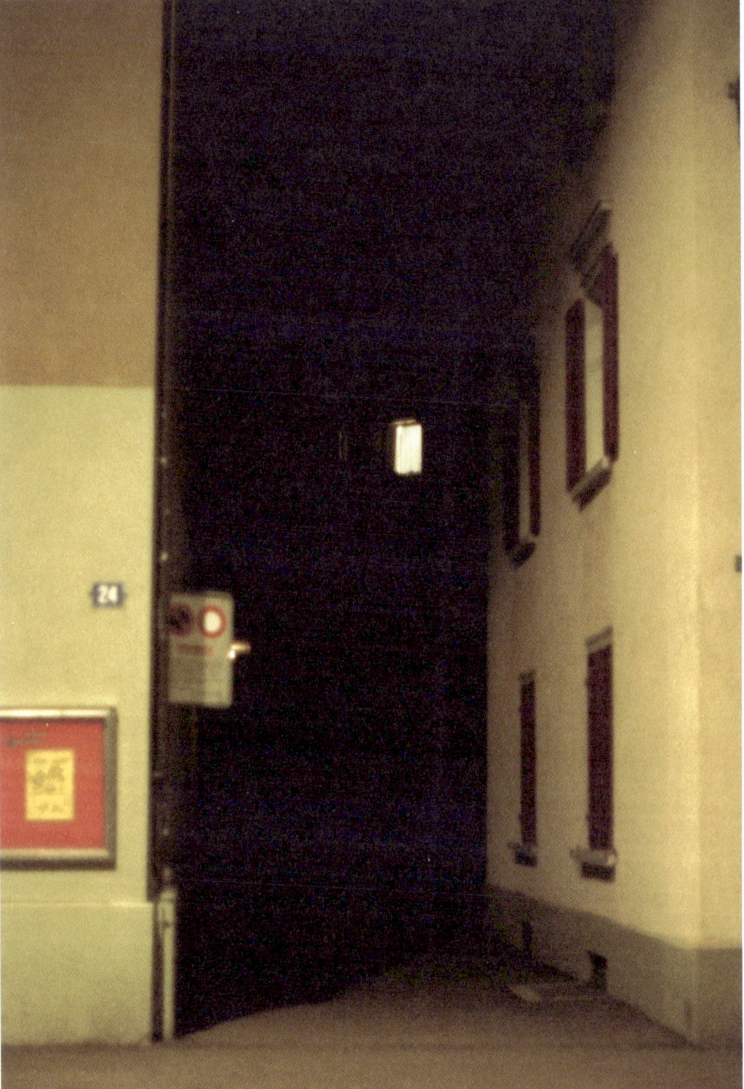

Las Vegas / Las Vegas

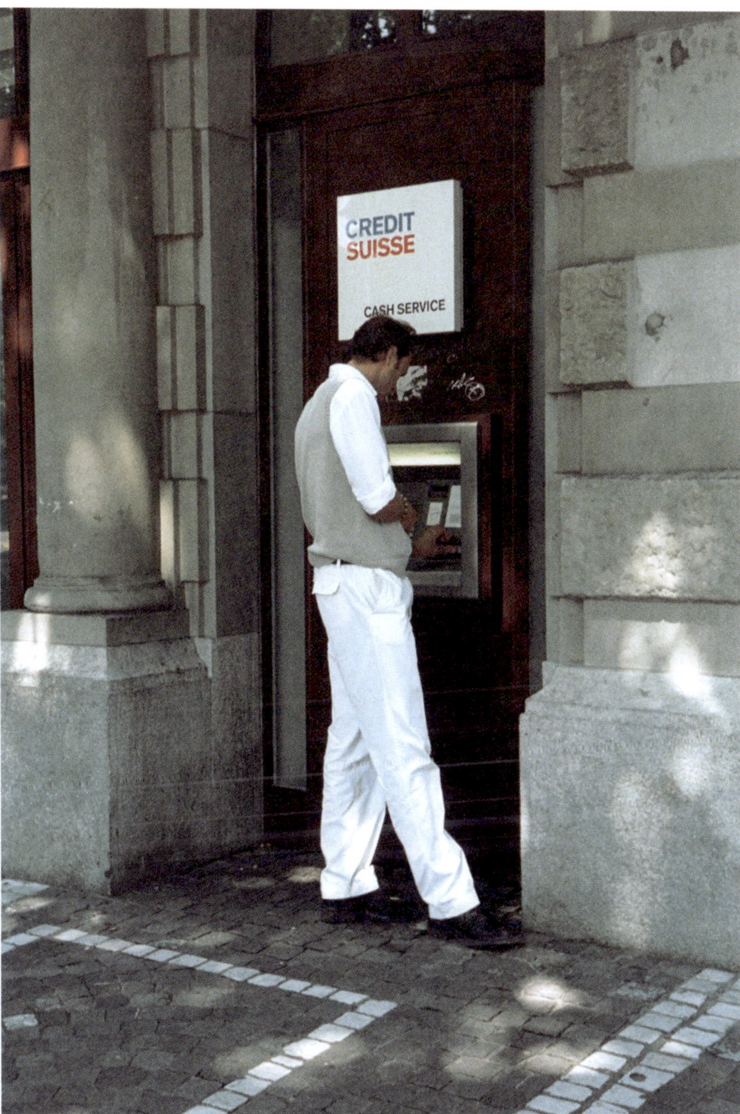

CREDIT
SUISSE

CASH SERVICE

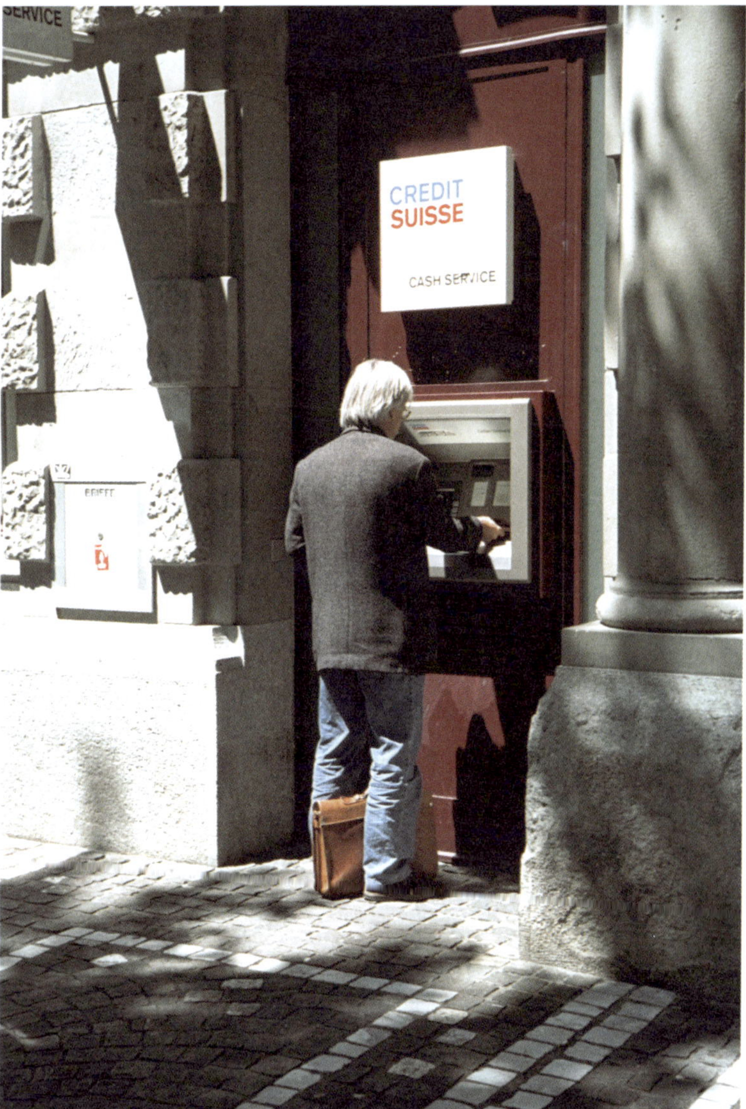
SERVICE
CREDIT
SUISSE
CASH SERVICE
BRIEF

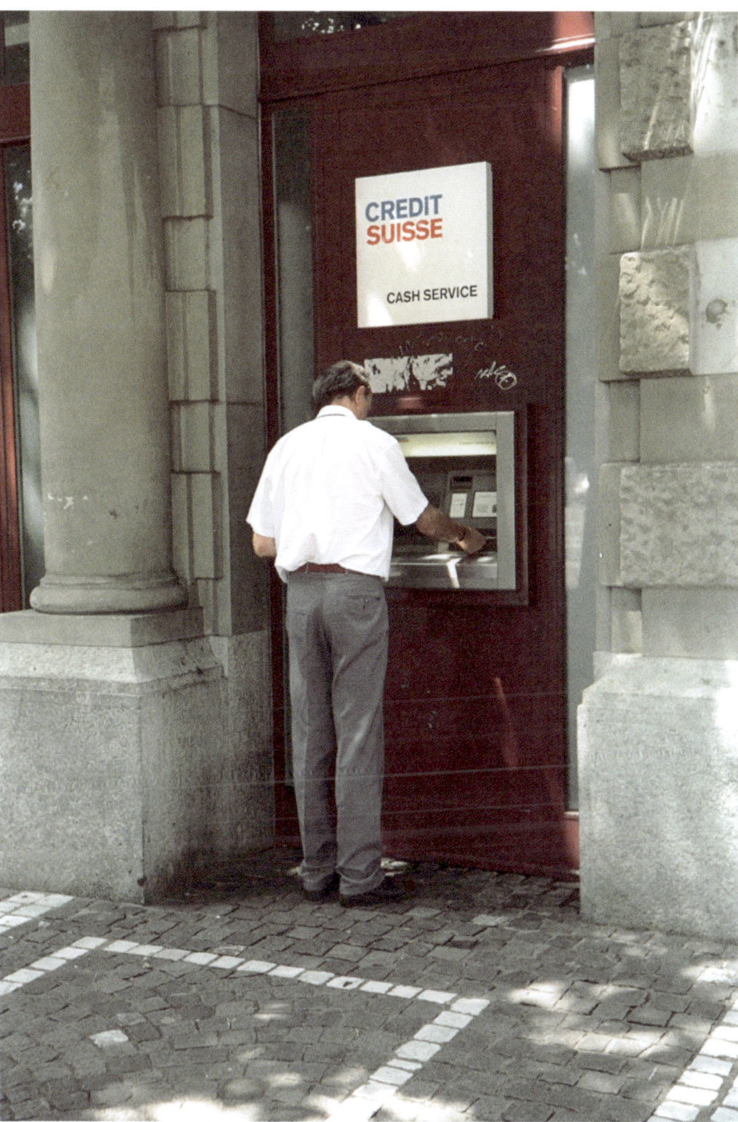

CREDIT
SUISSE

CASH SERVICE

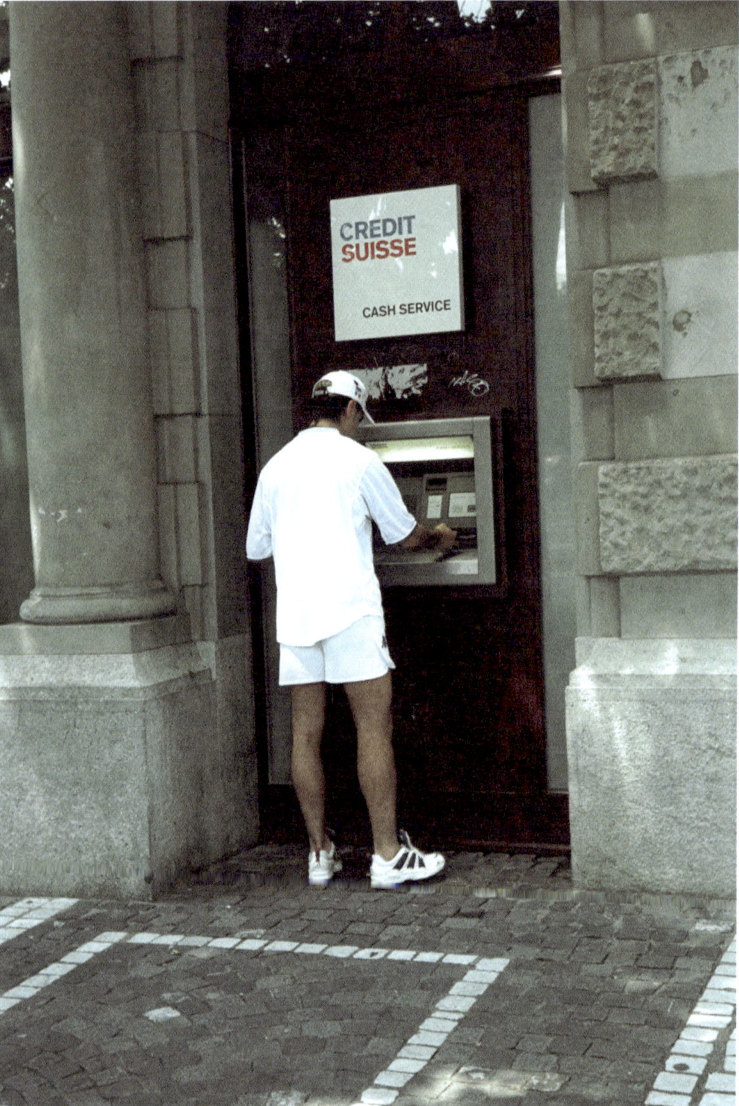

CREDIT
SUISSE
CASH SERVICE

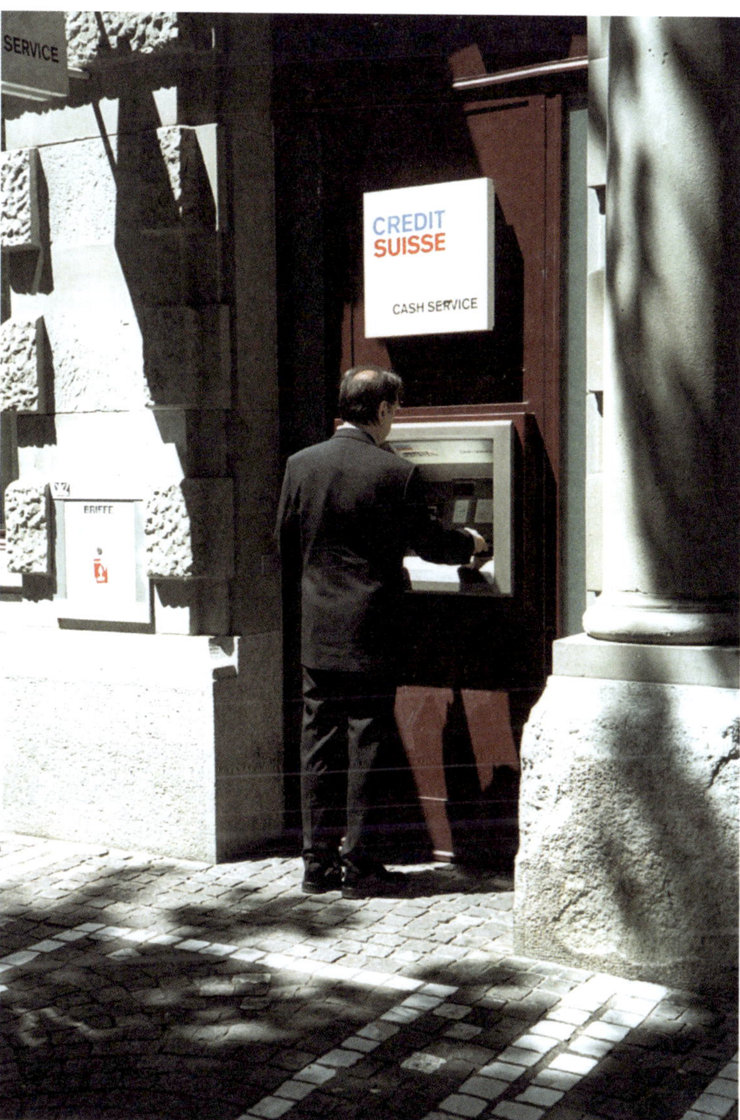
SERVICE
CREDIT
SUISSE
CASH SERVICE
BRIEFE

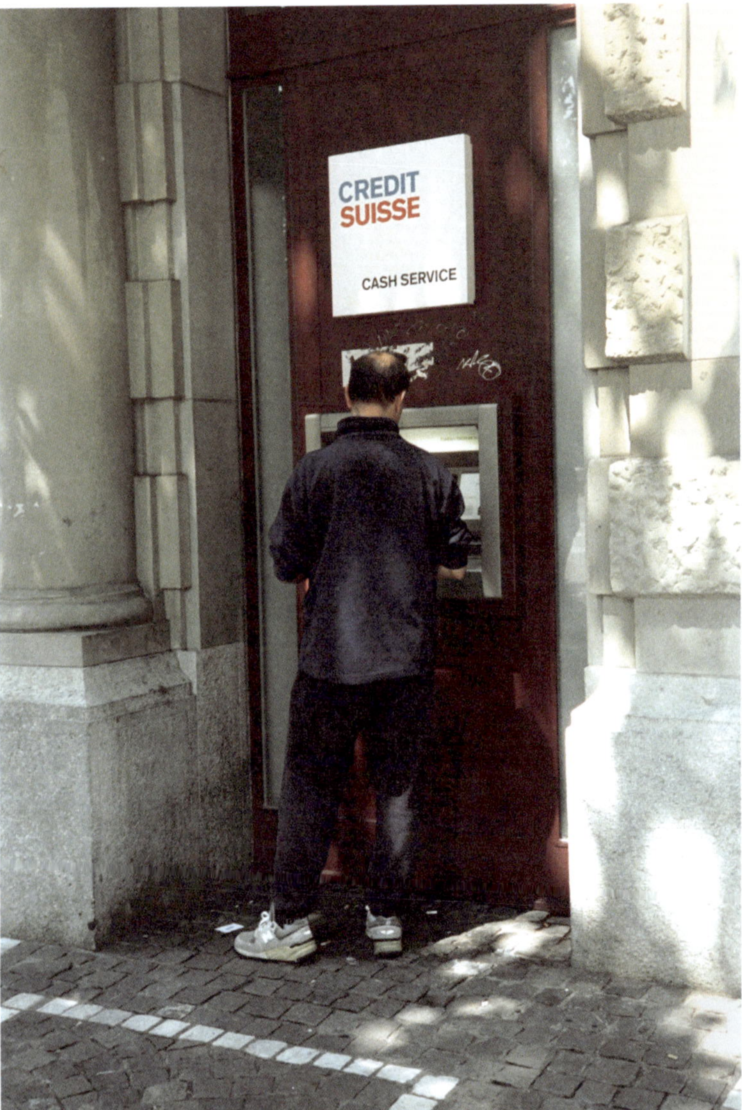

CREDIT
SUISSE
CASH SERVICE

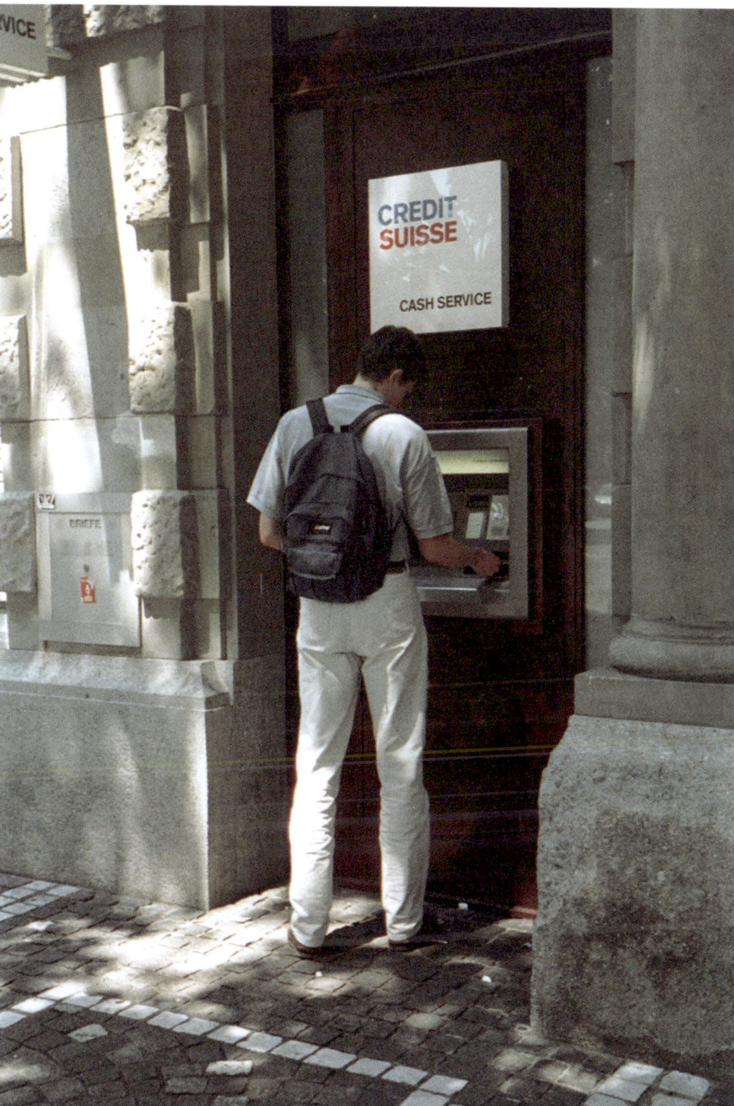

CREDIT
SUISSE
CASH SERVICE

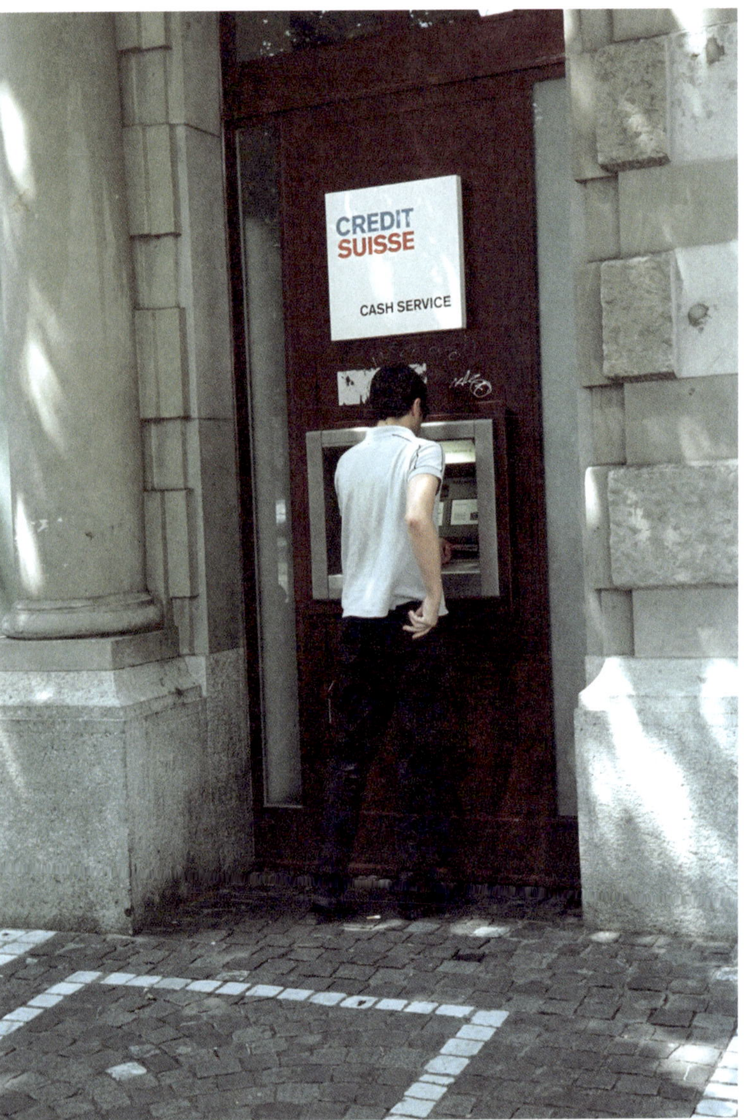

CREDIT
SUISSE
CASH SERVICE

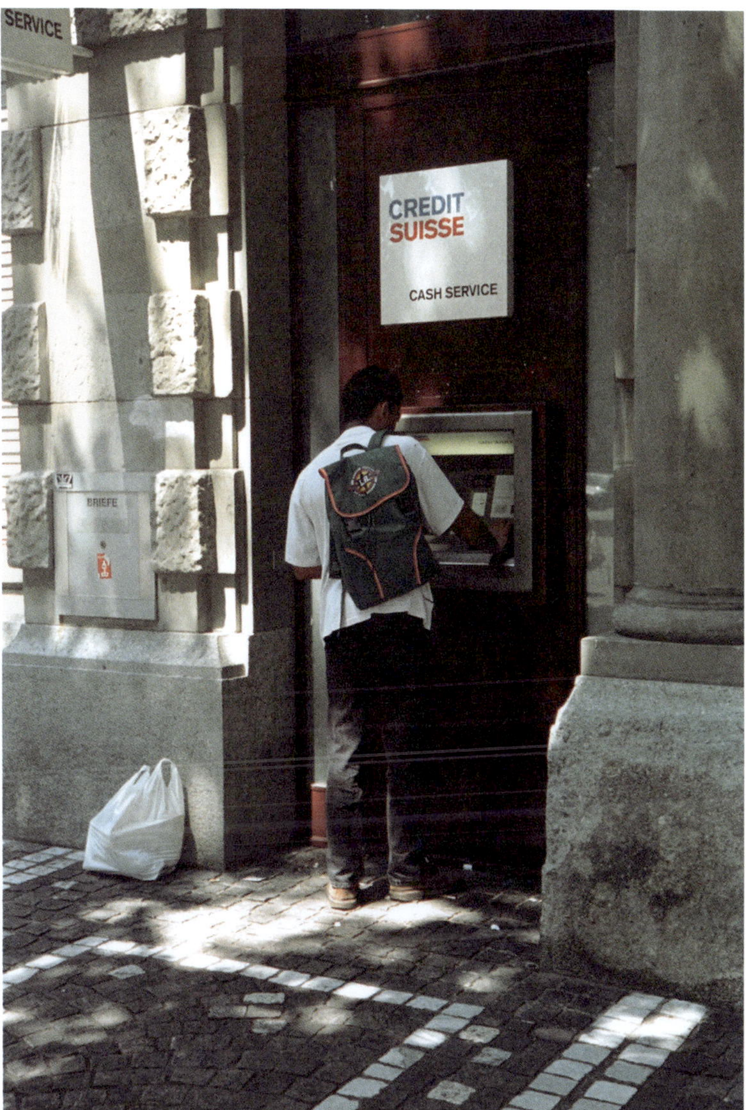
SERVICE
CREDIT
SUISSE
CASH SERVICE
BRIEFE

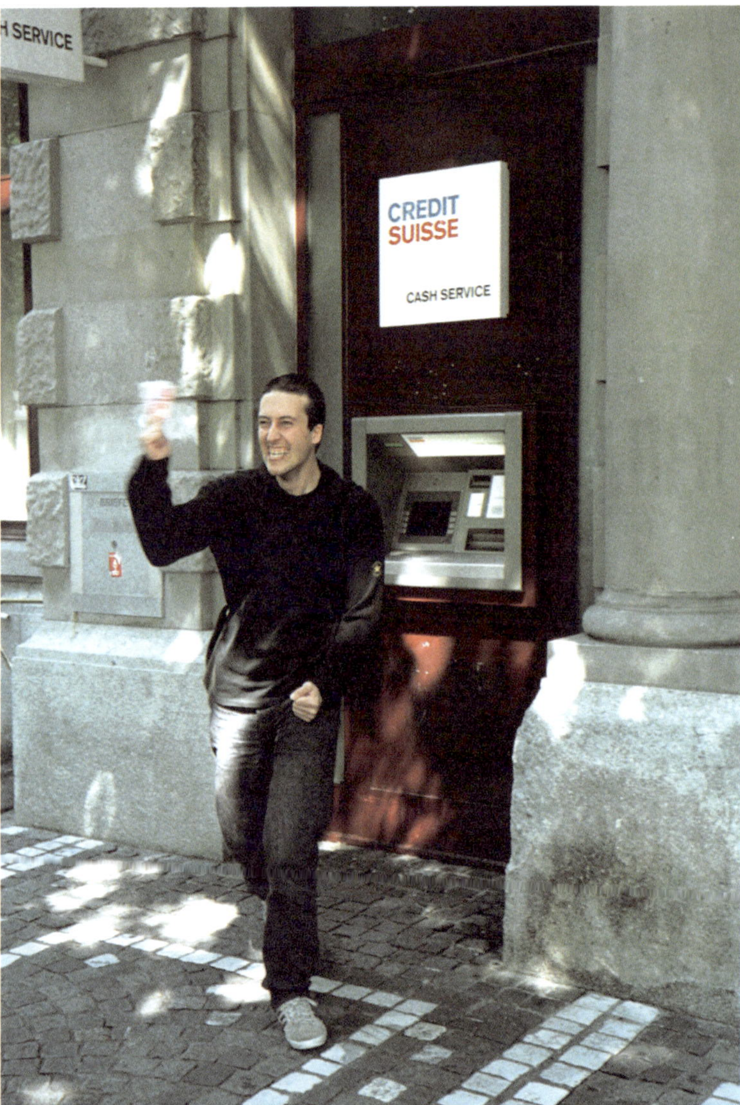
H SERVICE
CREDIT
SUISSE
CASH SERVICE

Kunst am Bau 2 / Art for Buildings 2

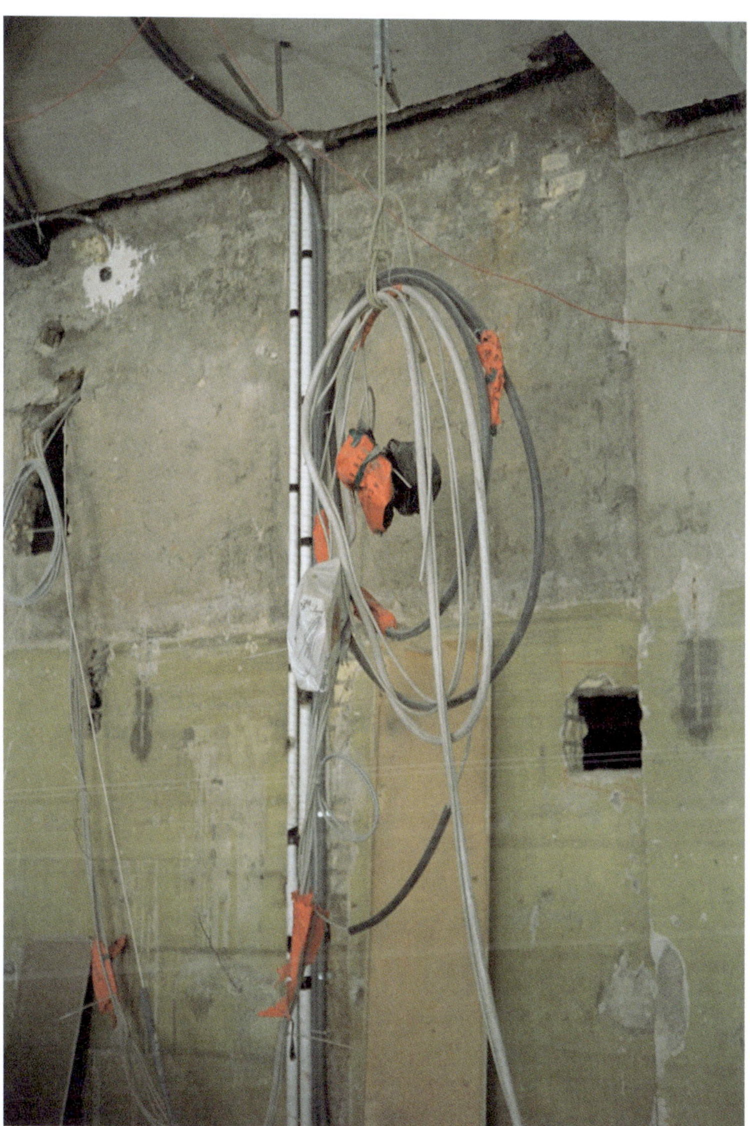

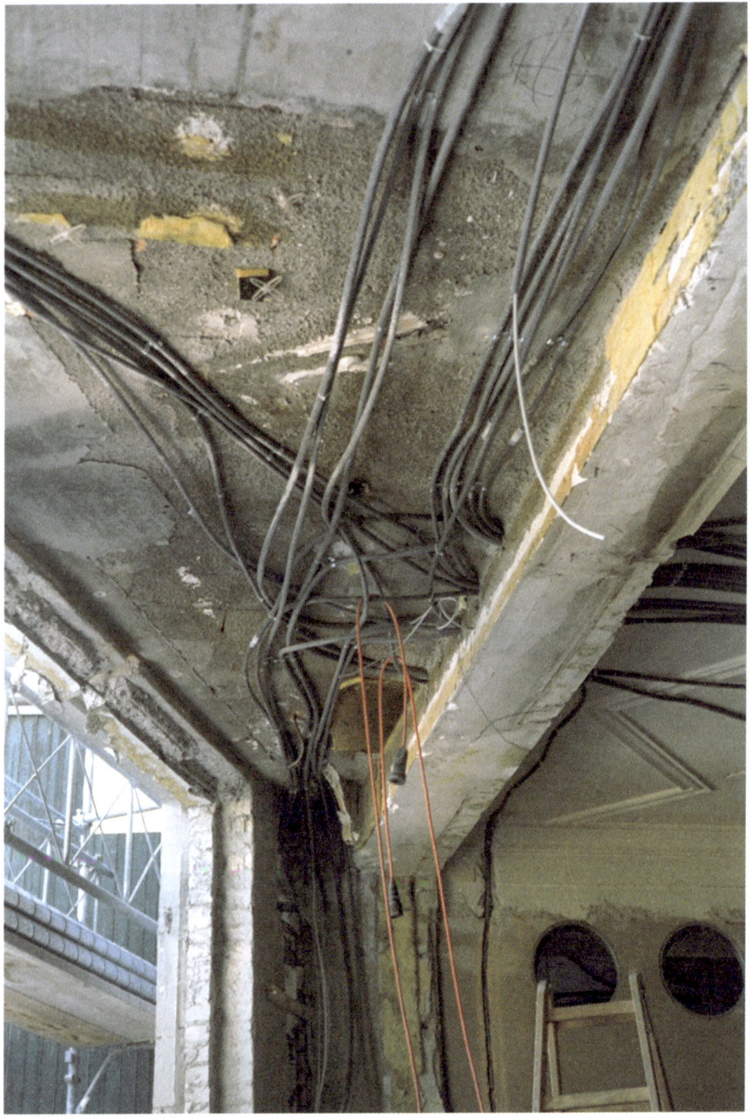

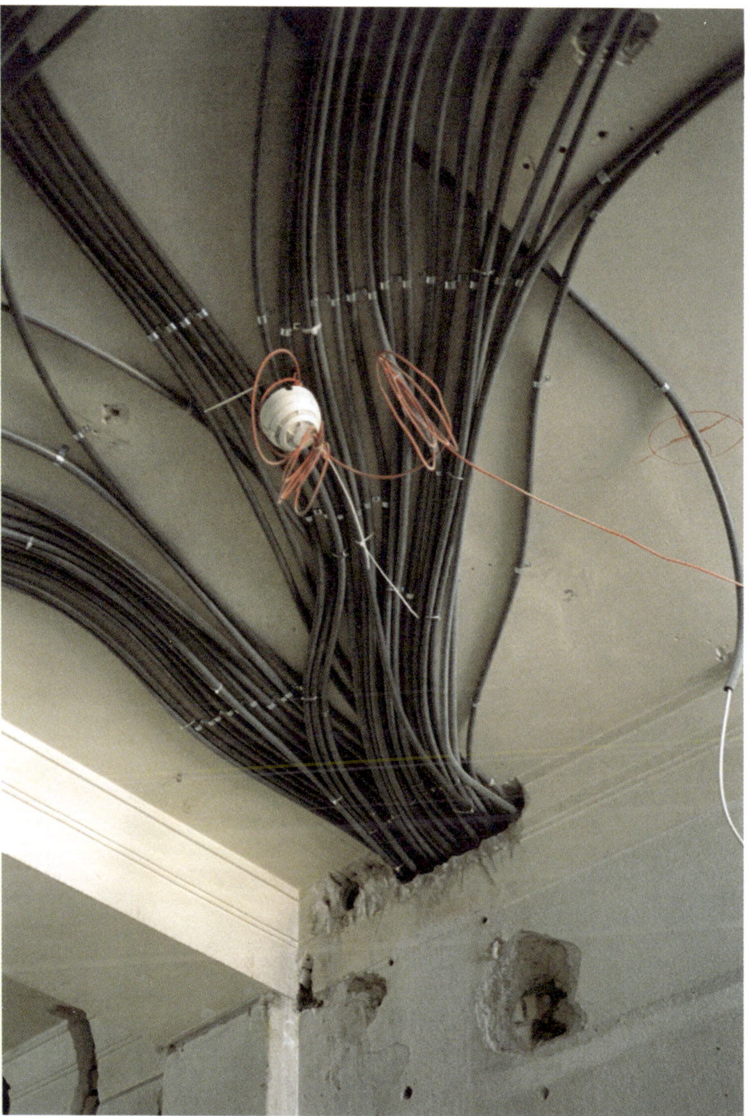

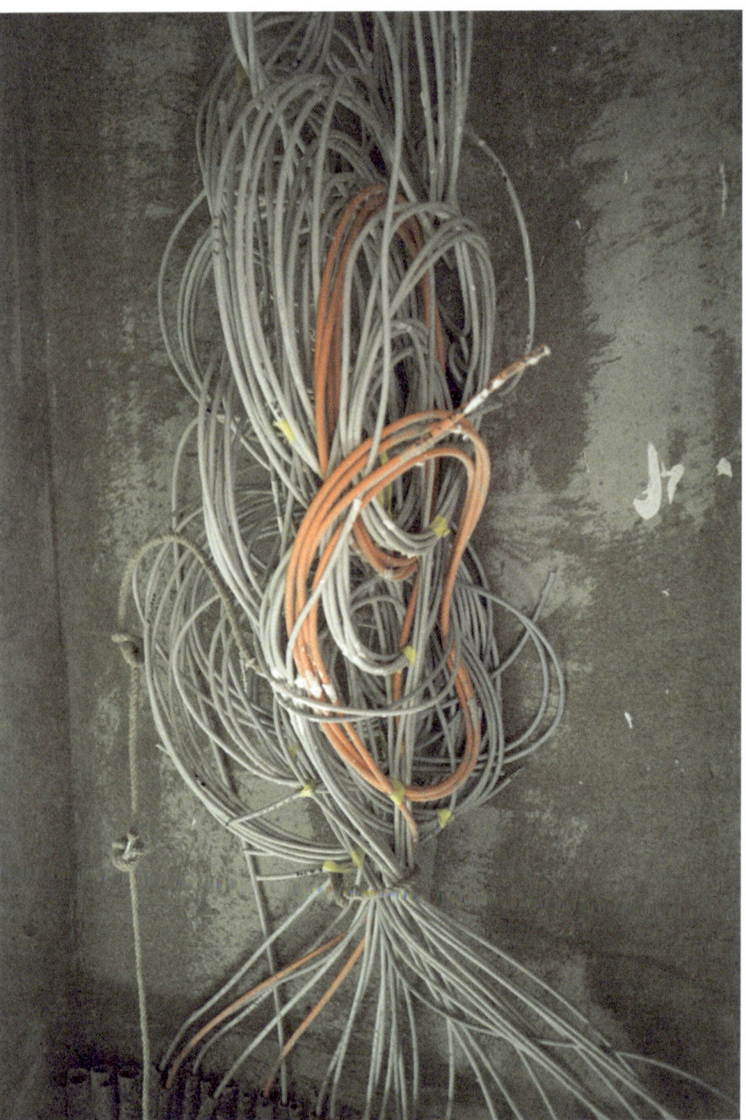

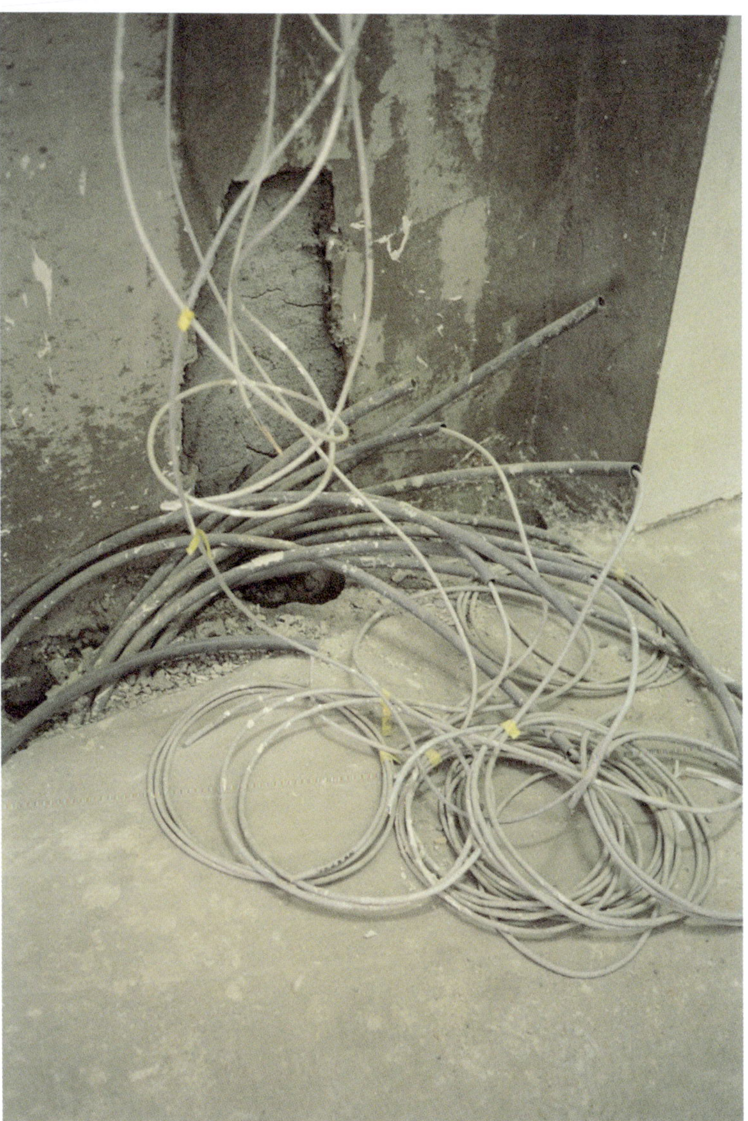

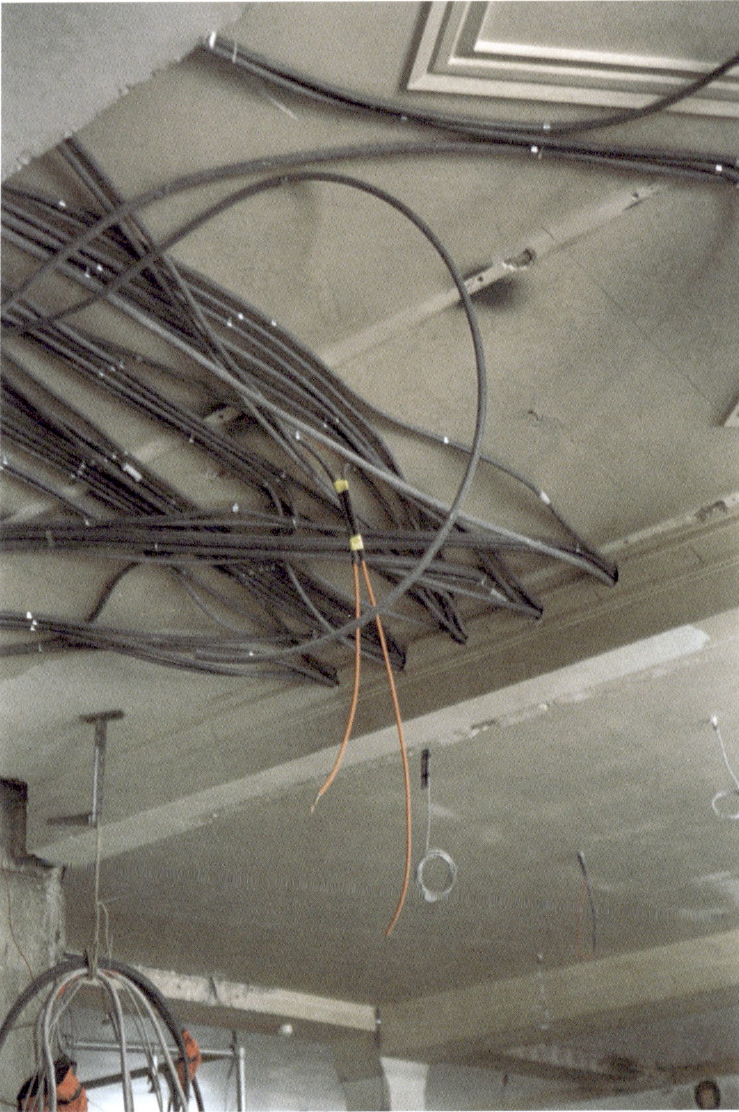

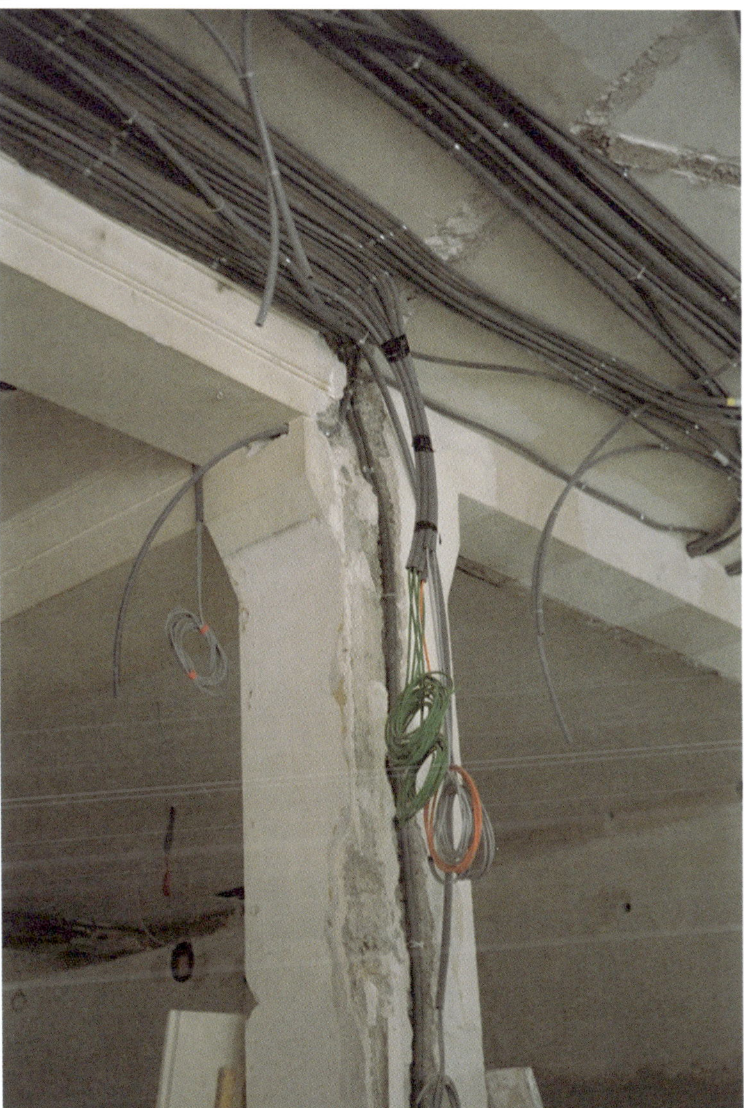

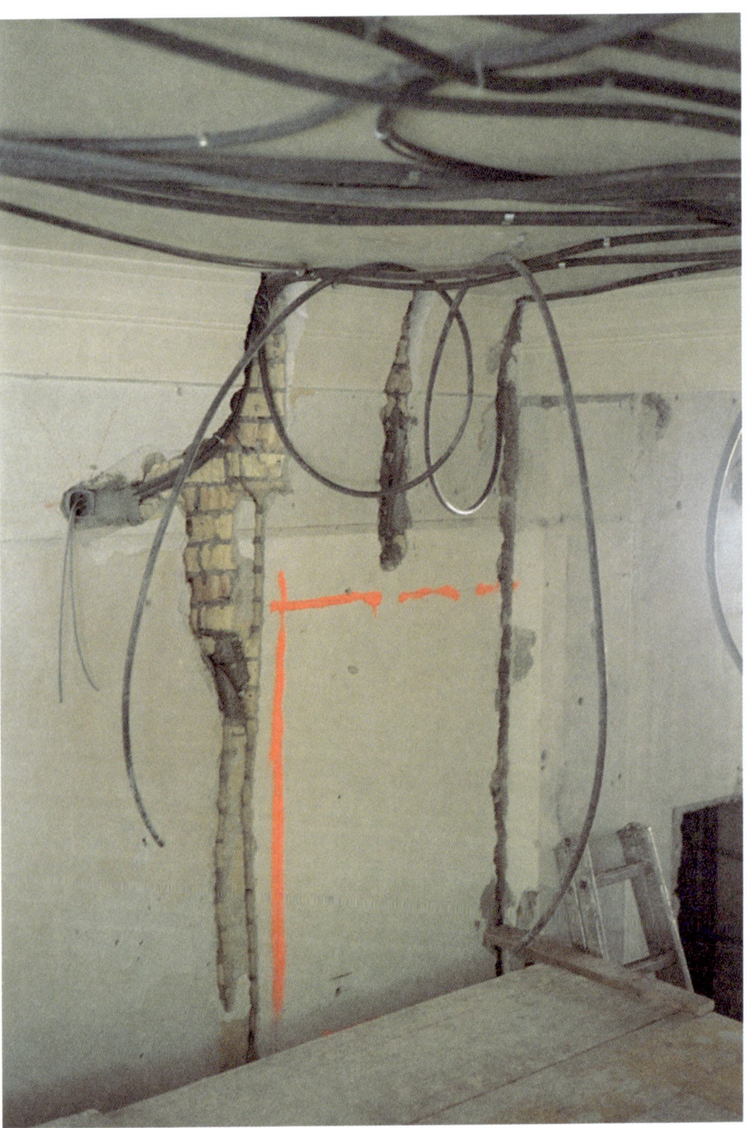

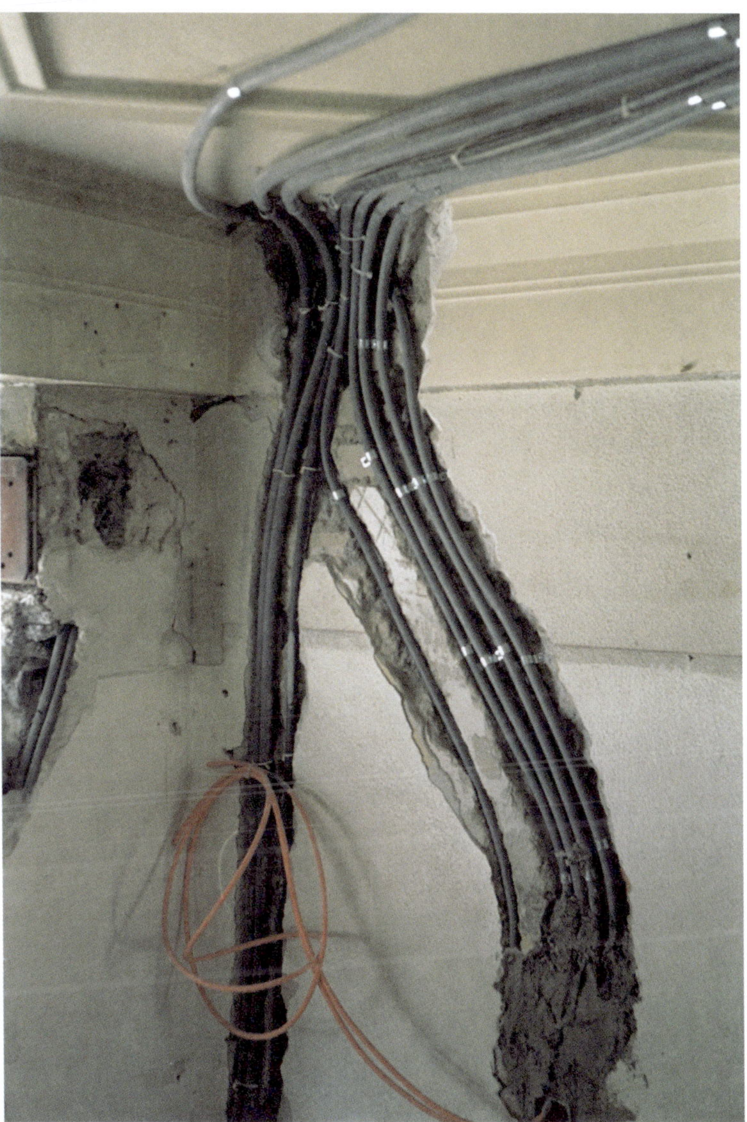

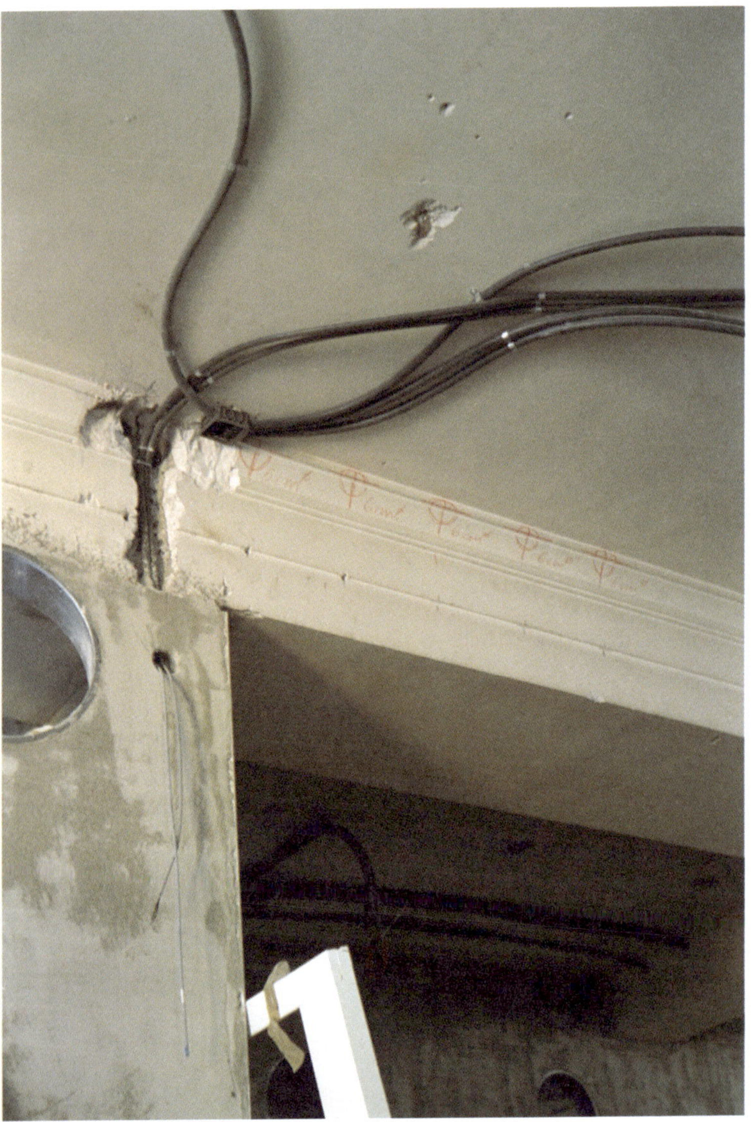

Verdächtige / Suspects

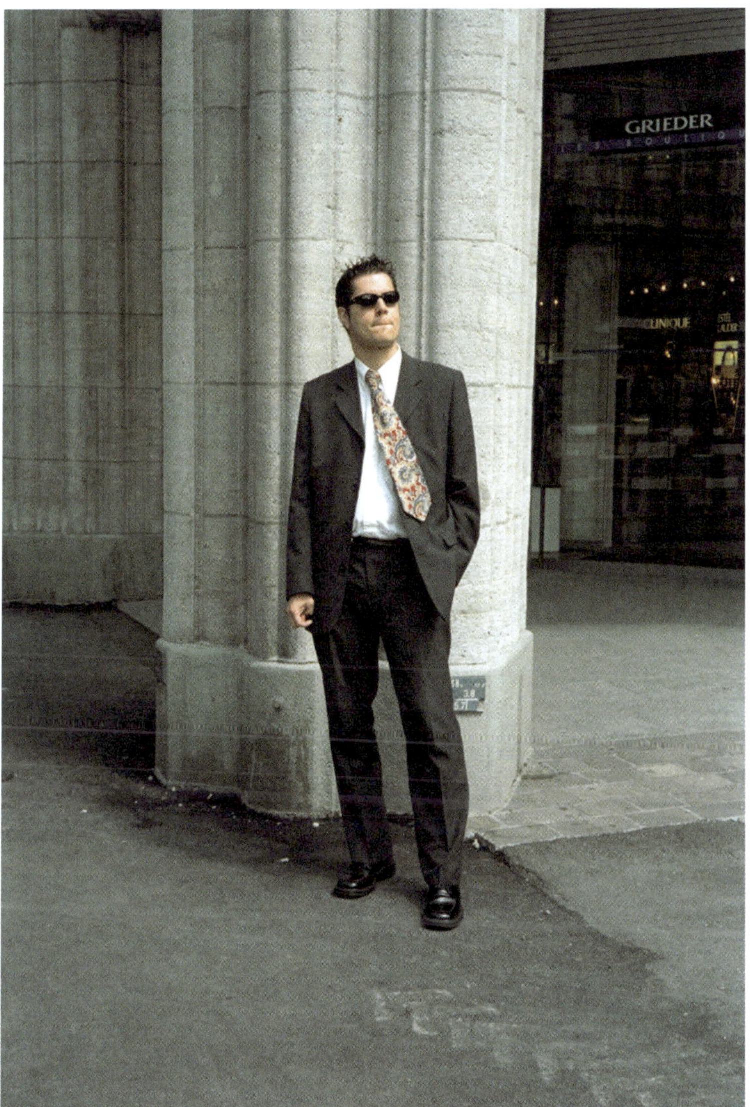

GRIEDER
CLINIQUE

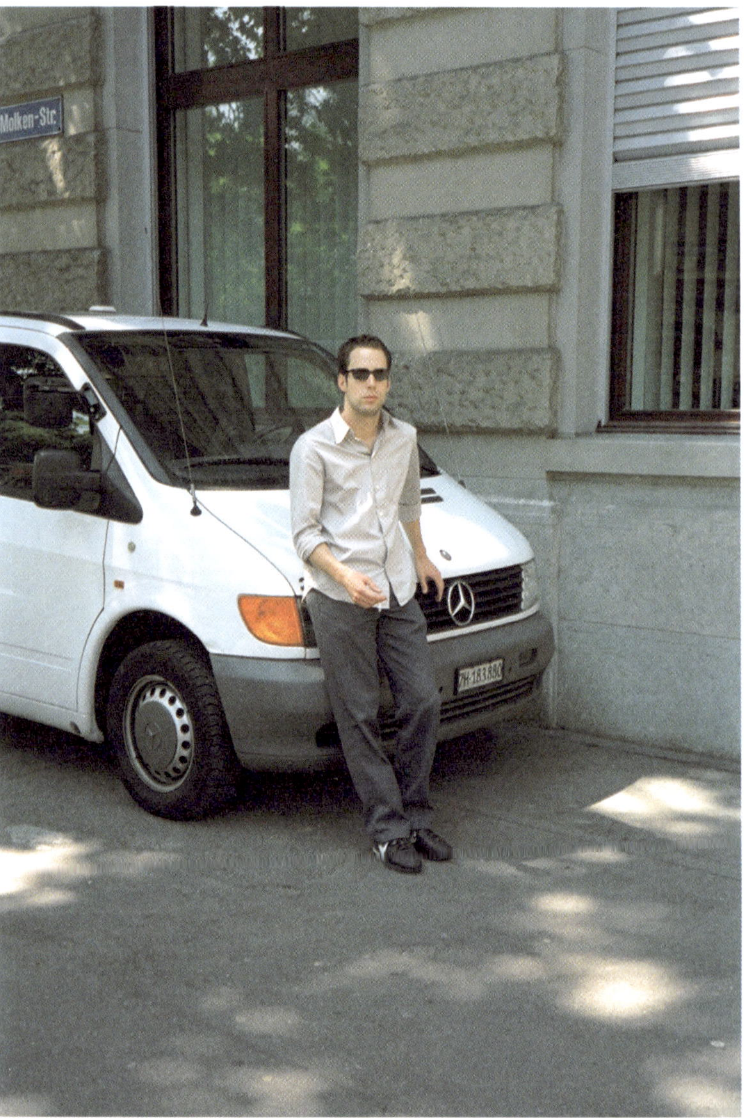

Molken-Str.
Molken-Str.

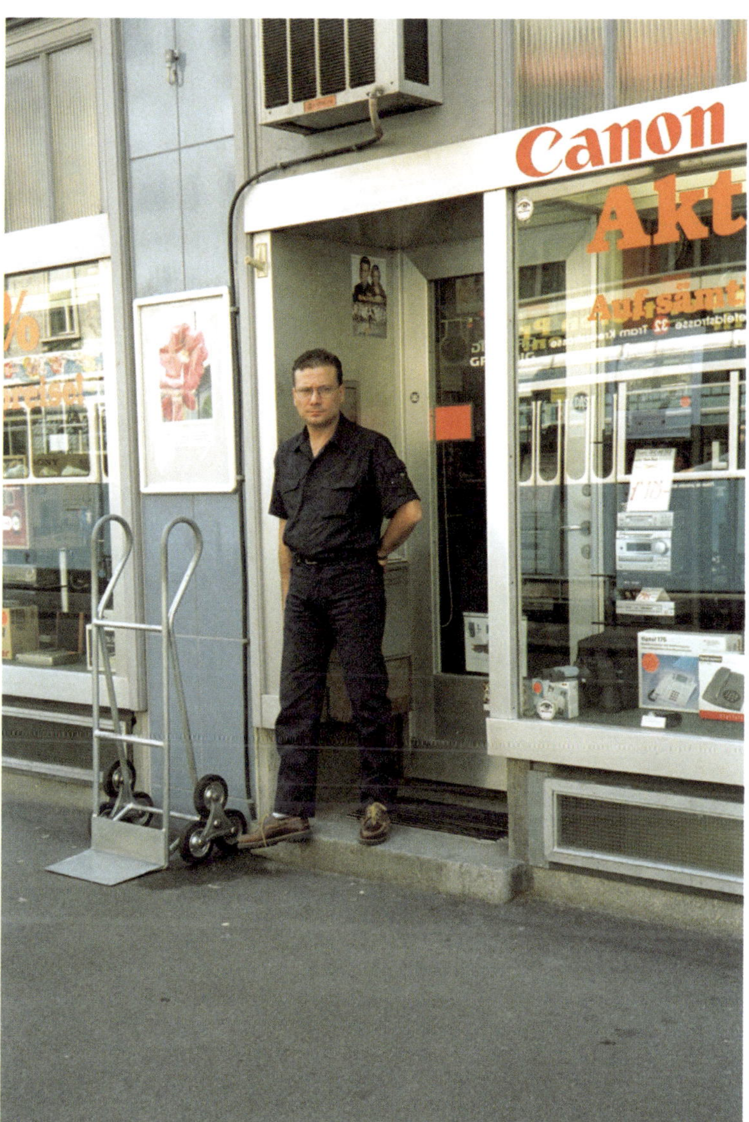

Canon
Akt
Auf sämt
%

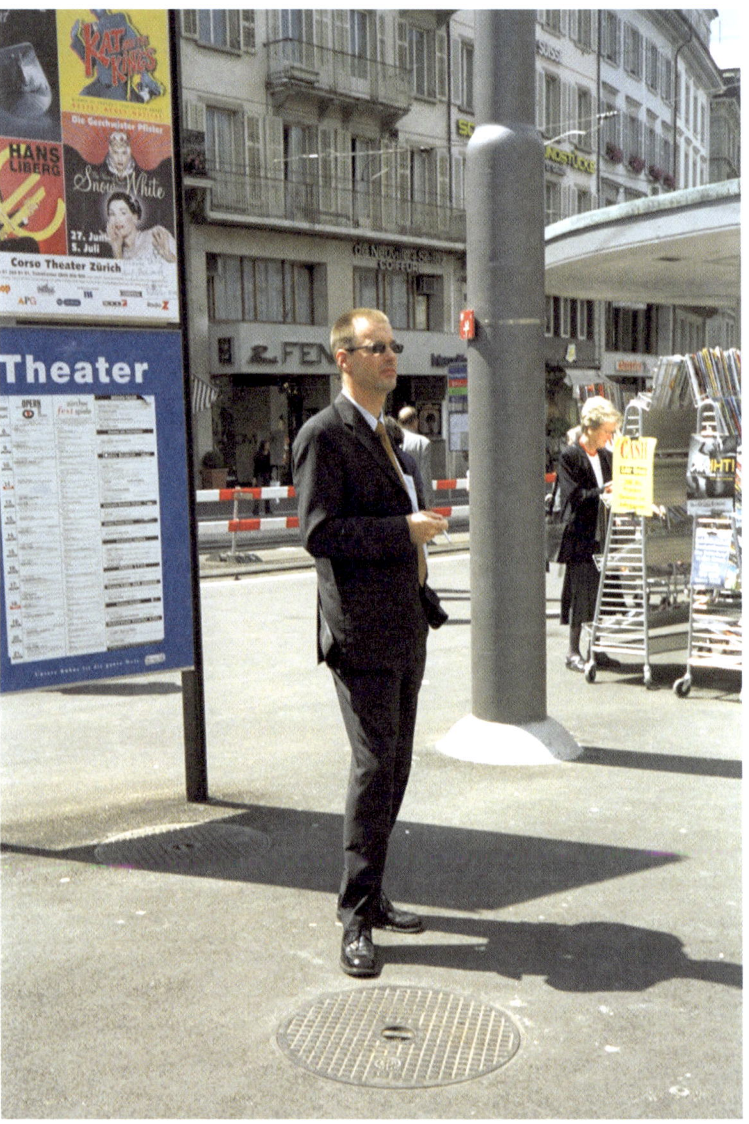
KAT AND THE KINGS
Die Geschwister Pfister
Snow White
27. Juni
5. Juli
Corso Theater Zürich
HANS LIBERG
APG
Theater
OPERN
zürcher
fest spiele
CASH
SUISSE

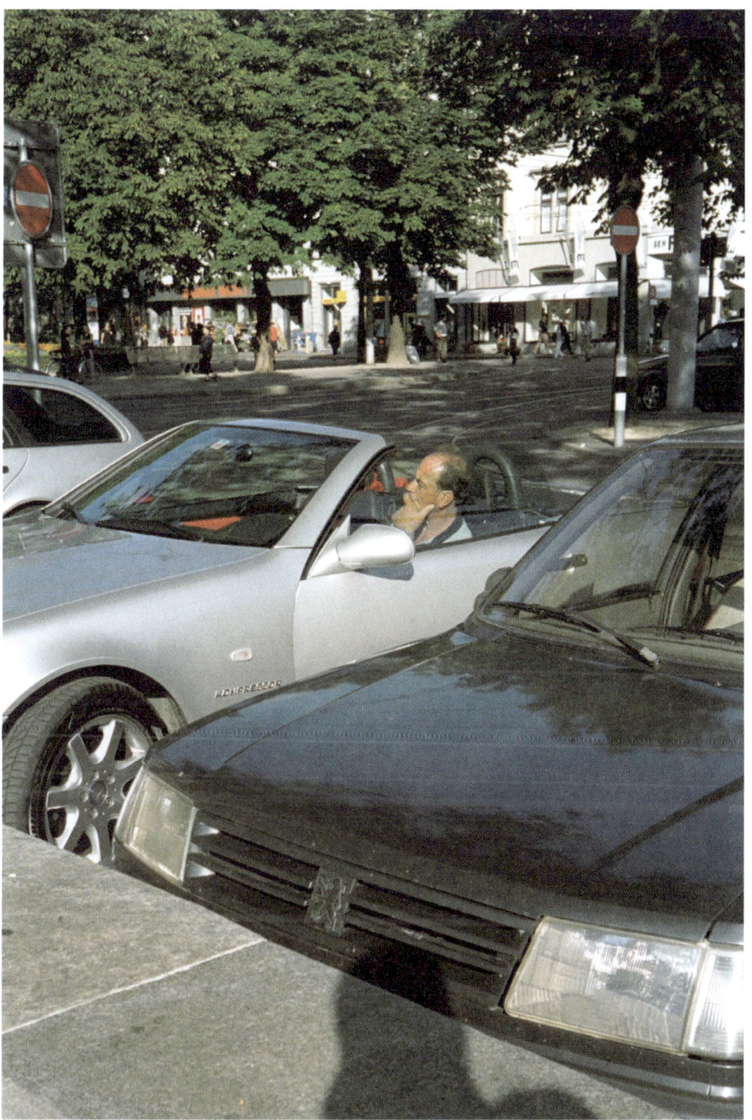

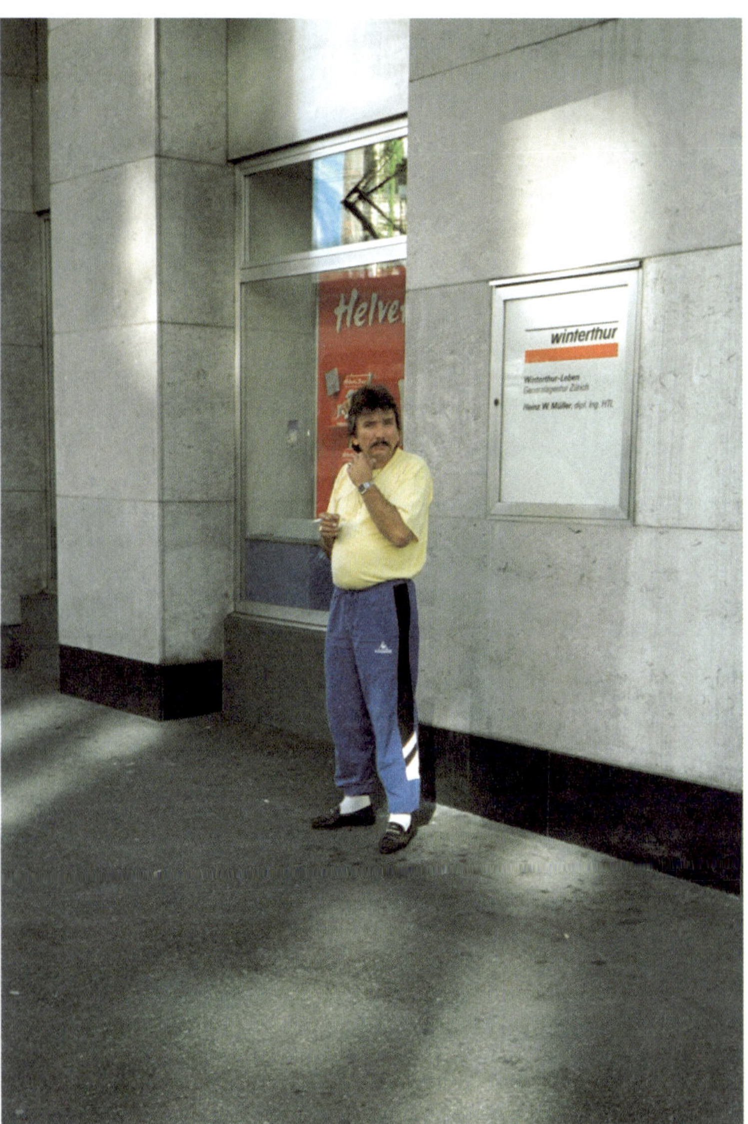
Helve
winterthur
Winterthur-Leben
Generalagentur Zürich
Heinz W. Müller, dipl. Ing. HTL

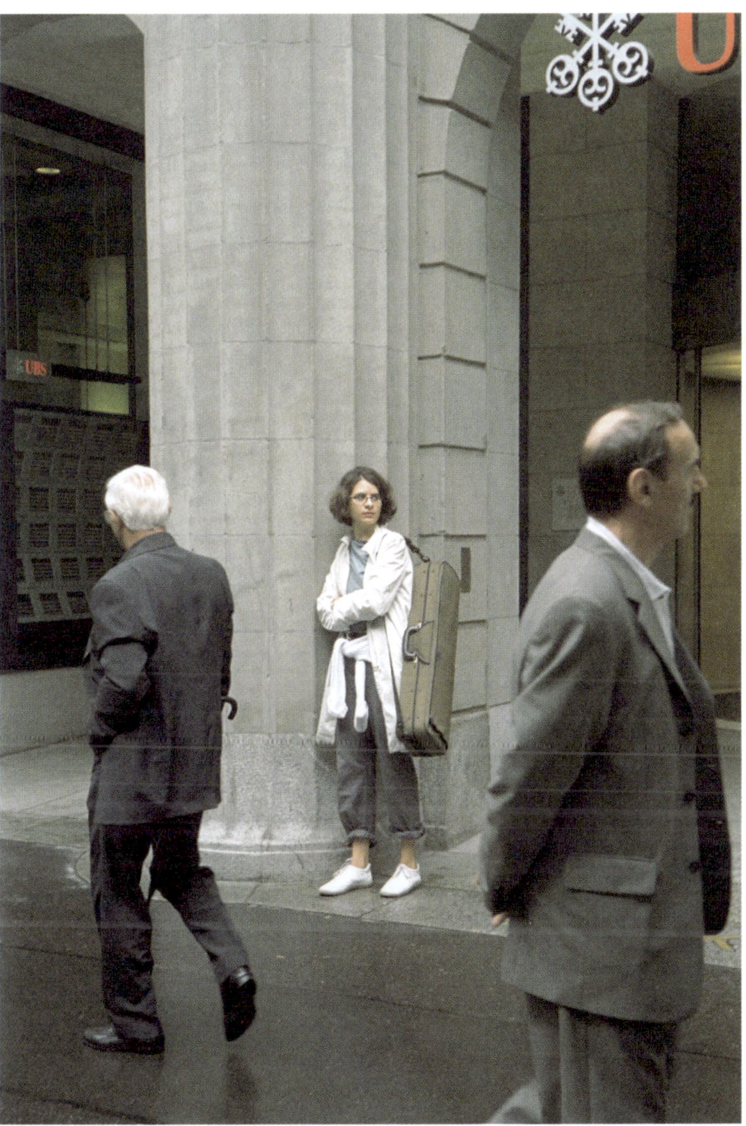

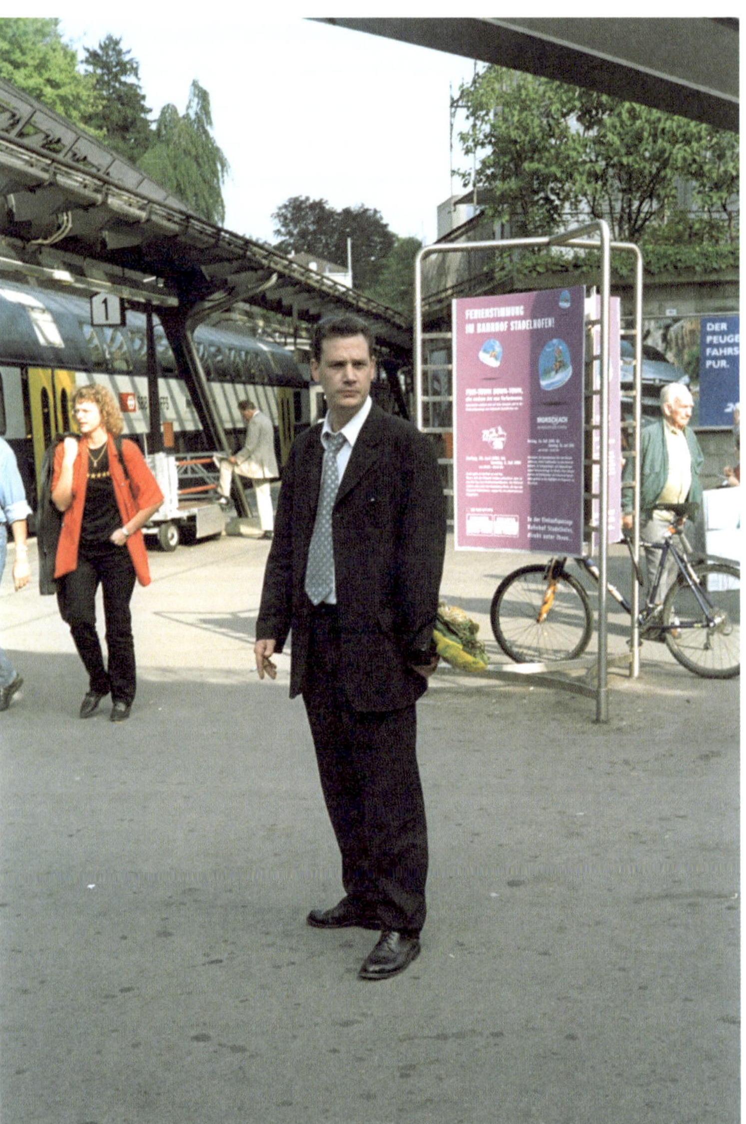

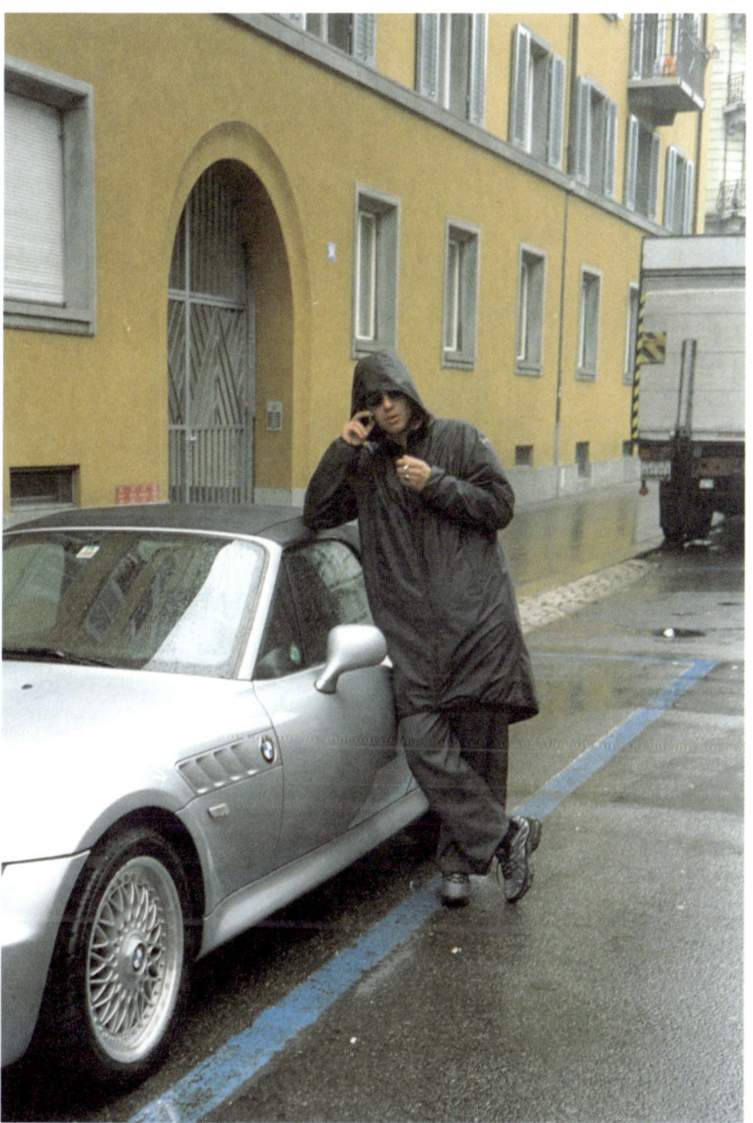

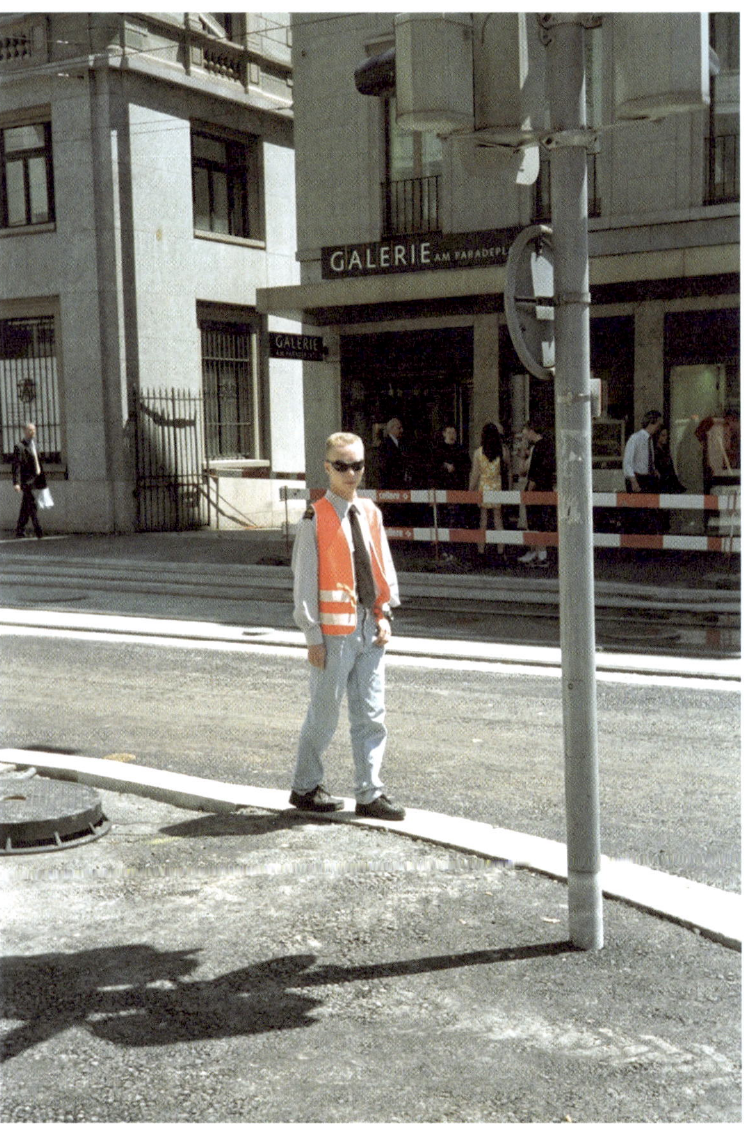
GALERIE AM PARADEPLATZ
GALERIE

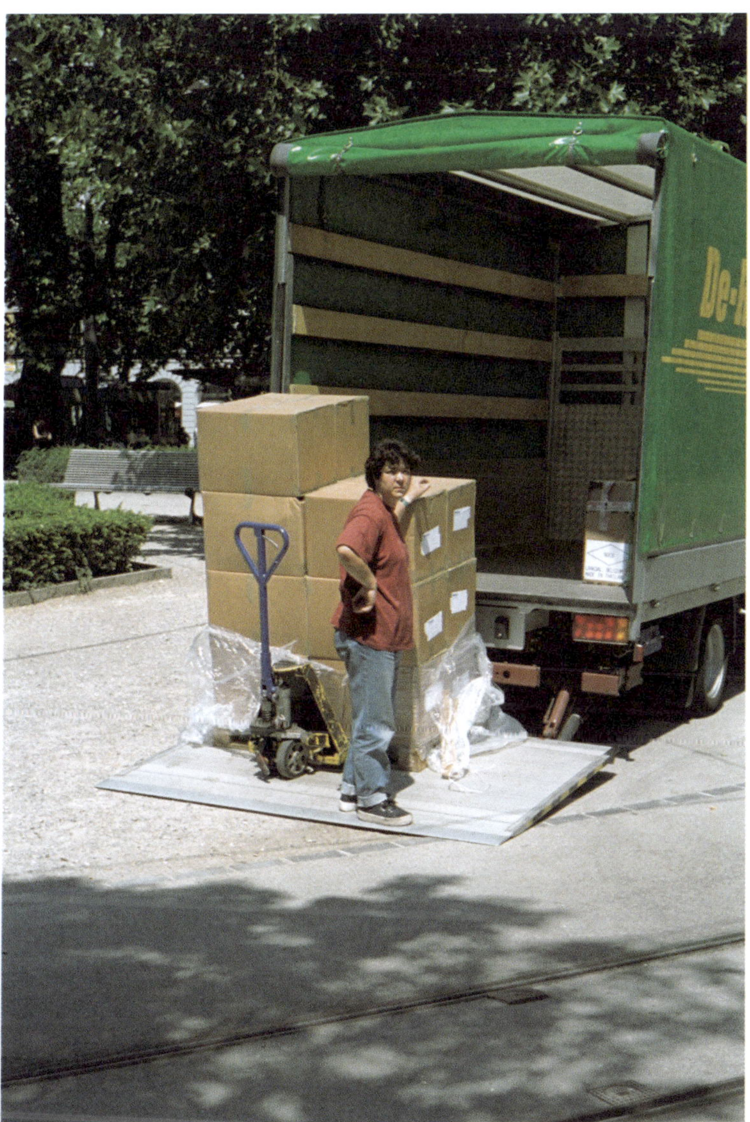
De-

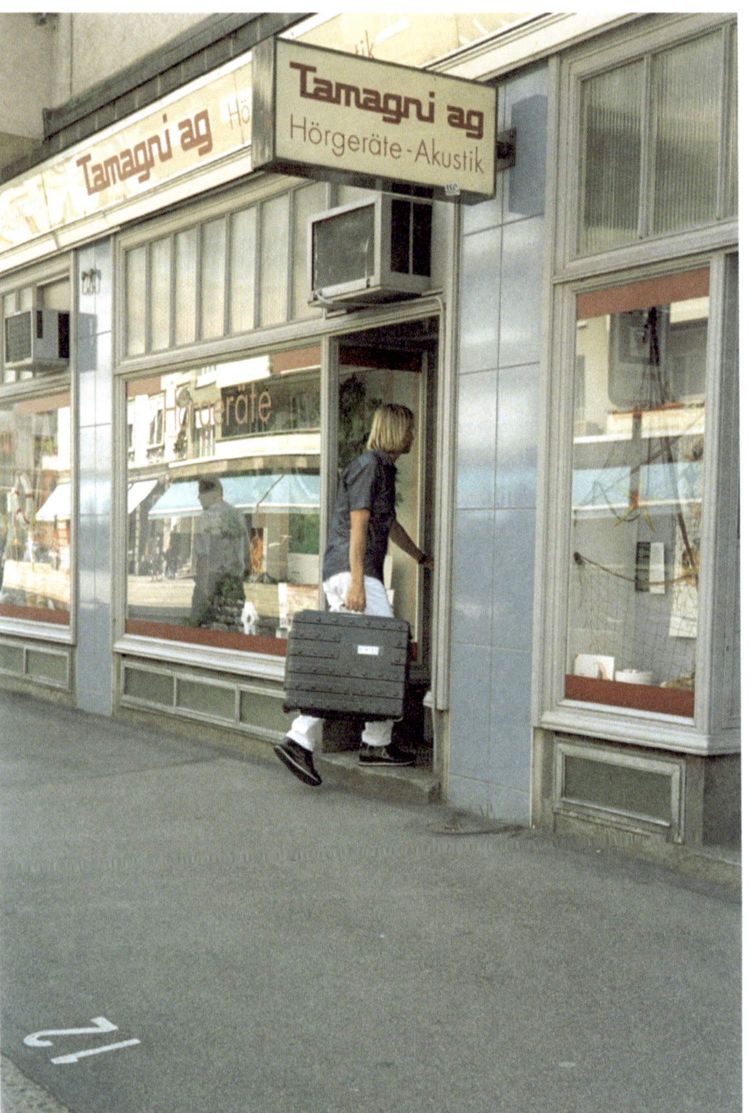

Tamagni ag
Tamagni ag
Hörgeräte - Akustik

Goldrausch 2 / Gold Rush 2

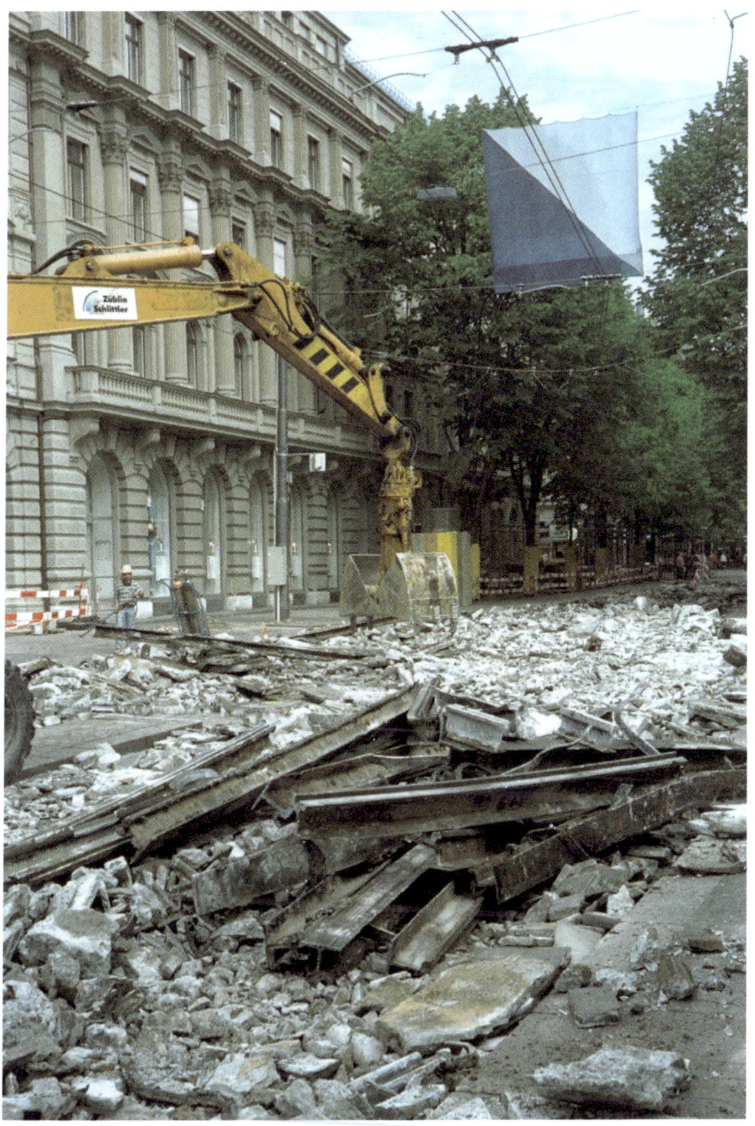
Züblin
Schlittler

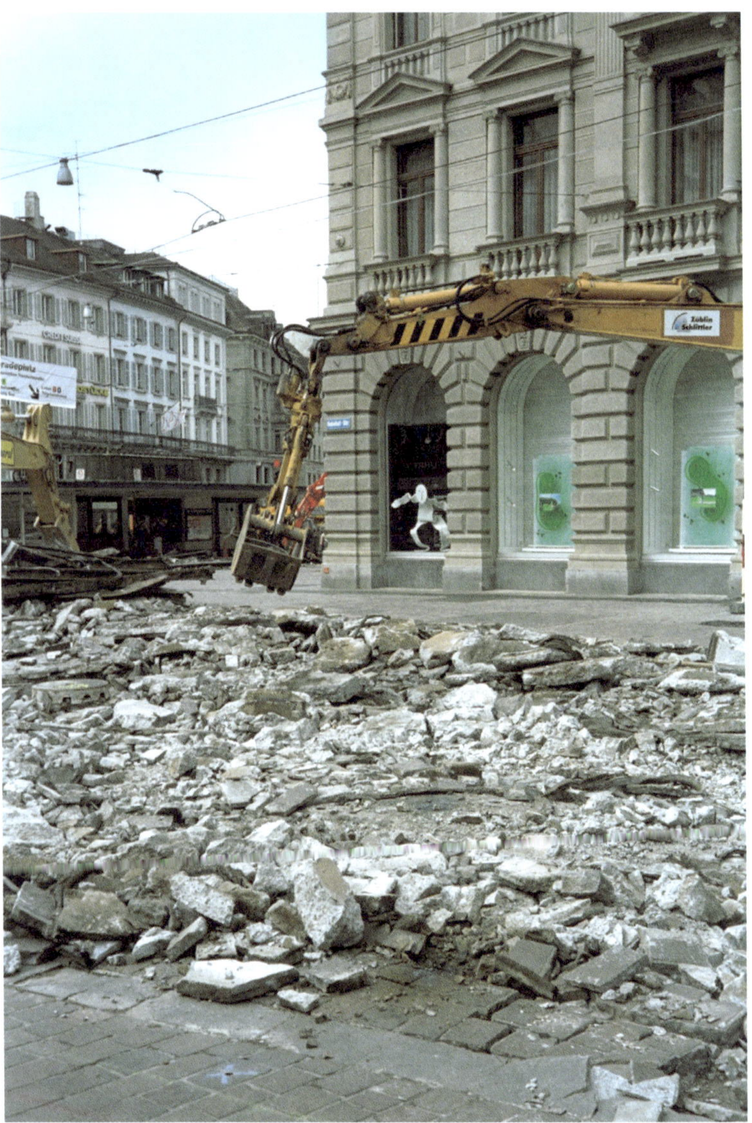

Züblin
Schlittler

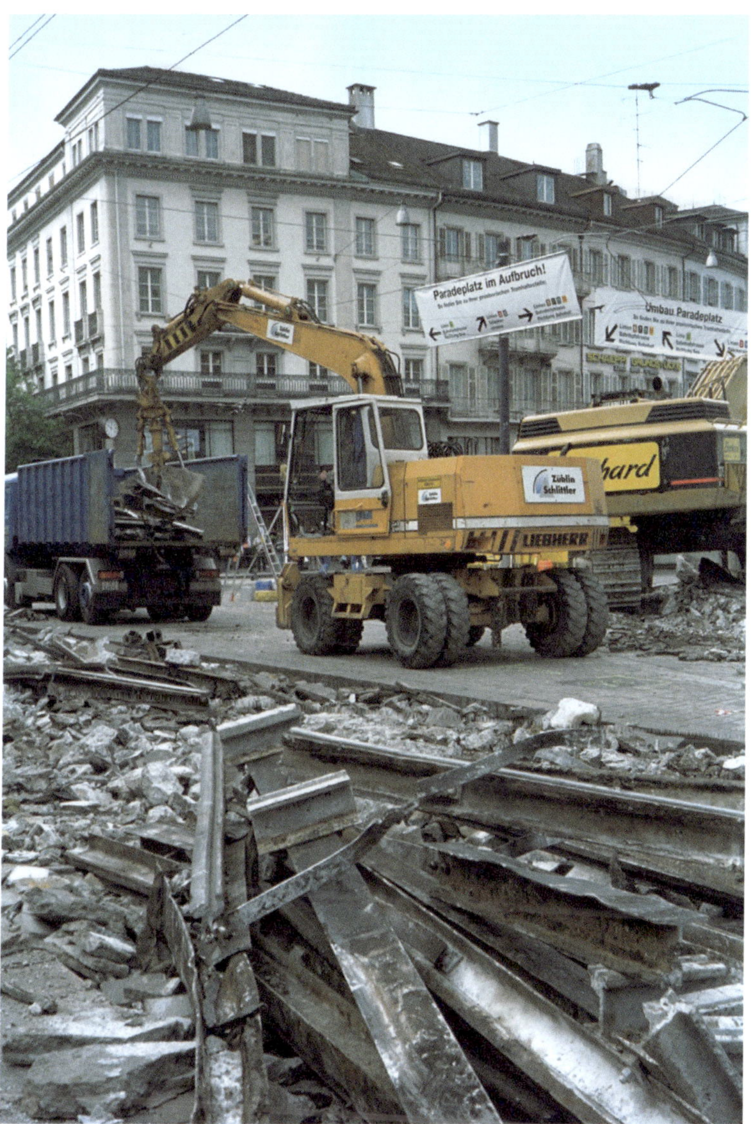
Paradeplatz im Aufbruch!
Umbau Paradeplatz
Züblin Schlittler
LIEBHERR

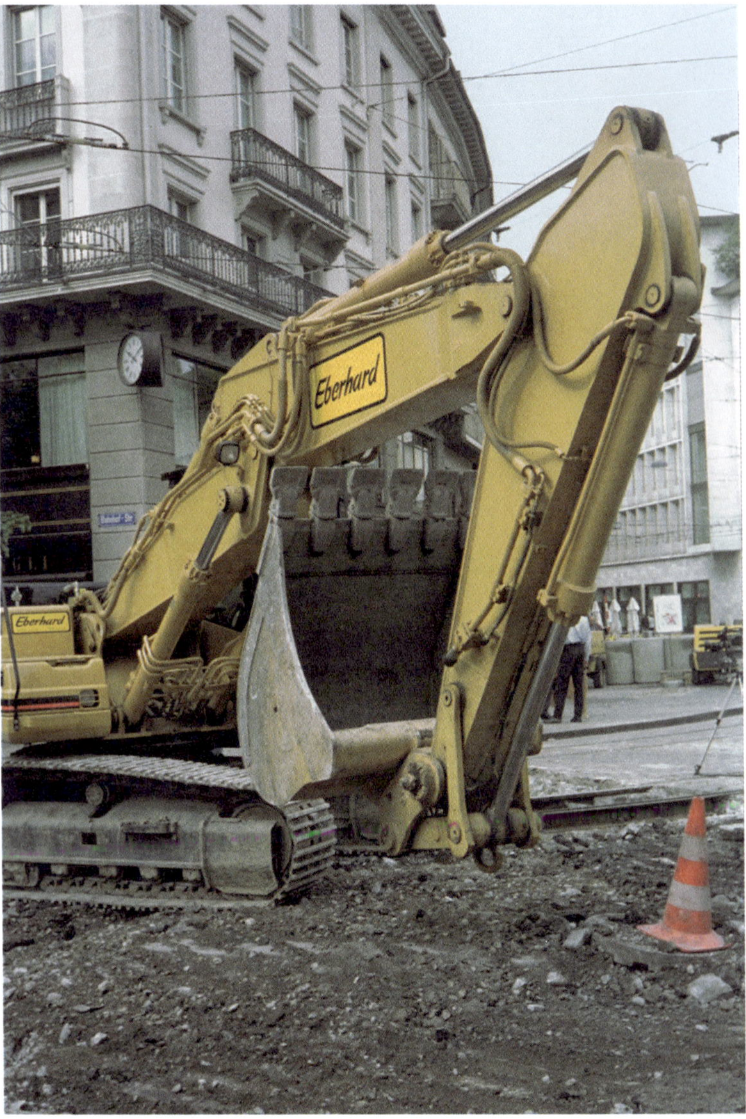
Eberhard
Eberhard

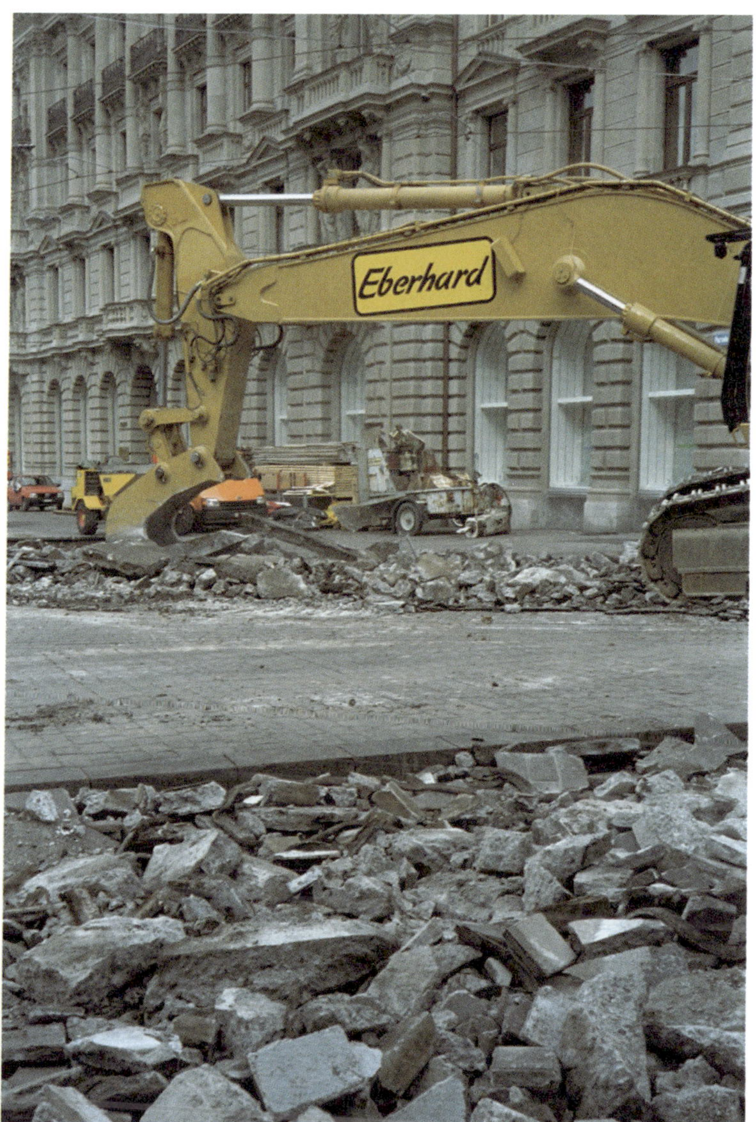

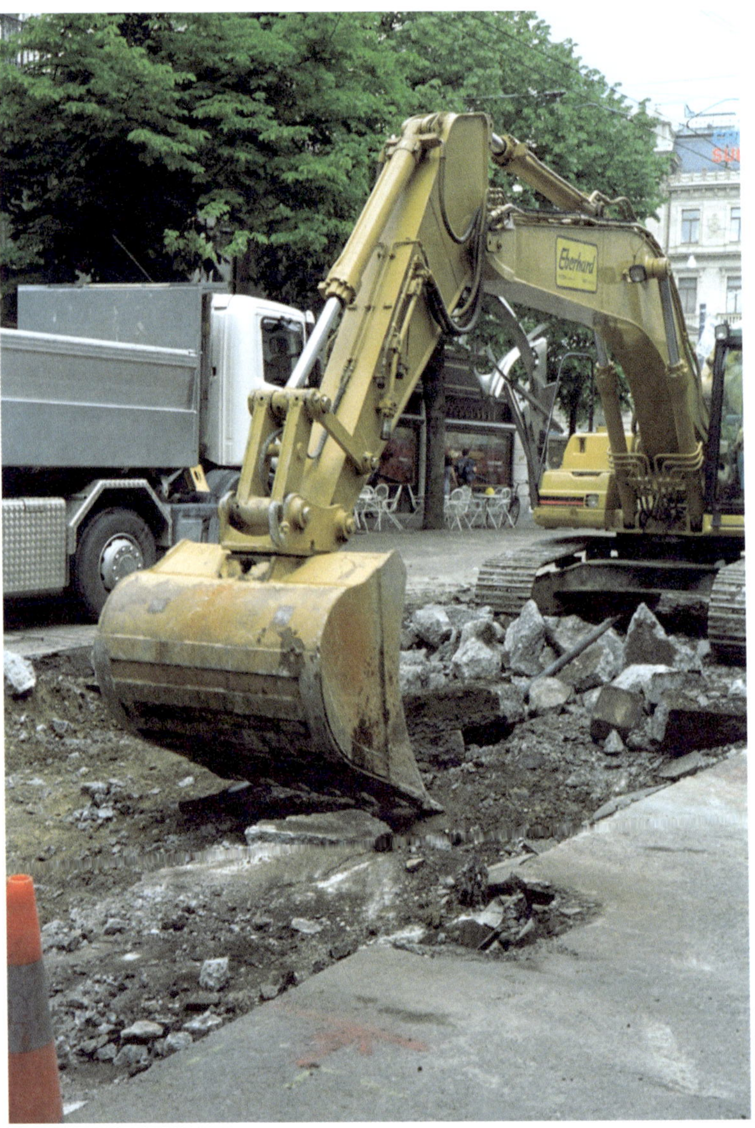

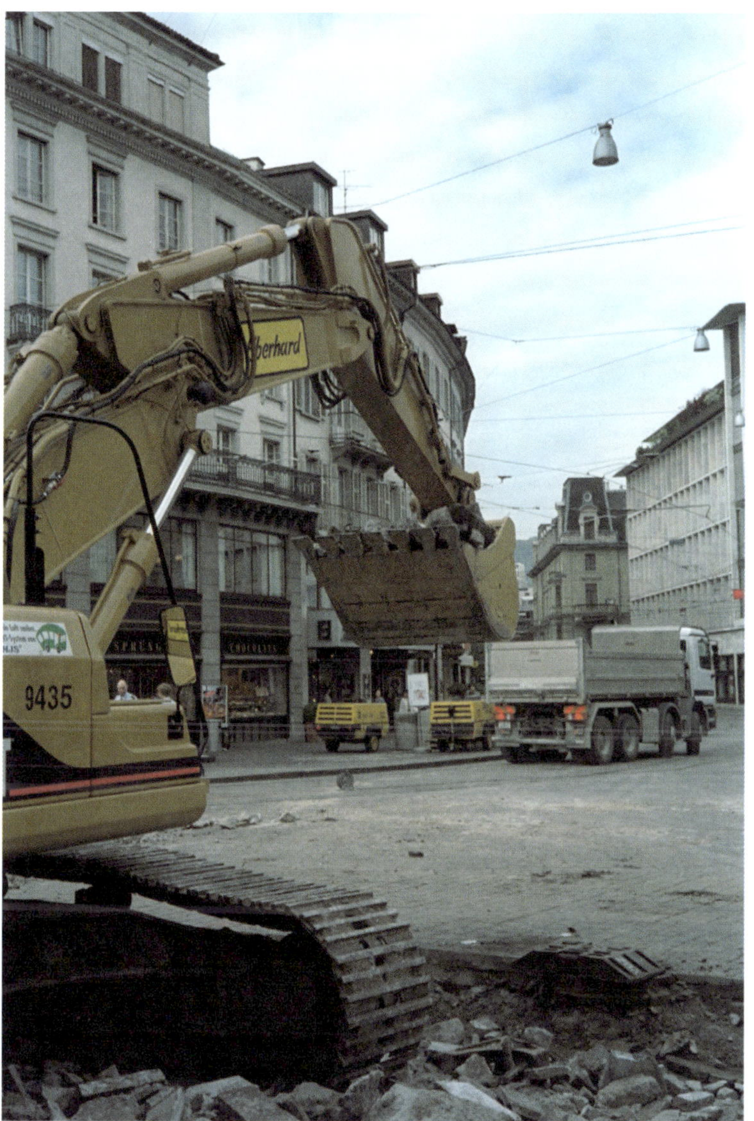
berhard
9435
SPRÜNGLI
CHOCOLATES

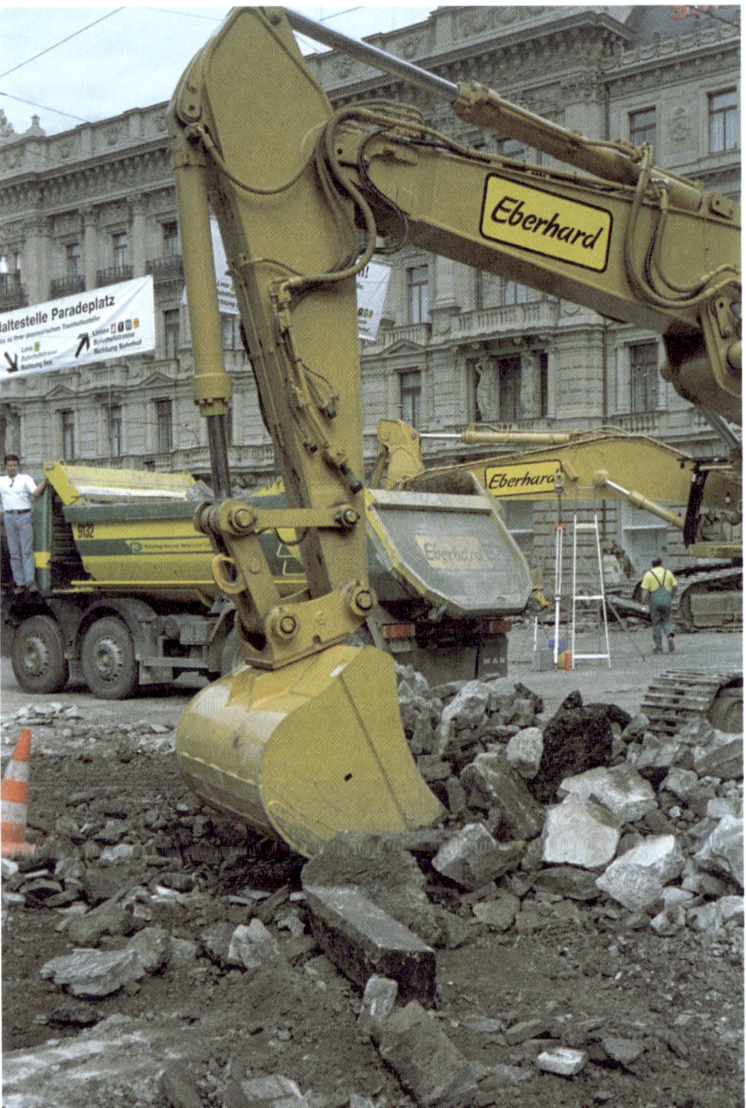
Eberhard
Eberhard
Eberhard
Haltestelle Paradeplatz
9132

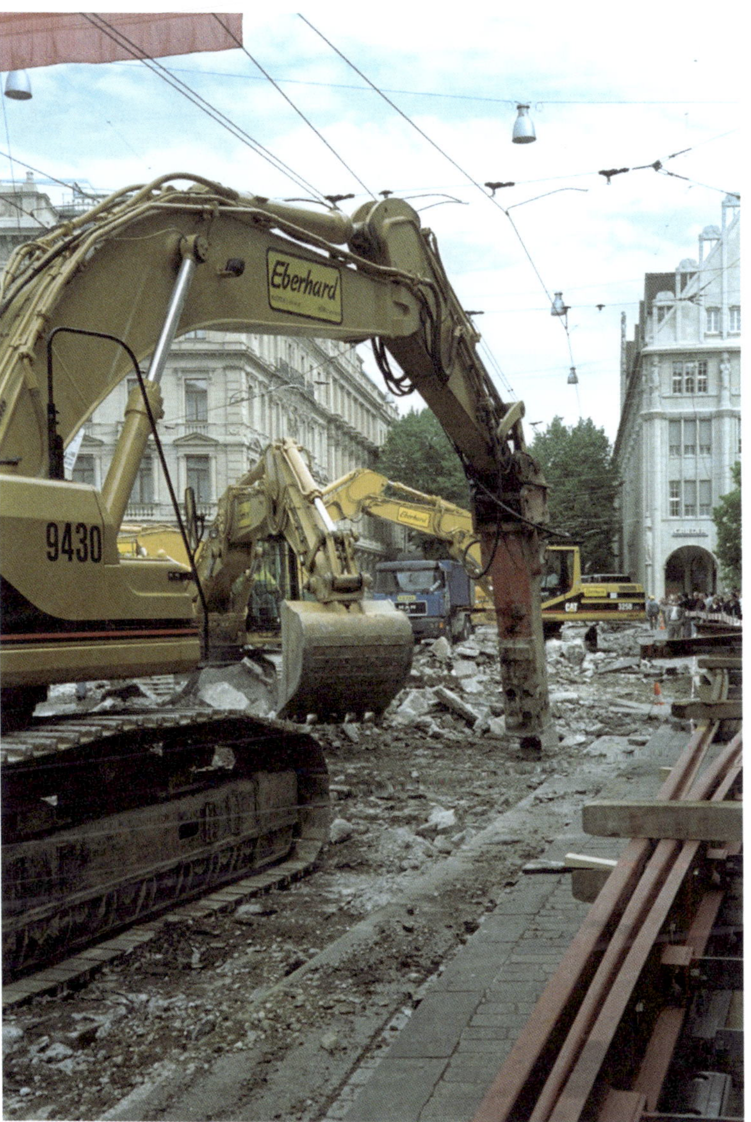

Eberhard
9430
Eberhard
CAT 325B

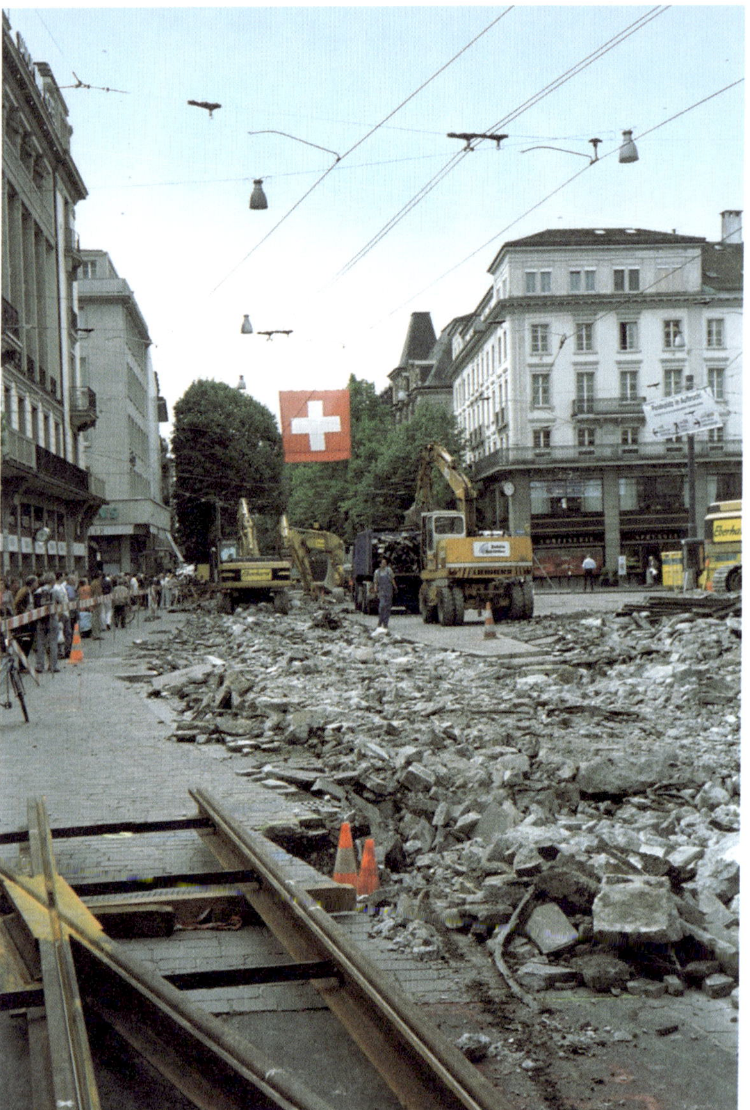

Degenerative Bilder 3/Degenerative Pictures 3

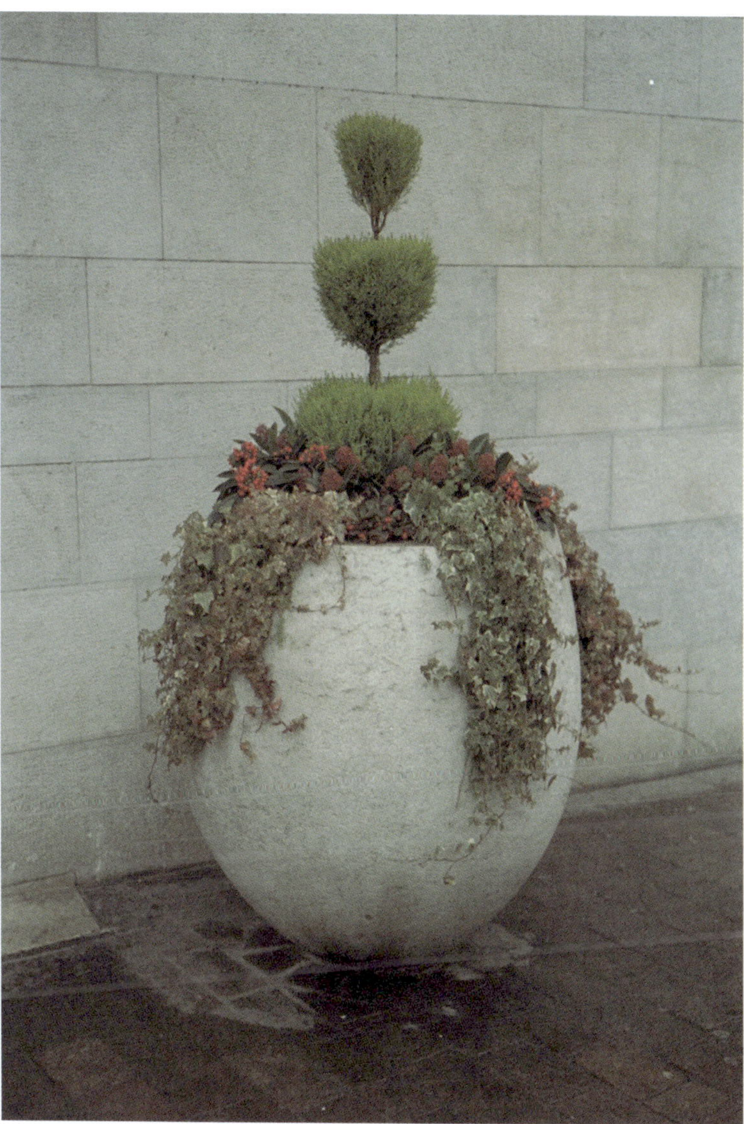

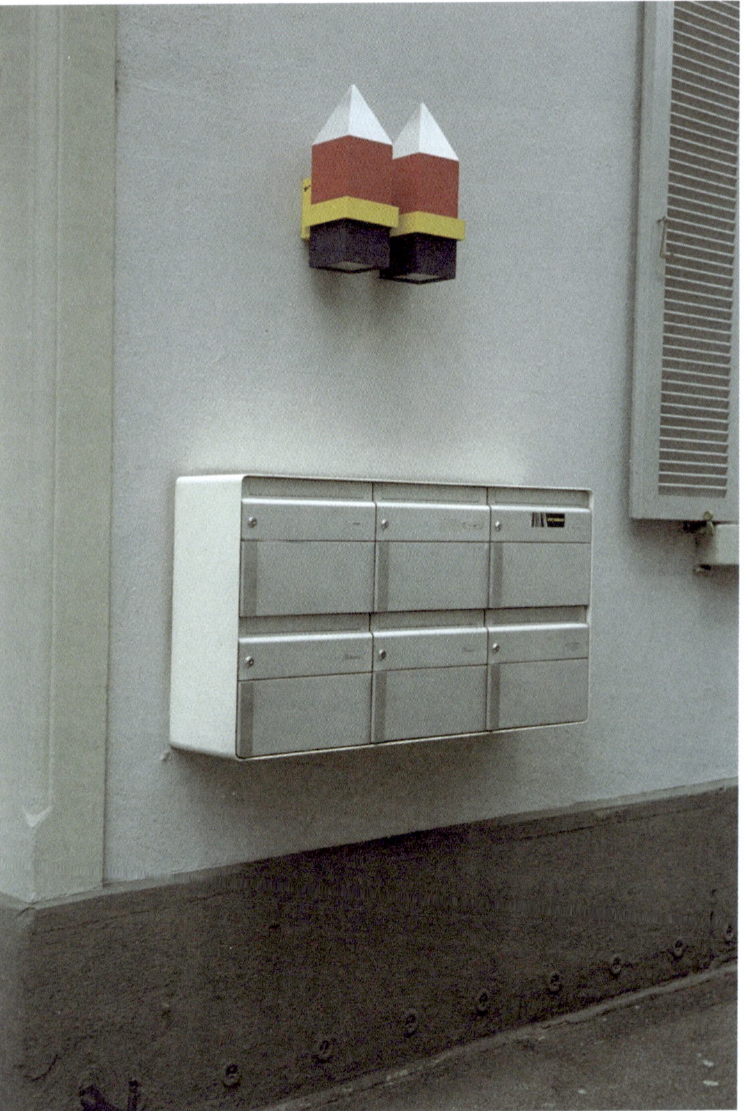

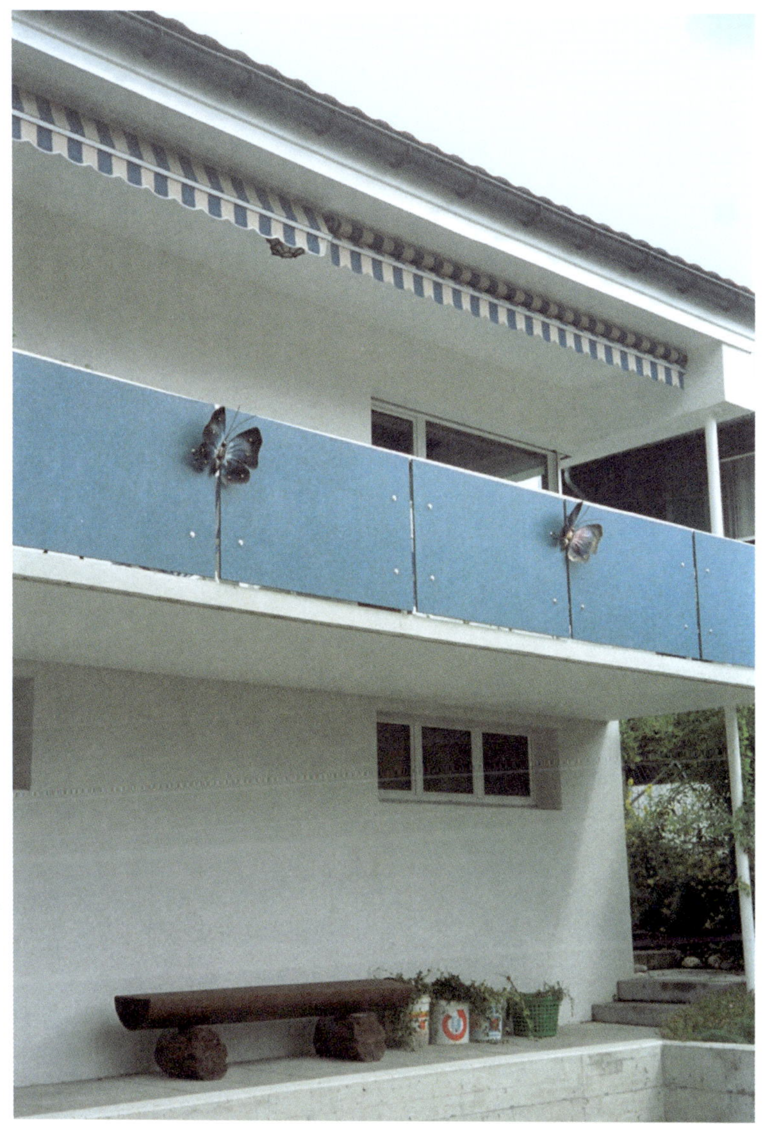

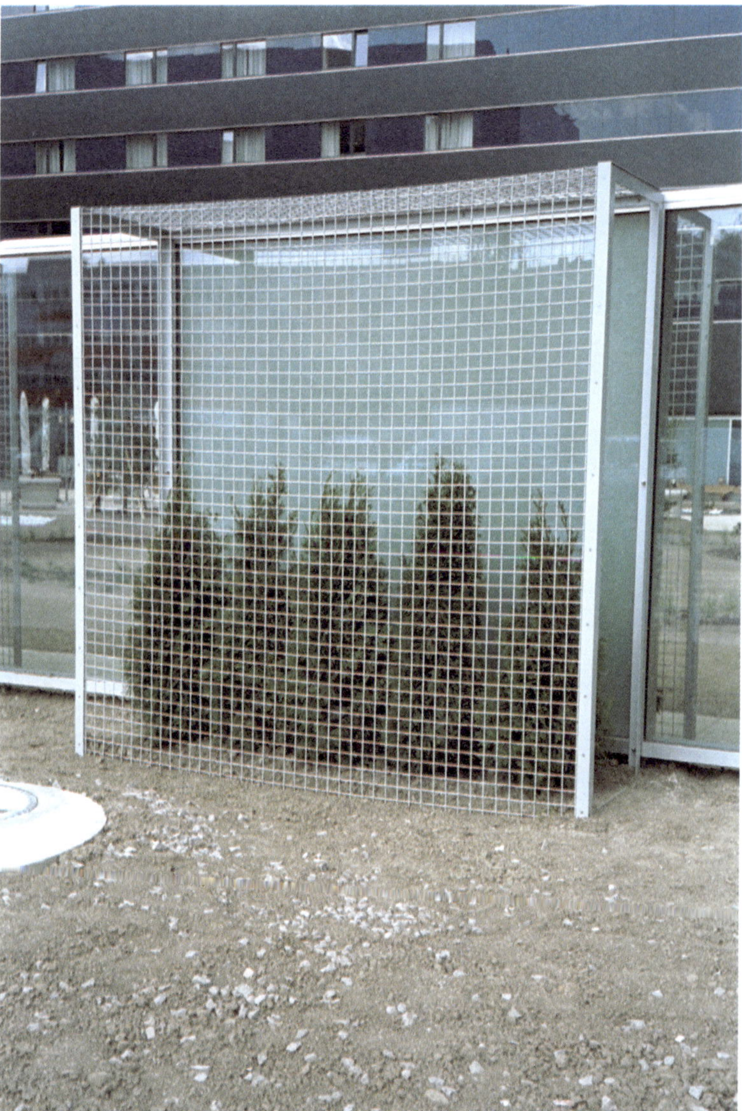

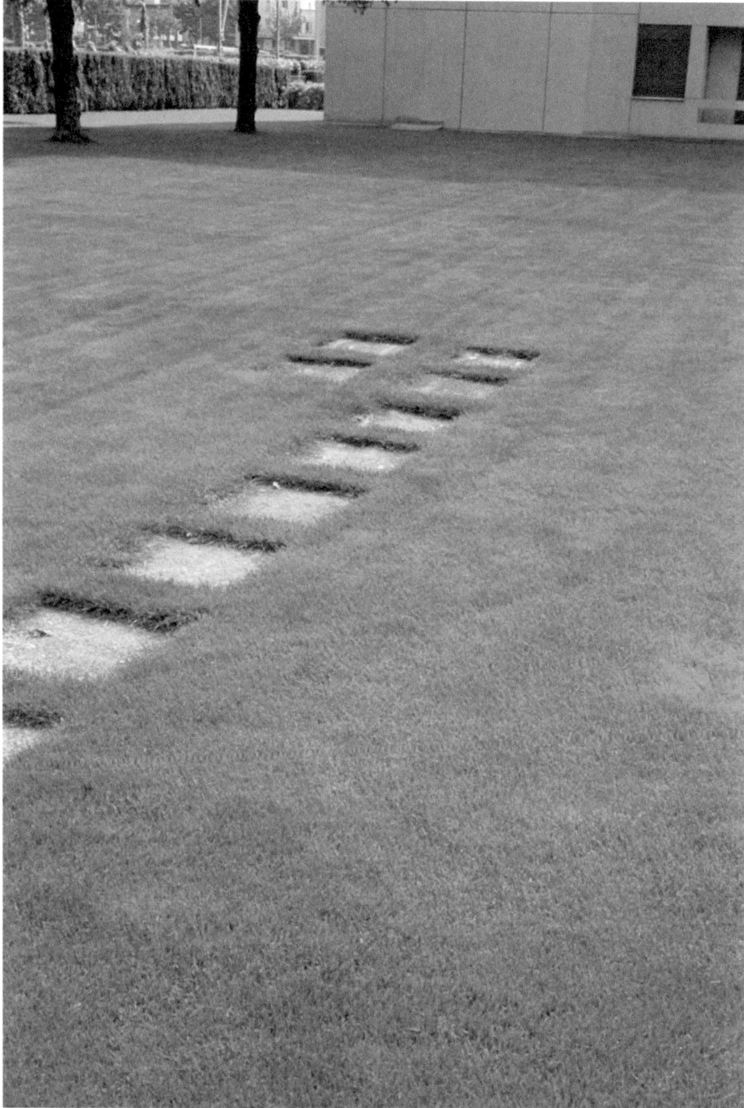

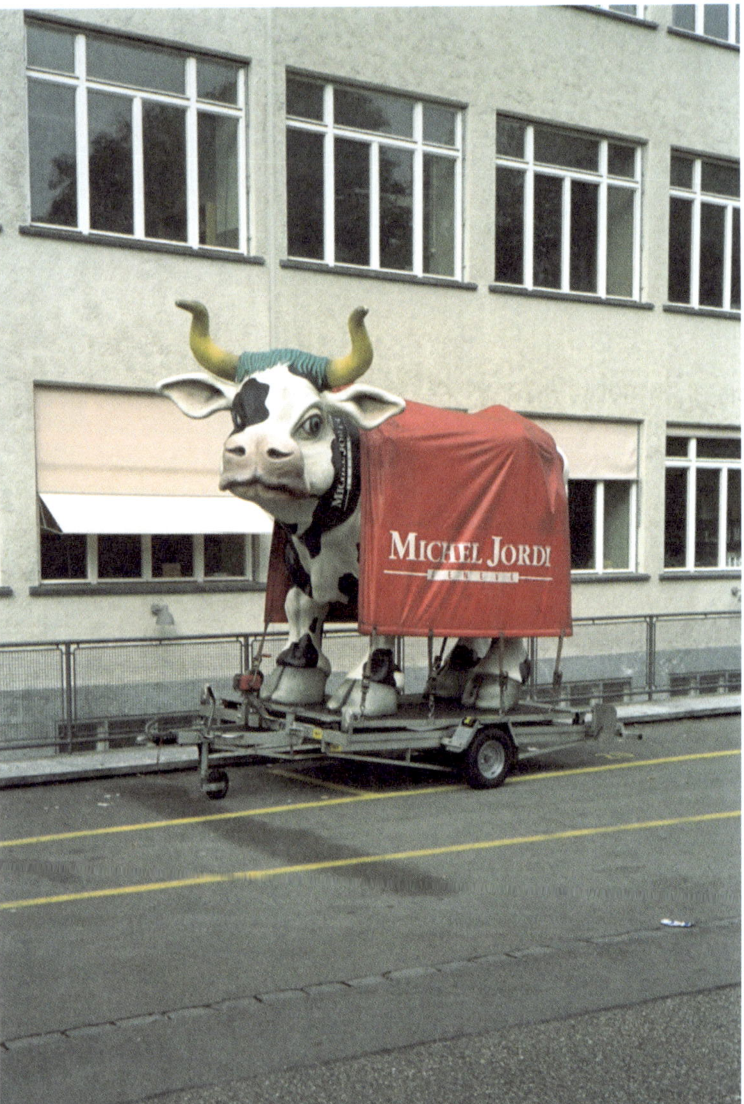

MICHEL JORDI

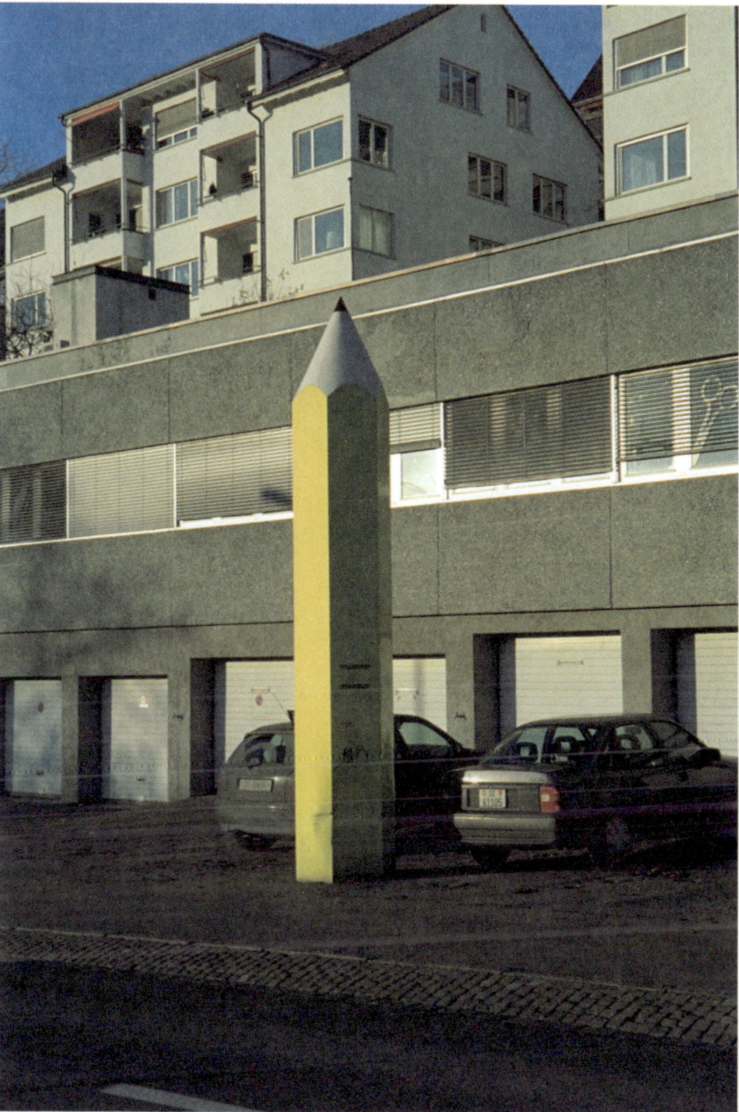

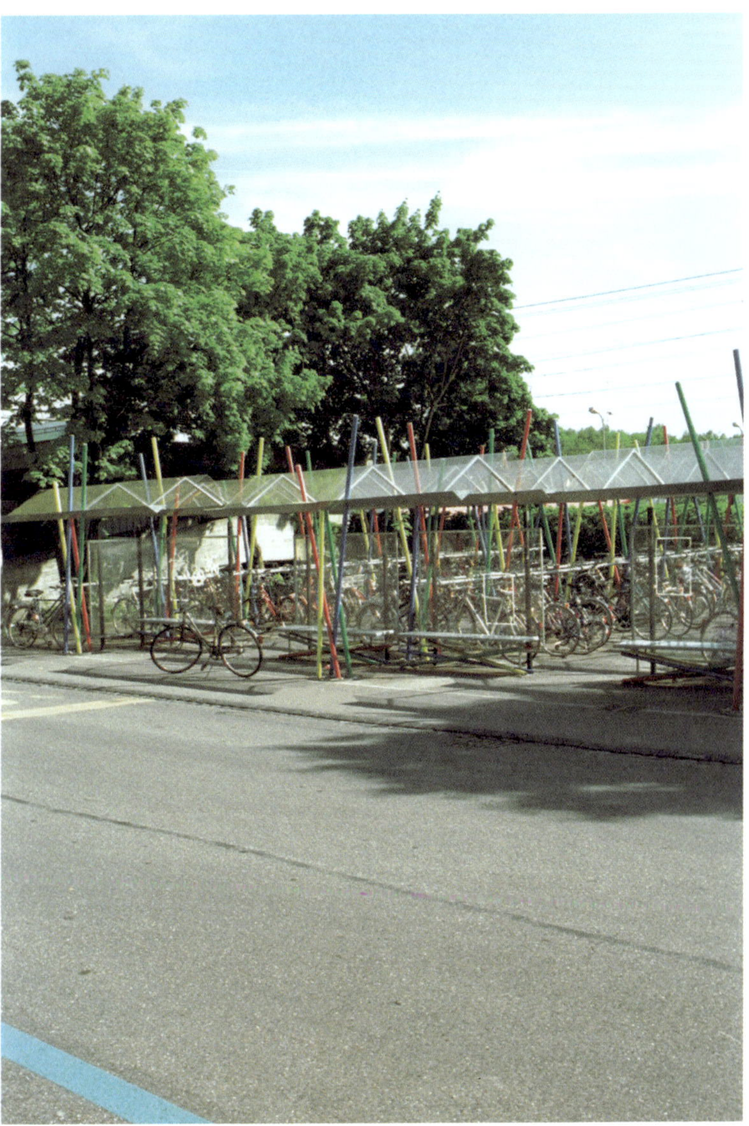

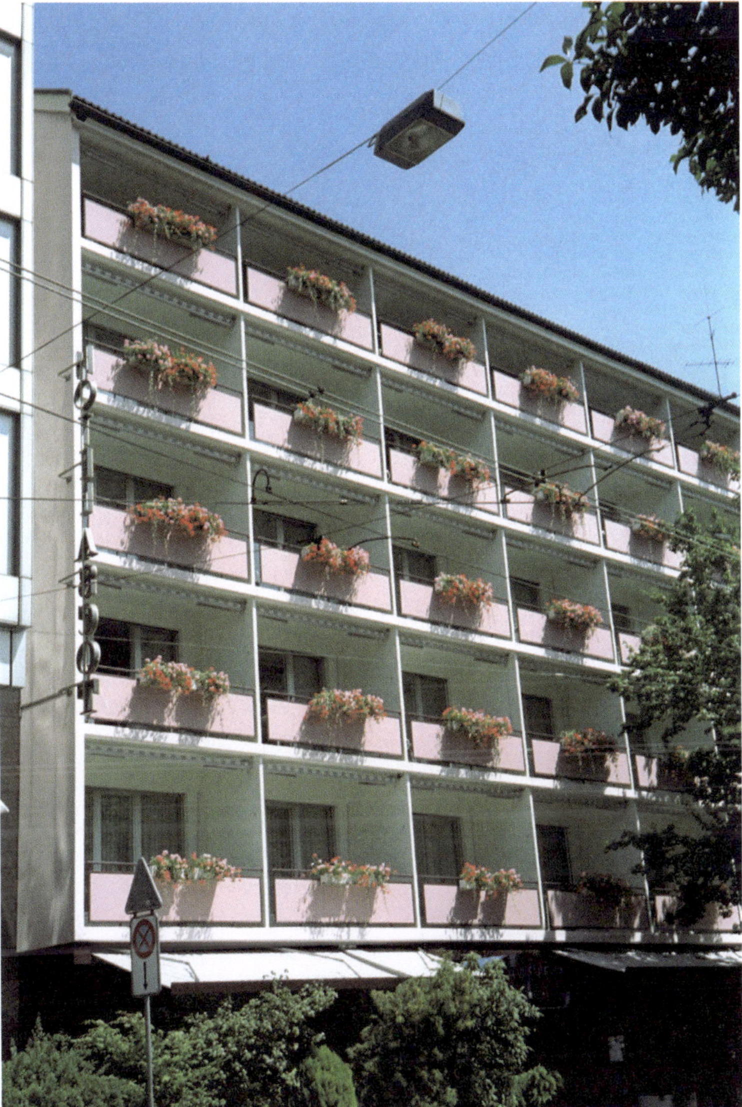

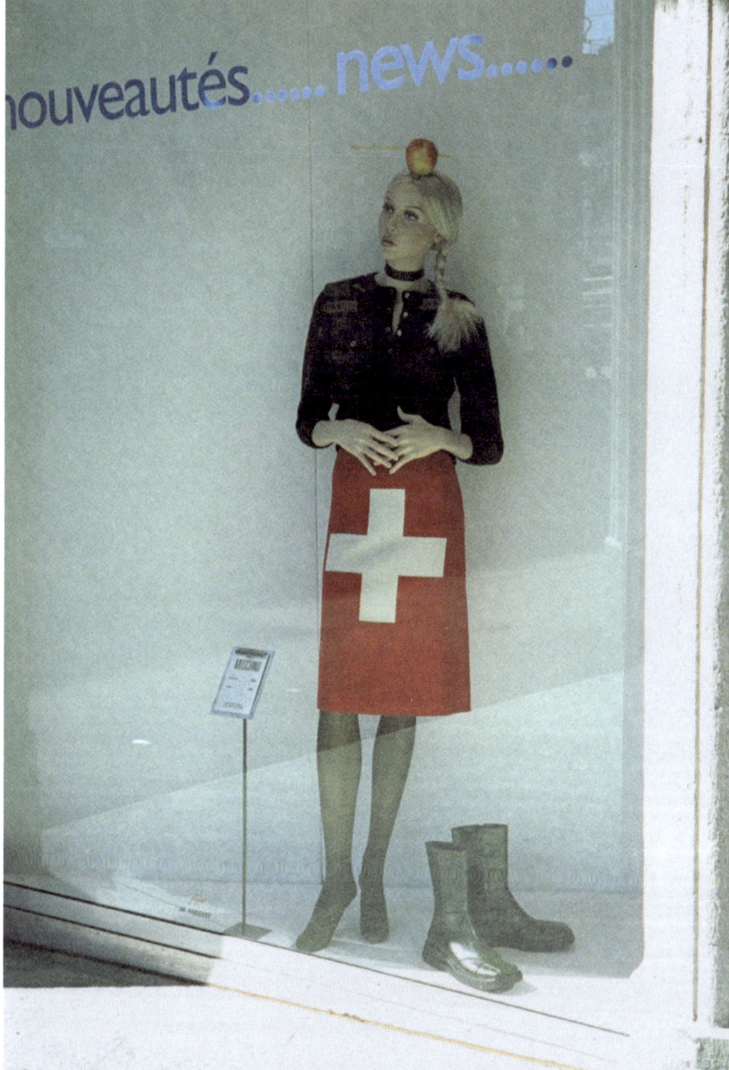

nouveautés...... news......

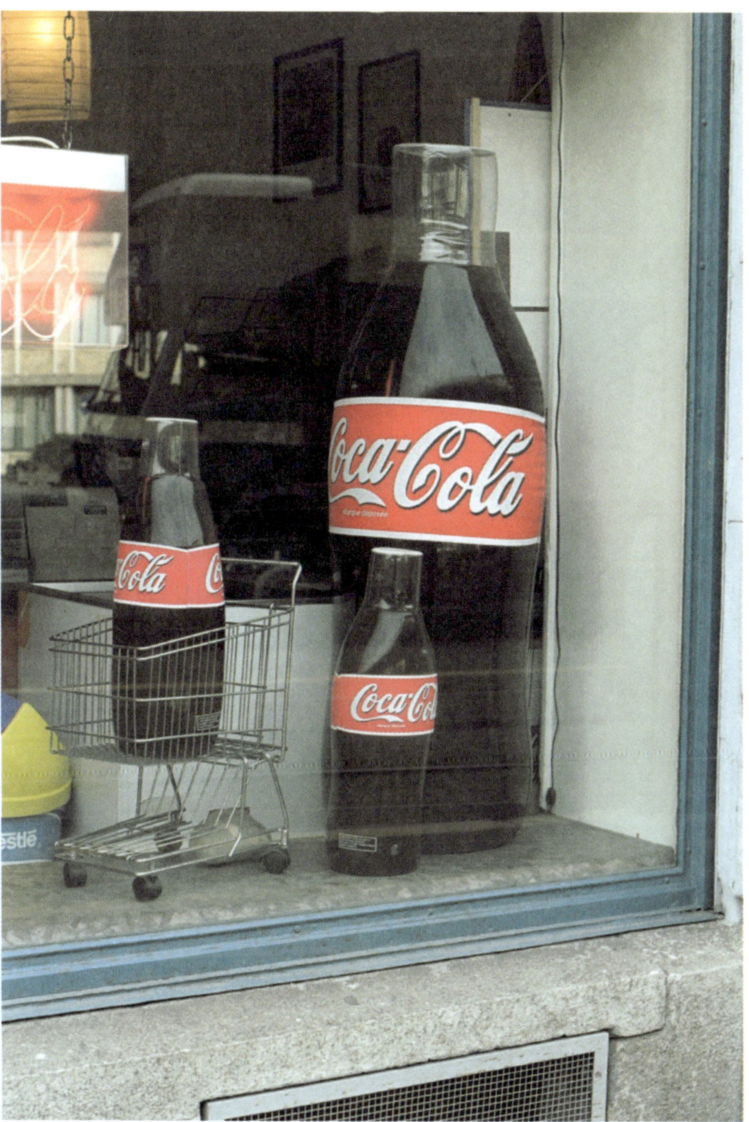

Coca-Cola
marque déposée
Coca-Cola
Coca-Cola
Nestlé

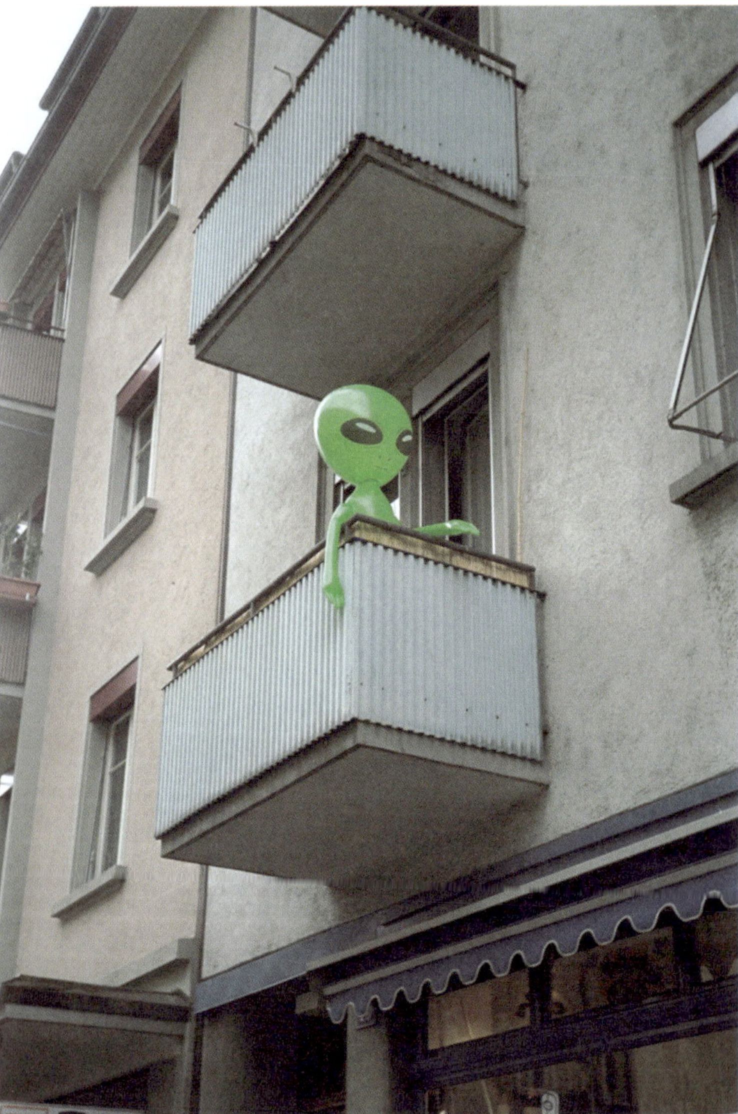

Schweigen ist Gold / Silence is Golden

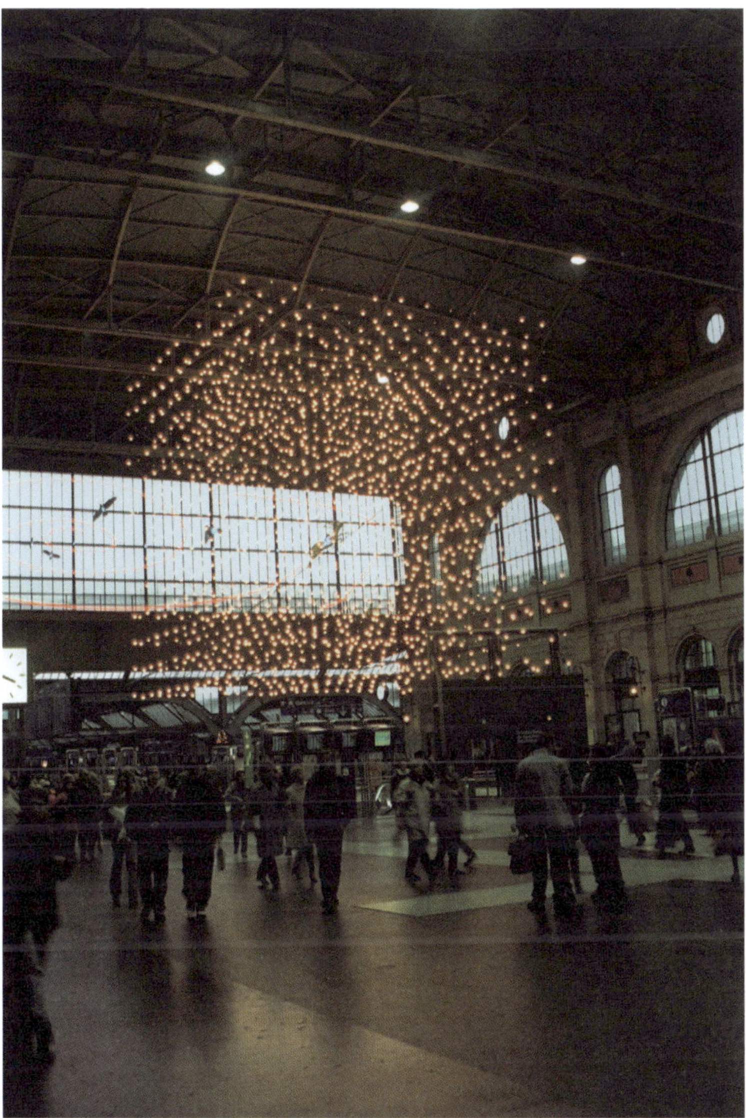

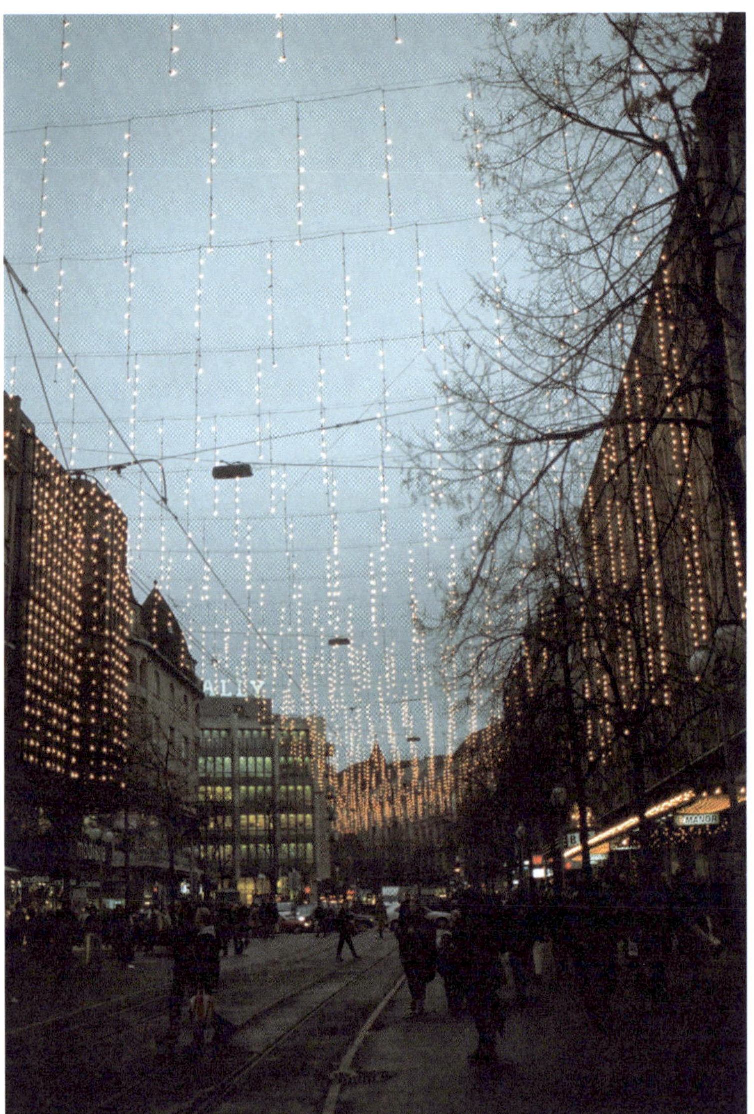

BALLY
MAJOR

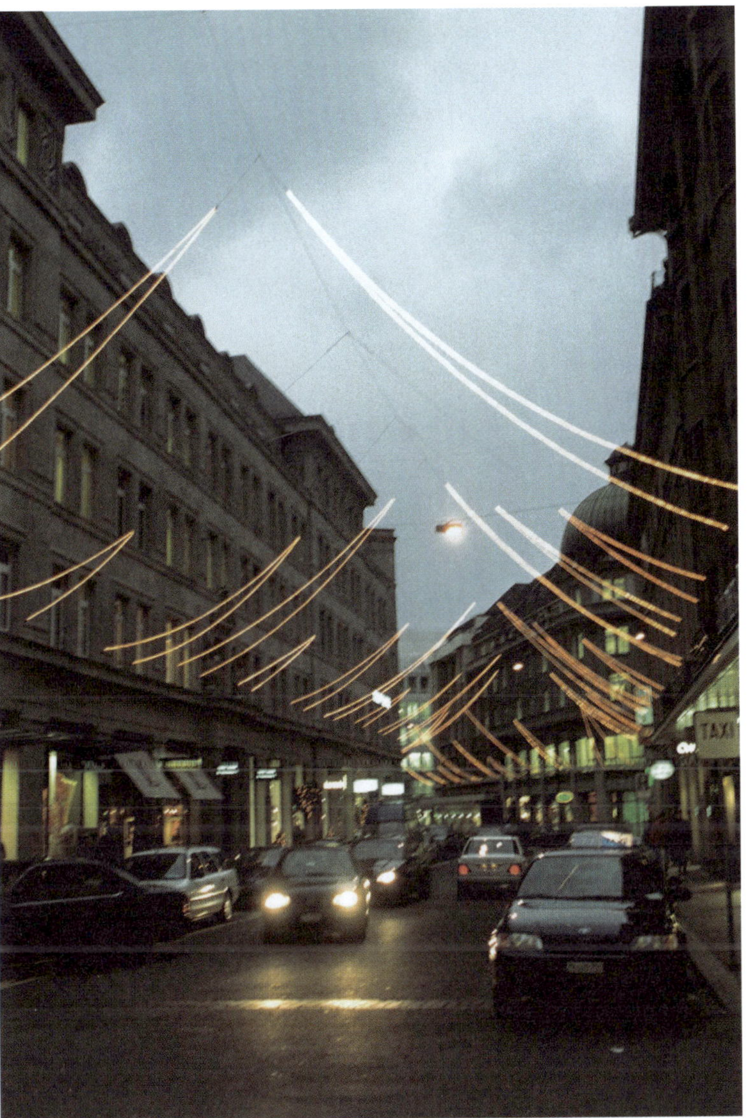

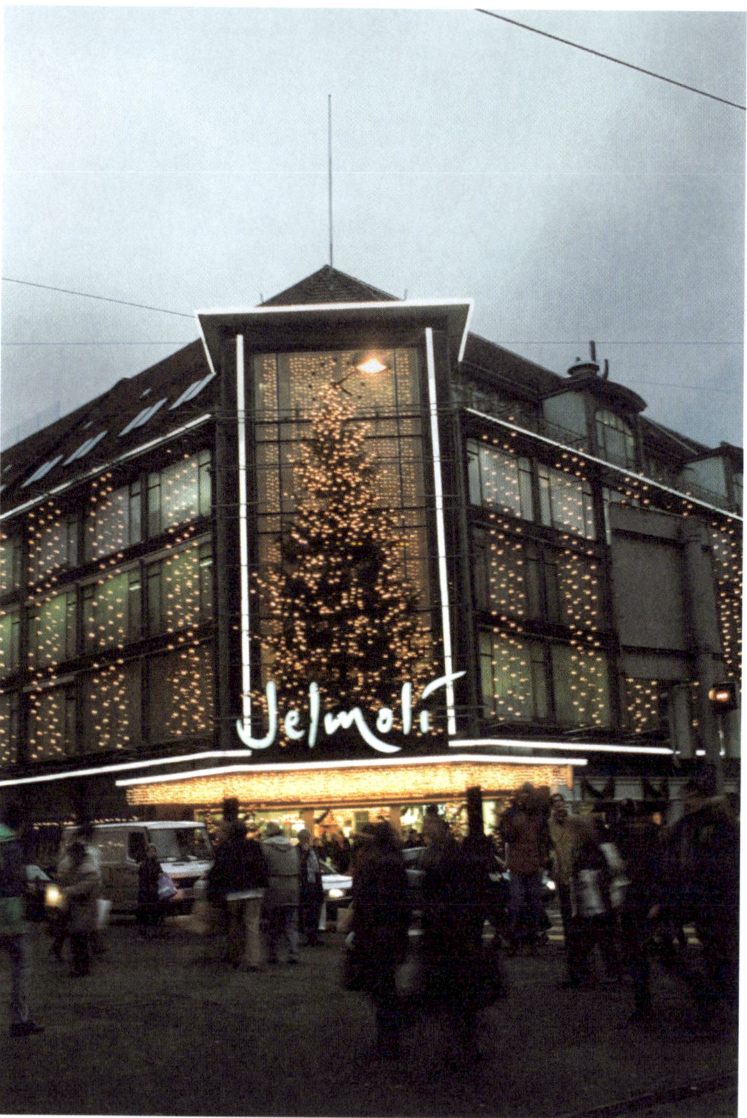
Jelmoli

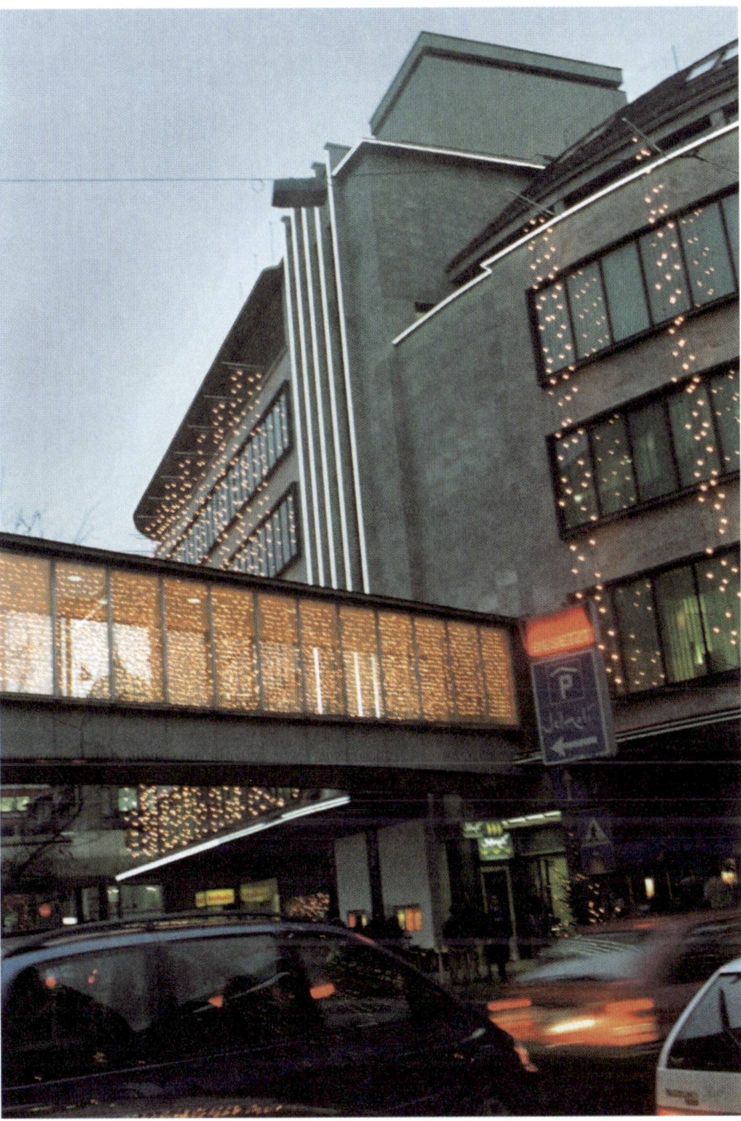

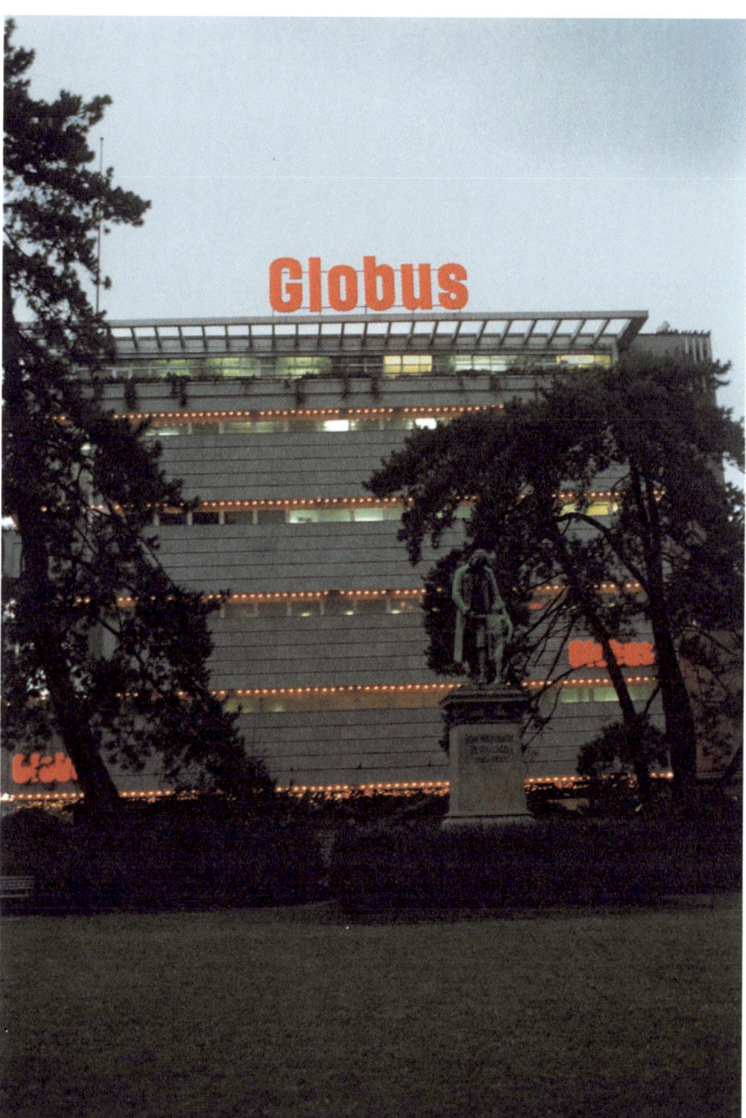
Globus

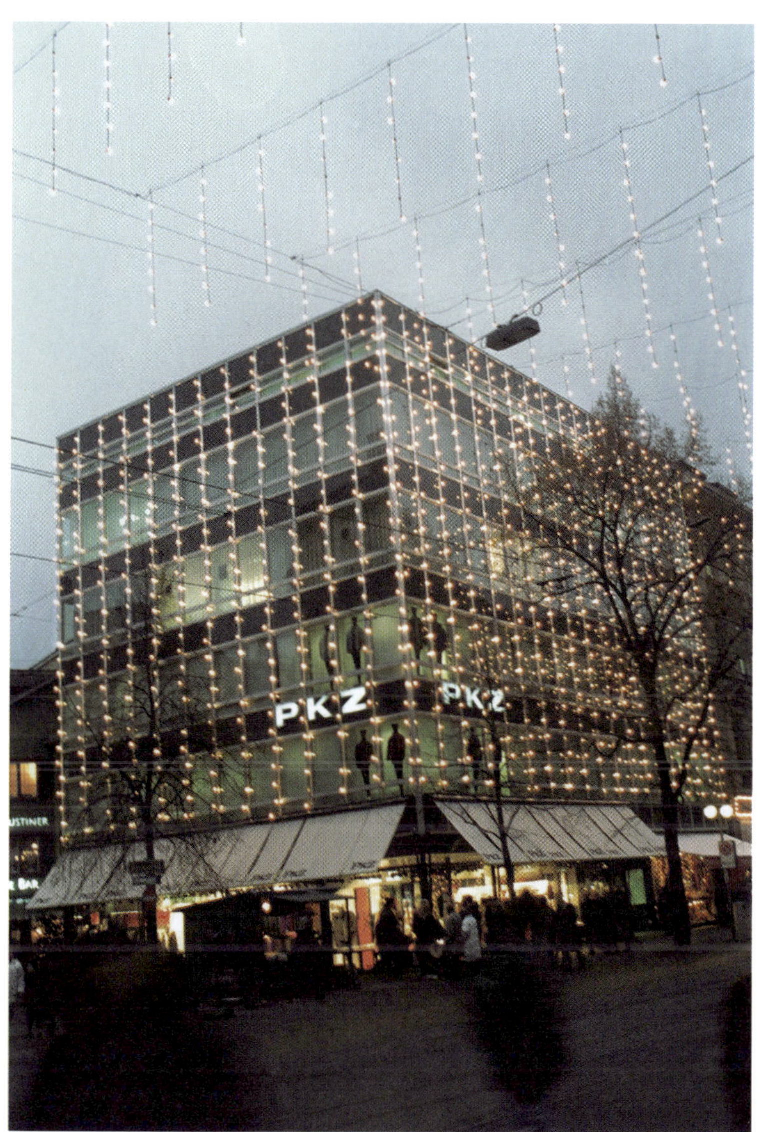

PKZ
PKZ
USTINER
BAR

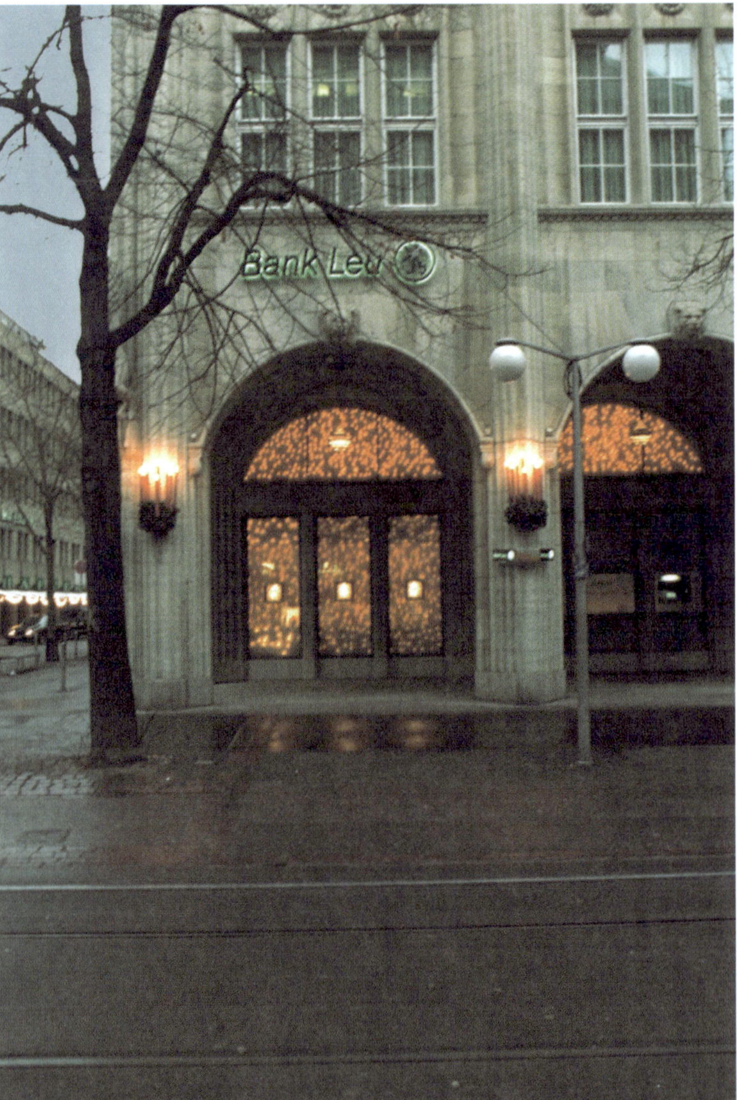
Bank Leu

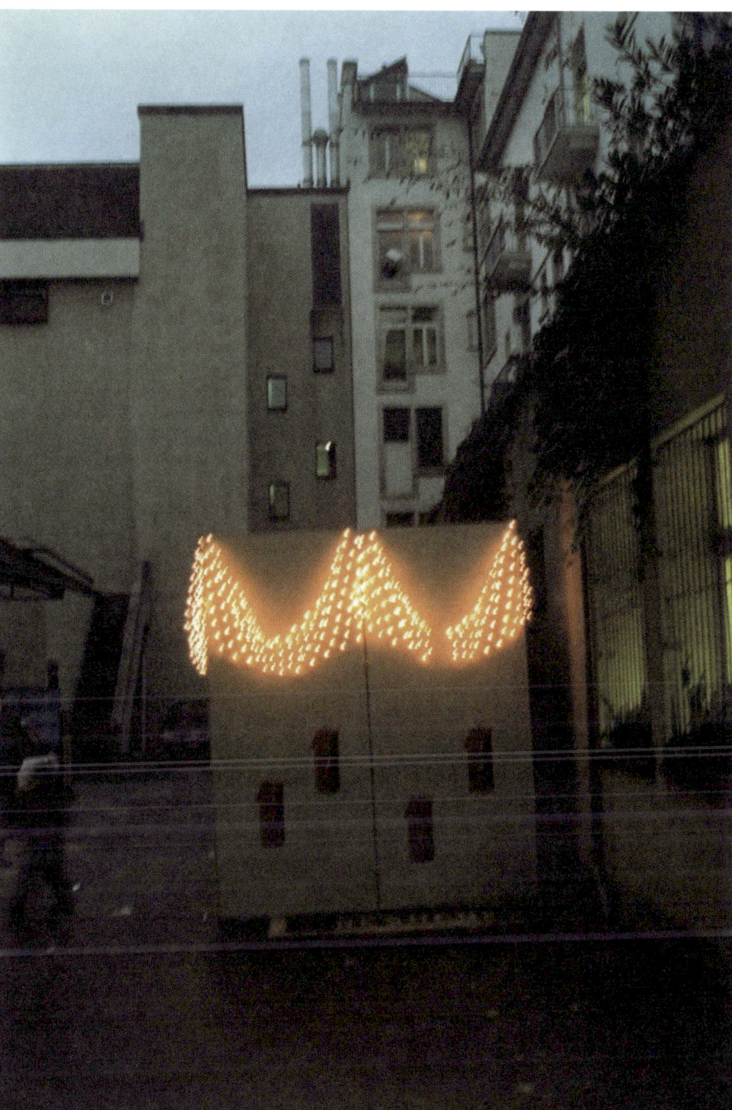

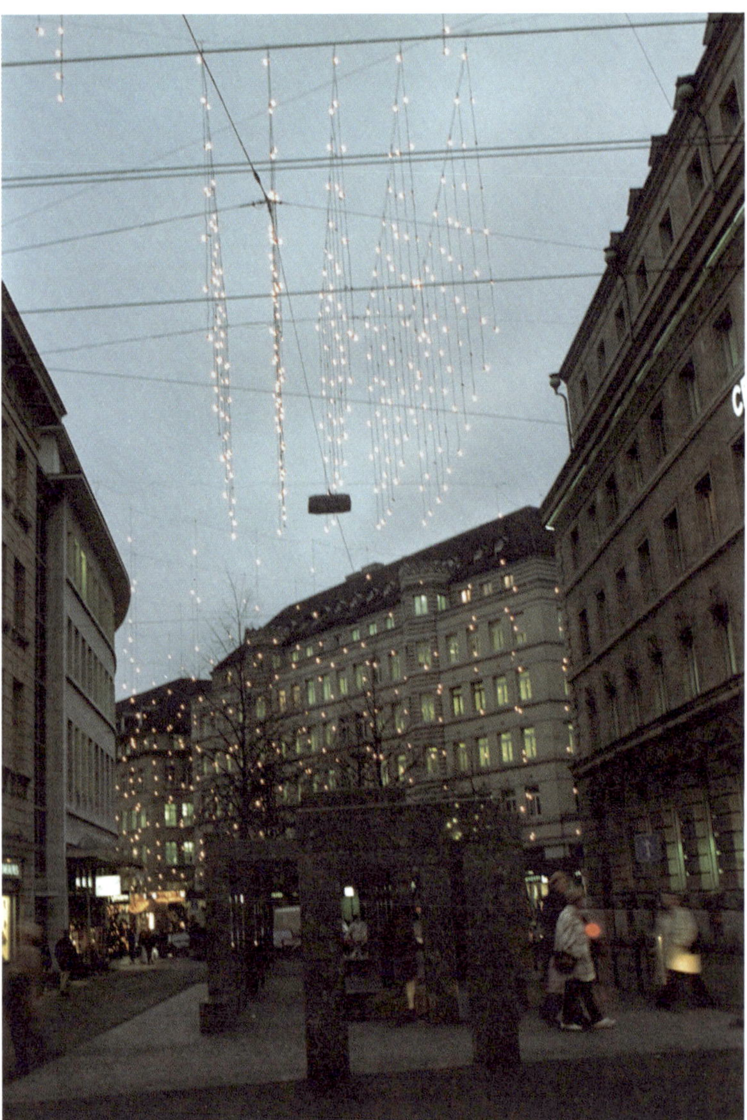

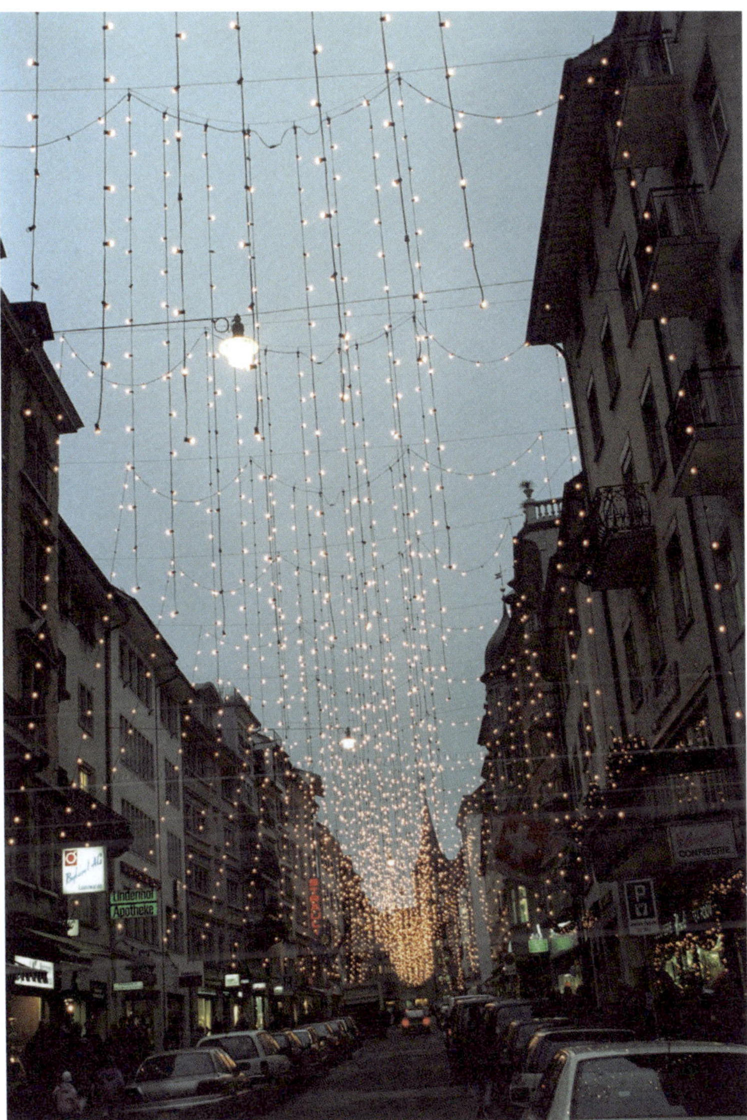
Lindenhof
Apotheke
CONFISERIE
P

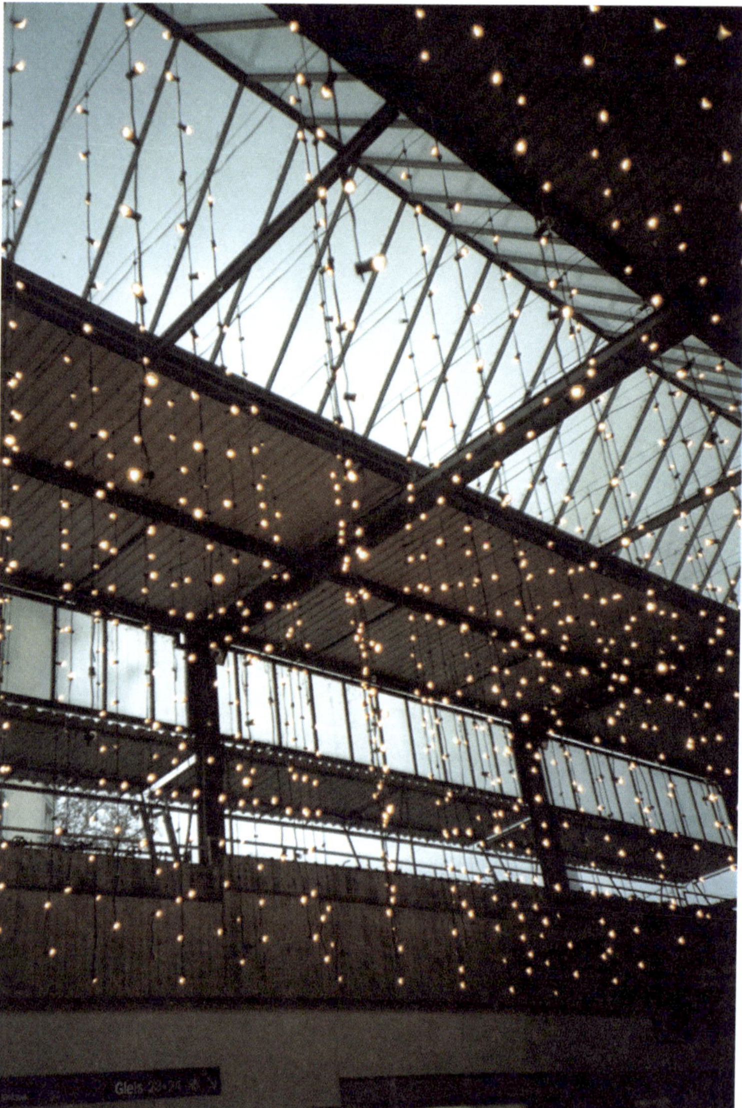

Gleis 23-24

Ziegler/Ziegler

Über eine Farbe jenseits der Moderne

Im Europa der Anekdoten und Gerüchte stehen die Alpenländer
auffällig heraus. Kaum hat man österreichischen oder
schweizerischen Boden betreten, trifft man Leute, die dem
Besucher ausführlich erklären, warum ihr Land ein schwieriges
sei, verengt, verbohrt, reaktionär; nicht wirklich Teil der Welt-
gemeinschaft. Man könnte das einen negativen Nationalismus
nennen, eine Obsession mit dem staatlichen Gebilde. Dabei
unterscheiden sich die Österreicher deutlich von den Schweizern.
Die österreichische alpine Geschichte ist dunkel, sprachlos,
hartgesotten, eingekesselt vom Ressentiment der Dörfler,
durchwoben von den Rachegelüsten des kleinen Mannes. Das
Bild der Schweizer Alpen und ihrer Refugien erscheint im Vergleich
eher hell, apollinisch, von wackerer Urwüchsigkeit. Selbst
der kauzigste Hirte entpuppt sich als guter alter Mann, wie man
in Johanna Spyris «Heidi»-Roman nachlesen kann. Der negative
Nationalismus der Schweiz handelt also nicht von dunklen Trieben,
sondern vom Pathos der Rechtschaffenheit.
Generationen von Aufklärern zwischen Tagerwilen und Genève
hätten nichts zu beleuchten, wenn es nicht auch in der
Schweiz eine dunkle Stelle gäbe; nämlich die Lichtlosigkeit der
Tresore. In einem einprägsamen Film (*Cría Cuervos*, 1975)
hat Carlos Saura das Bild der Lichtlosigkeit metaphorisch
ausgereizt. Der Patriarch einer reichen Familie sitzt im Rollstuhl.
Bei einem Unfall hat er sein Gedächtnis eingebüsst. In liebevoller
Aufmerksamkeit bemüht sich die Familie um die Erhellung
der dunklen Kammern seiner Erinnerung. Allerdings nicht ohne
eigene Interessen. Im erloschenen Teil des Hirns lagert nämlich
die Nummernkombination des Schweizer Kontos, und nur
dort. Geld ist ein abstraktes Tauschmittel, im Zweifelsfall eine
Zahl; Gold gehört zu den Elementen der Physik und des
Physischen. Es kommt als Barren, Münze oder Ehering. Seine
enorme Formbarkeit hat es prädestiniert, zum zentralen
Material einer individuellen Skulptur zu werden, nämlich des

Goldzahns. Gegossen und geprägt, brilliert es in Gestalt;
eingeschmolzen und amalgamiert gibt es sie für immer preis.
Deshalb stellt der Besitz von enteignetem, gestohlenem
und geraubtem Gold etwas ganz anderes dar als eine
Kompromittierung von Motiven im Geldkreislauf: Wer Gold
besitzt, hat möglicherweise physisch die Substanz in den
Händen, die Ausdruck persönlichen Glücks und Wohlstands
anderer Menschen war.
Anders als Silber ist Gold verwurzelt in einem Mythos, der
plötzlichen genauso wie dauerhaften Reichtum einschliesst. Alle
Geschichten vom Goldrausch handeln von der Anarchie, die
ausbricht, wenn das Begehrteste für alle zum Greifen nahe ist,
und von den Hierarchien, die begründet und gefestigt werden,
um das Begehrteste in die Hände der einen und nicht der
anderen zu schaufeln. Psychoanalytisch gesehen ist Gold also
verbunden mit der Konstitution des Gesetzes. Der Western
elaboriert den Konflikt, indem er zwei Gebäude von Autorität
in Entstehung zeigt: das private Vermögen und den Staat. Im
Zustand der Anarchie erscheinen beide in der Gestalt des Räubers.
Gold ist von den feudalen Gesellschaften an die industriellen
weitergereicht worden wie ein Platzhalter oder ein Pfand.
Die Währung, in vielen Ländern nicht zufällig «eine Krone», wurde
dem Untertanen als Tauschmittel an die Hand gegeben, wobei
er aufhörte, Untertan zu sein. Als Garantie der Konstruktion einer
nationalen Währung hat lange der staatliche Bestand an Gold
gegolten.
Sofern nicht die Thaler selbst mehr oder weniger aus Gold
geprägt waren, konnte man die Staatswährung in Gold tauschen;
nicht unbedingt ein verlockendes Angebot, wenn man be-
denkt, dass eben das Geld – und nicht das Gold – das Zahlungs-
mittel war. Die Währungs- und Börsencrashs des zwanzigsten
Jahrhunderts haben zu einer Abkopplung von Gold und Währung
in der Nationalökonomie geführt. Merkwürdigerweise ver-
schieben aber die Staatsbanken international weiterhin grosse
Mengen an Gold, um Währungsschwankungen unter Kontrolle

zu halten und Staatshaushalte zu schützen. Mit mehr oder
weniger Erfolg versucht man, den individuellen Handel mit Gold
bedeutungslos zu machen, weil die Nachfrage immer einen
Zweifel an den Währungen offenbart. Im unsichtbaren Transfer
von Goldreserven zeigt sich, dass die Erfindung freier Märkte
in der Vorstellung eines unhintergehbaren Wertes gründet. Auch
Demokratien ohne Könige leben weiter mit der goldenen Krone.
Der Mythos des Goldes erscheint ungebrochen. Gold ist
durch nichts anderes darzustellen als durch sich selbst; es hat
also ein verhindertes Verhältnis zur Repräsentation. Für die
Fürsten und Kaufleute der Renaissance war es eine Selbstver-
ständlichkeit, dass von Meistern gemalte biblische Szenen
in Goldrahmen platziert wurden, die ebenfalls der Werkstatt des
Meisters entstammten. Am Anfang des Quattrocento reichte
das Blattgold bis in den Bildraum selbst; wie viel davon zu
verwenden war, regelte ein Vertrag. Im Laufe des Jahrhunderts
verschwand das Gold aus dem Rechteck des Tafelbildes, und
an seine Stelle rückten Städte und Landschaften. Die Qualität
der Darstellung wurde als wichtig erkannt, weshalb die Auftrag-
geber darauf beharrten, dass das Bildfeld vom «Pinsel» des
Malers auszuschmücken war und nicht von seinem Assistenten.
Der Übergang bezeichnet die modernen Zweifel an substanziellen
Gütern – wo viel Gold ist, ist viel Wert – in die Hochachtung
von Dienstleistungen. Wer gut malen kann, steckt das Gold in die
eigene Tasche.
In den Verträgen zwischen den Malern und ihren Fürsten sind
die Farbe das eine und Gold ein anderes. Dabei findet in den
Bildern Blattgold sehr wohl als Farbe Verwendung, wenn es den
Engel mit einem Lichtschein oder den Ritter mit einer Rüstung
schmückt. Die Möglichkeit des Goldes, etwas anderes darzustellen als Gold, ist aber begrenzt. Der enorme Hang seiner
Oberfläche, als Tautologie in Erscheinung zu treten. «Und
zu wissen, es ist Platin…» war der Slogan einer jahrelangen
Schmuckkampagne, der auf Gold nicht anzuwenden gewesen
wäre. Man weiss es nicht, man sieht es. Gold ist resistent

gegen die Umwertungen im Prozess der Moderne, die die
Flexibilität von Formen höher schätzt als die Unverrückbarkeit
einer Substanz. Gold ist der reine Ausdruck einer Substanz –
im Reich des Materiellen etwa das, was in der Philosophie die
Wahrheit ist. Als Wort und Vorstellung allerdings hat Gold
eine reiche Karriere gemacht. Wie die Wahrheit umstellt ist von
der Wirklichkeit auf der einen Seite und von der Lüge auf der
anderen, ist alles, was golden genannt wird, anfällig für
Täuschungen. Es mag im Geheimnis der Sprache liegen – im
«Goldstaub des Signifikanten», mit Roland Barthes –, dass
sich das Gold überall eingenistet hat. Die Altklugen behaupten,
dass «Reden Silber und Schwelgen Gold sei»; eine Zigaretten-
werbung lockt seit Jahren «discover gold». Der ganze
Weihnachtsplunder ist gülden. Gold, jenseits seiner Substanz,
ist dann doch eine Farbe geworden, die mit anderen Farben
in unlauterer Konkurrenz steht. Man sagt von Metaphern,
die zu häufig gebraucht werden, dass sie aufhören, Metaphern
zu sein. So geht es dem Gold und dem Goldenen, als Unhinter-
gehbarem auf der einen Seite und nutzlosem Flitter auf
der anderen. Gold ist eine archaische Paradoxie der Moderne;
die das Gold als Rückgrat ihrer Konstruktion leugnet und vor
dem Goldenen das kritische Auge schliesst. Wie auch immer
man es betrachtet: Wer das Wort ins Spiel bringt, legt mit grosser
Wahrscheinlichkeit eine falsche Fährte aus.

Ulf Erdmann Ziegler

A Color Not Touched by Modernity

The alpine lands feature unusually prominently in the Europe of
anecdotes and rumors. One hardly has to enter into Austria
or Switzerland to be confronted with people who like to
explain to visitors at length why theirs is an especially problematic
country; narrow-minded, stubborn and reactionary, and not
really to be considered as part of the global community. One could
interpret this as a form of inverted nationalism, an obsession
with the national structures. Nevertheless, here the Austrians
prove to be quite different from their Swiss neighbors.
Austrian alpine history is dark, inarticulate, callous, suffused with
the pettiness of villagers, permeated with the vengeful desires
of the man in the street. The image projected by the Swiss Alps
and its refuges seems in contrast to be bright, Apollonian, full
of upright earthiness. Even the strangest shepherd turns out to
be a kindly old man, as is amply illustrated in Johanna Spyri's novel
"Heidi". Hence, the inverted nationalism of the Swiss does
not center around dark passions, but the pathos of righteousness.
Generations of upholders of the enlightenment between Täger-
wilen and Geneva would have had nothing to enlighten were it
not for one dark corner of Switzerland: namely the lightless interiors
of its safes. In one memorable film Carlos Saura (*Cría Cuervos*,
1975) metaphorically dissected the image of lightlessness.
The patriarch of a rich family is confined to a wheelchair and has
also been robbed of part of his memory as a result of an
accident. The family exhibits loving care in trying to cast some
light into the dark chambers of his memory. But they do so
not without some vested interest: that part of his brain affected
by amnesia also contained the combination number of their Swiss
bank account.
Money is an abstract means of exchange, or in case of doubt
just a cipher: gold belongs to the elements of physics and
the physical, it can assume the form of bars, coins or wedding
rings. The ease with which it can be shaped and formed destined

it to become the central material of that absolutely individual
sculpture, namely the dental crown. Cast and minted it shines
in every shape or form: melted down or mixed into an amalgam
it loses this property for ever. For this reason, the possession
of expropriated, stolen or plundered gold is something
entirely different to a financial scam: whoever owns gold might
have the physical matter in his hands that once expressed
the happiness and prosperity of other people. In contrast to silver,
gold is rooted in a myth that embraces both sudden and long-
standing wealth. All the stories of the gold rush relate the anarchy
that breaks out when that most sought-after material is put
within the grasp of all and tell of hierarchies that were founded
and built up to shovel this material into one pair of hands and
not another. From a psychoanalytical standpoint, gold therefore
can be seen as being closely related to the constitution of law.
Westerns elaborate this theme by illustrating the evolution
of structures of authority: private wealth versus the state. And
when anarchy prevails both appear in the form of the robber.
Gold was passed down from feudal to industrial societies, rather
like a substitute or pawn. The currency, which was not entirely
accidentally known as a "crown" in many countries, was placed
in the hands of vassals as a medium of exchange – allowing
them to progress beyond the state of being mere vassals. The
state reserves of gold long acted as a guarantee of the issue
of national currency. In so far as the thaler was not made of gold
anyway, the state currency might be exchanged for gold: not
exactly an attractive transaction, when one considers that money
– and not gold – was the legal tender. The currency and stock
market crash in the 20th century led to the abolition of parity
between gold and currencies in national economies. Strangely
enough, central banks still transfer large amounts of gold,
so as to control currency fluctuations and to protect domestic
budgets. And the attempt to relegate private gold speculation to
insignificance has met with varying success, as demand for
this material always reflects a certain doubt in individual curren-

cies. The invisible transfer of gold reserves reveals that the
invention of free markets is based on the idea of an incorruptible
value. Even democracies without kings tend to live on with
gold crowns.
The mythic fascination of gold remains seemingly unbroken. Gold
can be represented by nothing other than itself: it has a fraught
relationship with representation. For Renaissance princes
and traders it was a foregone conclusion that paintings by the
masters ended up in gilt frames that also originated from the same
masters' workshops. At the beginning of the quattrocento the
gold leaf even reached into the pictorial space and the amount to
be used was stipulated in written contracts. But over the course
of the centuries gold began to disappear from the rectan-
gular space of the painting to be replaced by towns and land-
scapes. The quality of the representation was now recognized as
being important, which led patrons to insist that the pictorial
surface was to be decorated by the master's own "brush" and
not by that of one of his assistants. The transition was
characterized by the modern mistrust of tangible assets – a lot
of gold signifying a lot of value – and the championship of services
instead. Anyone who could paint well could stuff gold into his
own pocket.
In the contracts between the princes and artists colors are one
thing and gold quite another. Nevertheless, gold leaf was
certainly used for coloristic effects when an angel was given a
halo or a knight decked out in armor. However, the ability of gold
to represent something other than just gold is rather limited.
The enormous pliability of gold is reflected by the propensity of its
surface to seem tautological. "And knowing it is platinum …" was
the slogan of a long-standing advertising campaign for jewelry
which would never be applicable to gold. One does not know it is
gold, it is to be seen.
Gold is resistant to the re-evaluation processes of modernity,
which valued the mutability of form higher than the immutability
of substance. Gold is the purest expression of substance –

the pendant to truth in philosophy in the sphere of the material.
Nevertheless, gold can look back on a rich and varied career
as word and idea. Just as truth has been surrounded by
reality on one side and by mendacity on the other, not all that
gleams is gold. This might arise from a secret of language – what
Roland Barthes referred to as the "golden dust of signifiers" –
which has allowed gold to settle everywhere. The more
precocious claim that "silence is golden," while an ad campaign
for cigarettes has long been beckoning consumers with
the exhortation "discover gold." The whole Christmas tinsel is
golden. Gold, beyond its mere substantiality, has in fact become
a color that competes unfairly with other colors. It is said
of metaphors that the more often they are used, the more they
cease to be metaphors. The same is true of gold and its
"gleam": being incorruptible on the one hand and useless glitter
on the other. Gold is an archaic paradox of modernity, which
eschews gold as the backbone of its construction and closes its
critical eyes in the presence of the gleam. Which ever way
one looks at it: anyone who introduces the word is most probably
laying a false trail.

Ulf Erdmann Ziegler

Translation: David P. Gogarty

Peter Tillessen wurde 1969 in Hanau a.M./BRD geboren. Nach dem Grundstudium der Agrarwissenschaften studierte er an der FAMU in Prag und an der HGK in Zürich Fotografie. Seit seinem Abschluss arbeitet er in diversen Projekten im Grenzbereich zwischen Kunst und Fotografie. Mit seiner Dauerfotobuchserie «Serienkiller», gewann er im Jahr 2000 den Schweizer Preis für Berufsfotografie «The Selection». Seit 1994 war er international an zahlreichen Ausstellungen beteiligt.

Die hier gezeigten und unter dem Namen «Gold» zusammengefassten 22 Serien sind Teil der ständig wachsenden Arbeit «Serienkiller» die mittlerweile aus 48 Einzelbüchlein besteht. «Serienkiller» existiert in einer Kleinstauflagen von 5+2 Exemplaren.

Die derzeit 48 Serien sind:

1 Mobile Skulpturen	35 Bilderbuch 2
2 Speiselokale	36 Degenerative Bilder 2
3 Parachutisme	37 Freunde der Nacht
4 Bilderbuch 1	38 Goldvreneli
5 Swiss Safari	39 Auslaufmodelle
6 Guadeloupe	40 Kunst am Bau 2
7 Goldrausch 1	41 Inhalt und Form
8 Wiederholungstäter	42 Trockenfleisch
9 Tête-à-tête	43 Degenerative Bilder 3
10 Gute Zeiten, schlechte Zeiten	44 Las Vegas
11 Schweigen ist Gold	45 Verdächtige
12 Frauen	46 Goldrausch 2
13 Alreadymades	47 Elektrosmog
14 Generator	48 Bilderbuch 3
15 Sherpas	
16 Die Welt ist gross	
17 Luscht zum Läbe	
18 Gruppenausstellungen	
19 Schlechter Verkehr	
20 Fesche Mädels	
21 Crème de la Crème	
22 Träumereien	
23 Selbstreferenzielle Bilder	
24 Goldmäuse und Goldhamster	
25 Fleisch und Blut	
26 Degenerative Bilder 1	
27 Architekturfotografie	
28 Baywatch	
29 Vom falschen Gebrauch der Dinge	
30 Es darf keinen Spass machen	
31 Konzeption	
32 Aktionskünstler	
33 Kunst am Bau 1	
34 Mobile Iglus	

Peter Tilllessen was born in Hanau a.M./Germany in 1969. Following a foundation
course in agronomy, he took up photography at FAMU in Prague and the Zurich School
of Design. Since completing his studies, he has worked on a number of projects
that cross the border between art and photography. He was awarded the Swiss Prize
for Professional Photography in 2000 for his ongoing volumes of "Serial Killers."
He has been represented in numerous international exhibitions since 1994.
The 22 series shown here under the heading "Gold" have been selected from
his "Serial Killers". He has produced 48 small volumes to date, published in tiny runs
of 5+2. They are titled as follows:

 1 Mobile Sculptures
 2 Eateries
 3 Parachutisme
 4 Picture Book 1
 5 Swiss Safari
 6 Guadeloupe
 7 Gold Rush 1
 8 Recidivist
 9 Tête-à-tête
10 Good Times, Bad Times
11 Silence Is Golden
12 Women
13 Alreadymades
14 Generator
15 Sherpas
16 Big World
17 Lust for Life
18 Group Shows
19 Traffuck
20 Smart Chicks
21 Crème de la Crème
22 Roveries
23 Self-referential Pictures
24 Golden Mice and Golden Hamsters
25 Flesh and Blood
26 Degenerative Pictures 1
27 Architectural Photography
28 Baywatch
29 Of the False Use of Things
30 It Mustn't Be Fun
31 Conception
32 Action Artists
33 Art for Buildings 1
34 Mobile Igloos

35 Picture Book 2
36 Degenerative Pictures 2
37 Friends of the Night
38 Gold Piece
39 Last Year's Models
40 Art for Buildings 2
41 Content and Form
42 Dried Beef
43 Degenerative Pictures 3
44 Las Vegas
45 Suspects
46 Gold Rush 2
47 Electrosmog
48 Picture Book 3

Goldmäuse und Goldhamster/Golden Mice and Golden Hamsters

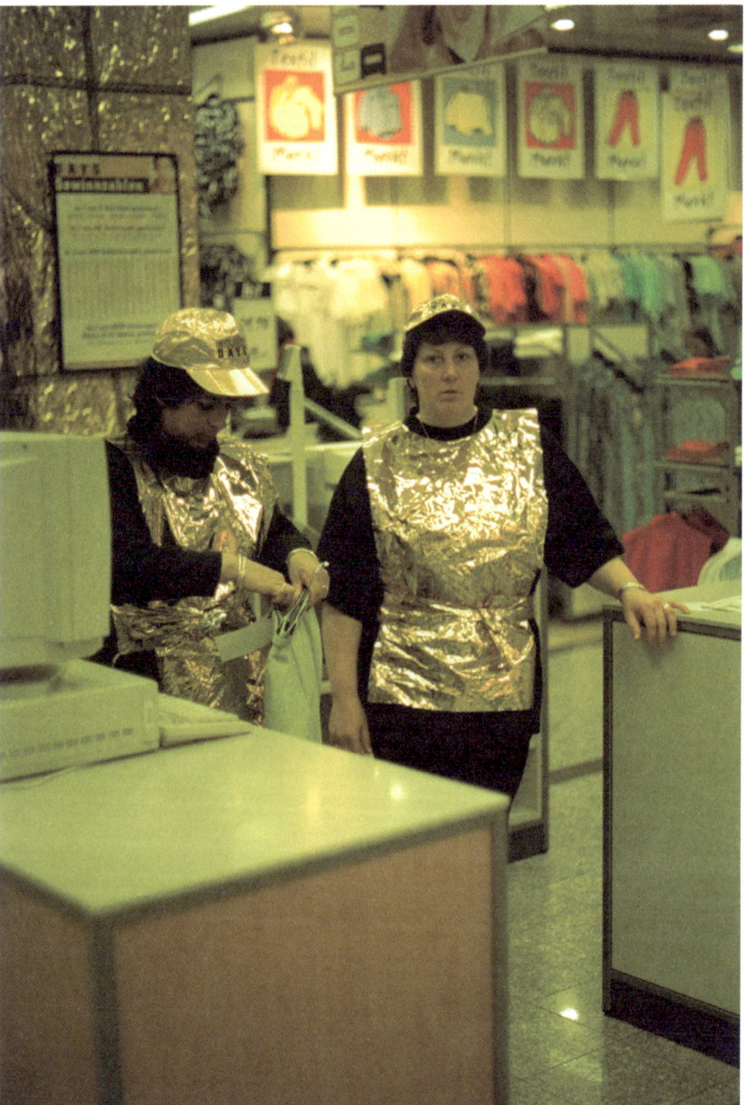

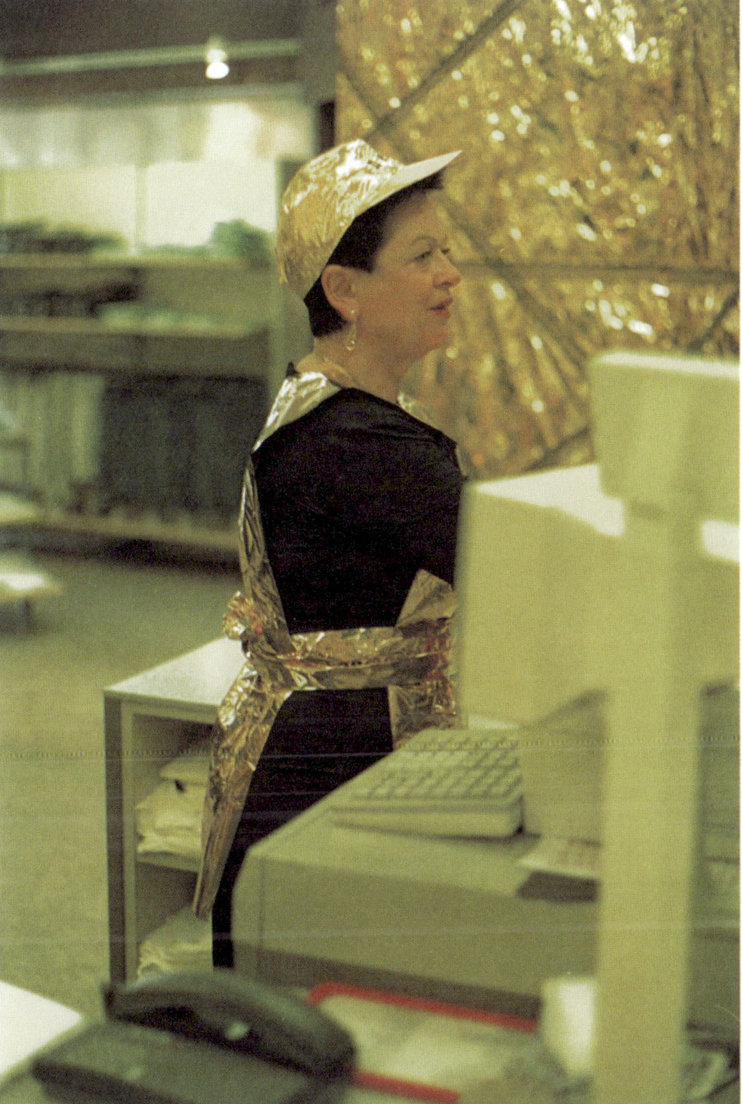

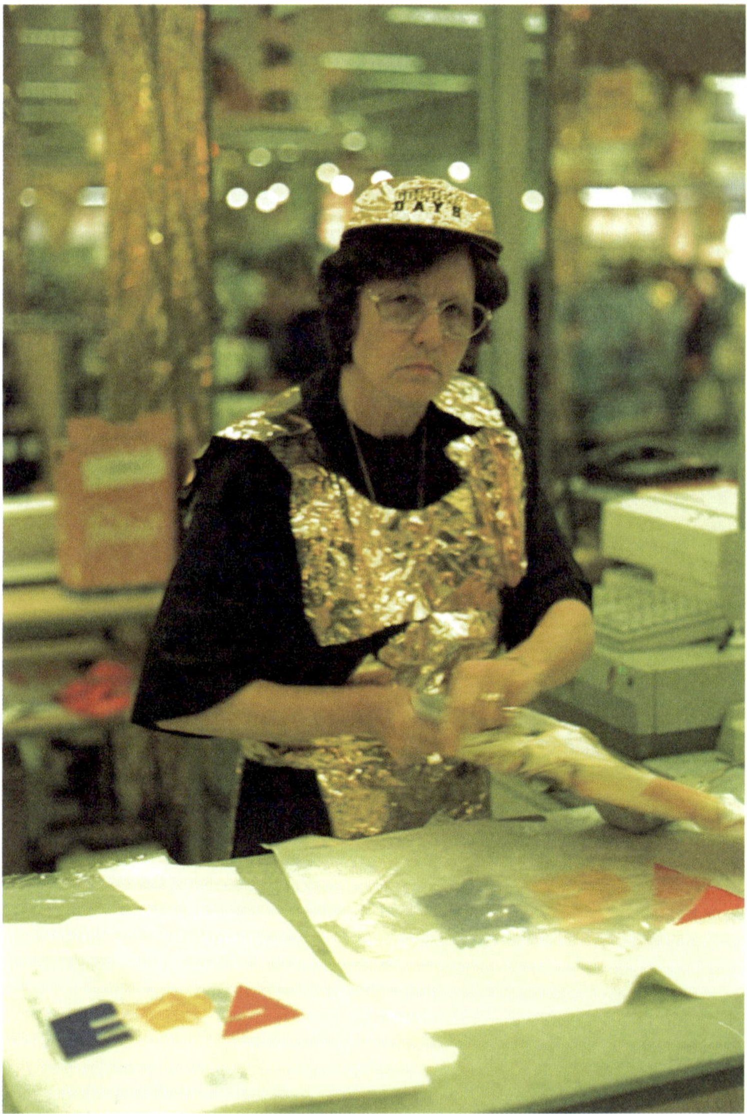
DAYS

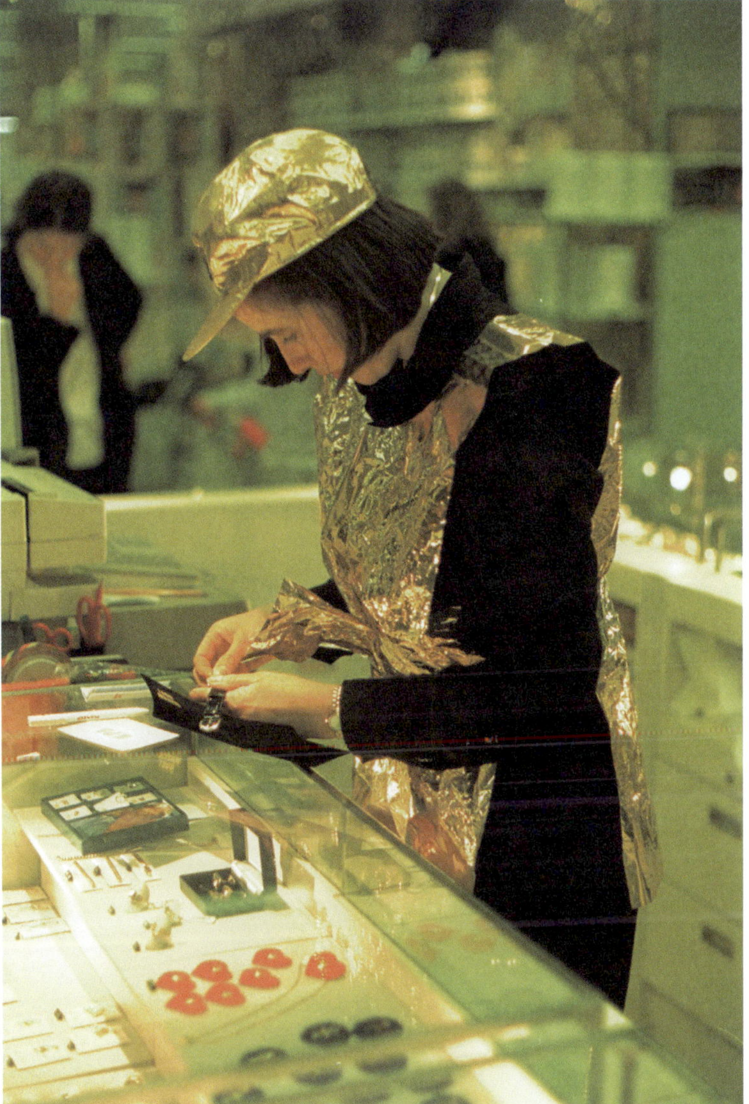

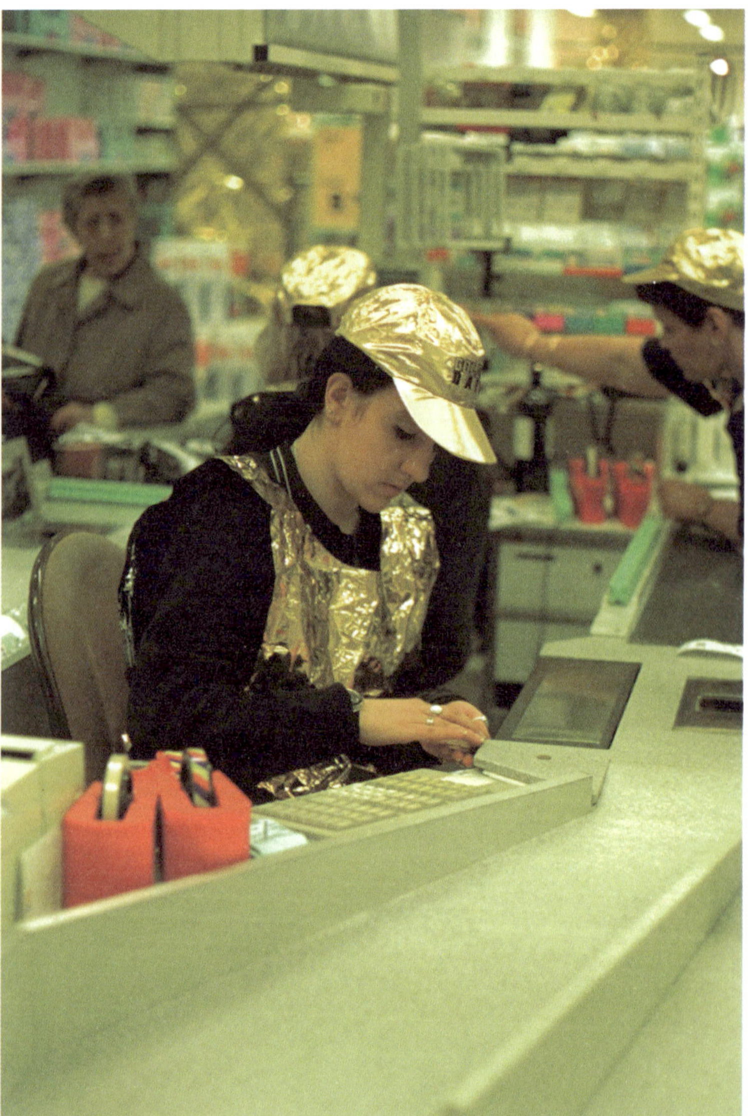

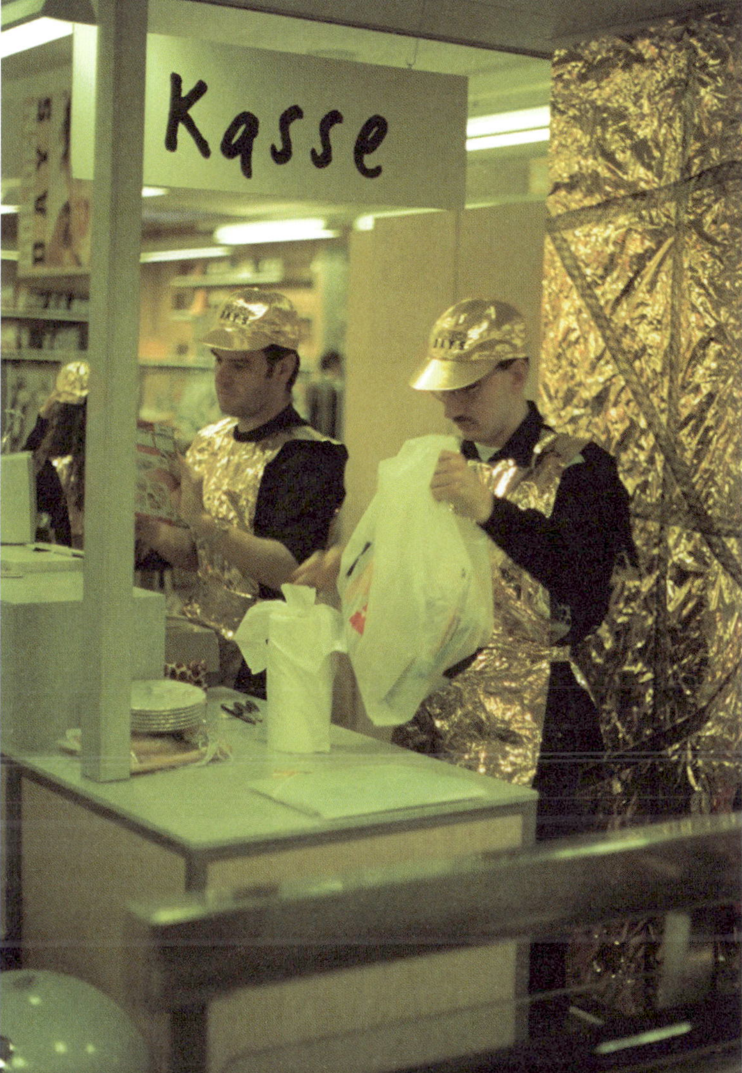
Kasse

Peter Tillessen
Gold

Spezieller Dank für Rat und Schlag geht an/
Special thanks to Muriel, Lukas, Laurent,
Cat-Tuong, Bruno, Christof, Lars und/and Nele

Photographs: Peter Tillessen
Design: Integral Lars Müller mit Peter Tillessen
Text: Ulf Erdmann Ziegler
Lithography: Ast & Jakob AG, Köniz
Printing: Stämpfli AG, Bern
Binding: Buchbinderei Burkhardt AG, Mönchaltorf

© 2000 by Peter Tillessen and
Lars Müller Publishers

Lars Müller Publishers
CH-5401 Baden/Switzerland
books@lars-müller.ch

ISBN: 3-907078-27-6

Printed in Switzerland